SAY WE WON AND GET OUT

SAY WE WON AND GET OUT

GEORGE D. AIKEN AND THE VIETNAM WAR

Stephen C. Terry

Student Researcher Louis D. Augeri

Center for Research on Vermont
University of Vermont

White River Press
Amherst, Massachusetts

Say We Won and Get Out
George D. Aiken and the Vietnam War

© 2020 Stephen C. Terry

All rights reserved.

First published by White River Press, PO Box 3561, Amherst,
Massachusetts 01004 whiteriverpress.com

ISBN: 978-1-887043-64-9 paperback
978-1-887043-63-2 ebook

Designed by Sophia Trigg

Cover photo: U.S. Senate Historical Office

Library of Congress Cataloging-in-Publication Data

Names: Terry, Stephen C., author.
Title: Say we won and get out : George D. Aiken and the Vietnam War /
   Stephen C. Terry ; research by Louis D Augeri.
Description: Amherst, Massachusetts : White River Press, 2020. | Includes
   bibliographical references and index.
Identifiers: LCCN 2019041516 (print) | LCCN 2019041517 (ebook) | ISBN
   9781887043649 (paperback) | ISBN 9781887043632 (ebook)
Subjects: LCSH: Aiken, George D. (George David), 1892-1984. | Mansfield,
   Mike, 1903-2001. | Vietnam War, 1961-1975--Political aspects--United
   States. | Legislators--United States--Biography. | United States.
   Congress. Senate--Biography. | United States--Politics and
   government--1945-1989.
Classification: LCC E748.A193 T47 2020 (print) | LCC E748.A193 (ebook) |
   DDC 328.73/0922 [B]--dc23
LC record available at https://lccn.loc.gov/2019041516
LC ebook record available at https://lccn.loc.gov/2019041517

Contents

Author's Note 9
Acknowledgements 13
Preface 17

Part I – Vietnam: Substance and Shadow

Introduction 25
1. Aiken Joins Foreign Relations Committee 33
2. Aiken During the Kennedy Presidency 44
3. Aiken During the Johnson Presidency 51
4. Aiken During the Nixon Presidency 80
5. Conclusions on Aiken and Vietnam 135

Part II – George D. Aiken's Life and Legacy

6. Early Life 145
7. Vermont Political Career 153
8. Early Senate Career 170

Part III – Author's Perspective

What Would George Aiken Do Today?
   Stephen C. Terry 179

Appendix

Speeches and Interviews:
   Lincoln Day Address (Feb. 12, 1938) 189
   Lend-Lease Speech (Feb. 1941) 196
   Vietnam Analysis: Present and Future (Oct. 19, 1966) 209
   "Impeach Him or Get Off His Back" (Nov. 1973) 214
   Cabot High School Graduation Speech (June 17, 1969) 227
   "Aiken of Vermont" Interview by Bernie Sanders (Spring 1973) .. 234

Post Script: Jeff Danziger 247
Chronologies:
  Vietnam War Timeline 251
  George D. Aiken Chronology 263

Bibliography 275
Index 281

"The men the American people admire most extravagantly are the most daring liars; the men they detest most violently are those who try to tell them the truth."

- H.L. Mencken (1924)

George D. Aiken, a hillside farmer and a liberal Republican Depression-era Governor, rose to national prominence as a leading GOP U. S. Senator and enduring critic of the Vietnam War from 1962-1975. Aiken's long-standing friendship with Senate Majority Leader Mike Mansfield, an unheard of political alliance in today's sharply divided Washington, forged bi-partisan opposition to the war. Aiken was neither "hawk" nor "dove", but a "wise owl" who spoke his mind forcefully and bluntly to all against the war. He advised President Johnson to declare that the U. S. won the Vietnam War and to get out. Later, Aiken told President Nixon to stop bombing in Cambodia or he couldn't be elected "dogcatcher." This is pure Aiken speaking truth to power for ending America's most controversial war, a common-sense voice that the Nation sorely needs today.

This book demonstrates that bi-partisan Senate leadership has worked in the past and must be present in order to solve urgent national problems. Senator Aiken was a catalyst for forging consensus on issues from civil rights to foreign policy by being open-minded to all ideas that would help his constituents. Aiken's philosophy was always to help people first. He never made decisions based on his party, a lost art in the current political environment. A Senator like George Aiken today would help show how to restore bi-partisanship.

Author's Note

This book on Senator George D. Aiken and the Vietnam War had its origins more than 50 years ago when I was a reporter for the Vermont Press Bureau, the State House bureau for the *Rutland Herald* and the *Barre-Montpelier Times Argus*. I would interview Senator Aiken to get his views on matters that impacted Vermont, as well as his work on the Senate Foreign Relations Committee.

More often than not these conversations were either early in the morning, or later in the evening. The early morning calls were made as I knew that up until 7:45 a.m. you could always reach Aiken in his Senate office, and he would take a call from a Vermont reporter. The late evening calls would usually be after major Presidential speeches like the State of the Union, or pronouncements on the war. He would then be at his Washington apartment which was located next to the Supreme Court building overlooking the East Front of the Capitol.

In those days the *Herald* had a very late deadline, and as a reporter you could get breaking news into the paper up until 1 a.m. for the morning paper that would hit the streets about 5 a.m.

In these conversations, Aiken was always direct, blunt and usually responsive.

My first face-to-face meeting with Aiken was in June 1965 at the annual Dairy Days Parade in Enosburg. I spent about thirty minutes interviewing him on a street corner as a parade of fire trucks and tractors were winding their way down Main Street. We talked mostly about Vermont and dairy farmers, but there were passing references to Vietnam, enough so that I realized it was a topic on his mind.

My real insight into Aiken's personality and his thinking came after I joined his staff in April 1969 where I remained until Aiken retired from the Senate on Jan. 2, 1975. During this period, I often took notes on the events I witnessed. In some cases, I would write myself a memo. More often than not I would tuck away in my memory the events that transpired. After Aiken retired from the Senate and returned to Vermont, where he lived another 10 years before his death in 1984, I would keep in touch with the Senator and Lola, who lived until her 102nd birthday before her death in 2014, 30 years after the death of her husband.

I had always aspired to do a book on Senator Aiken. The first effort was in 2004 when I co-edited with the late University of Vermont Prof. Samuel Hand, "The Essential Aiken" which was a compilation of some of Senator Aiken's important speeches during his long political career.

Earlier on my long-time friend, Bill Porter of Adamant, and former Managing Editor of the *Barre-Montpelier Times Argus*, and before that an editor at the *Rutland Herald* during the years I was in Washington, would often talk about the events of the day, especially during the Vietnam War.

These conversations have remained with me for many years, and in some respects, they formed early drafts of this book in my head before I started writing it in early 2018.

I did write a version of the Cambodia chapter soon after I left Aiken's staff in 1974 as Lola had provided some important running commentary on the evening of April 30, 1970 when President Nixon delivered a nationally television speech on the topic. I was struck in 2019 when I watched a replay of the Cambodia invasion speech on YouTube. I had forgotten that Nixon did not use a teleprompter but read the speech from a text he held in his hands. The hot lights caused him to pause and wipe sweat from his chin. It was a vivid reminder of Nixon's persona.

Another important, and recent contribution for this book came from

Author's Note

Tony Marro, former colleague of mine at the Vermont Press Bureau in the 1960s, who once served as an intern for Senator Aiken, before his long and distinguished career in newspapering at Newsday, and before that, *The New York Times*. Tony read early drafts of this book and helped me put some aspects of Aiken's life into context, as well as to provide sage editorial advice.

Acknowledgements

This book would not have been possible without the strong support and encouragement from Richard Watts, the Director of the Center on Research for Vermont. Watts, a former resident of Putney, George Aiken's hometown, arranged to have two students serve as research assistants for this book. They were David Brandt, who was then a senior, and Louis Augeri, a sophomore. After David had graduated in June of 2018, Louis remained with me until this book was completed in late summer of 2019. Louis and I would meet each week to review the Aiken papers that are housed in Special Collections at the UVM Library or go over drafts of the book.

Louis has made a very valuable contribution to this book in countless ways, not the least of which was his keen eye for language, and his Generation X technology skills.

The contribution made by Louis is the reason this book cover carries a "student researcher Louis D. Augeri" under my by-line. I simply could not have done this book without him. Thank you, Louis. You have a brilliant academic career ahead of you! Please know readers, any mistakes in this book are all mine.

The staff at the University of Vermont's Special Collections were invaluable for much of the research conducted prior to the writing of the book. Prudence Doherty, Chris Burns, and the rest of the Special Collections staff were exceptionally helpful.

A special mention and shout out for the work of the division of Continuing and Distance Education for its generousity, as well as for its stalwart support for the George D. Aiken Lectures. The annual lecture series, named after Senator Aiken, is one of the most prestigious UVM events to honor the memory of Senator Aiken and his work on foreign policy, agriculture, energy and economic development.

The collective staff at the Center for Research on Vermont was crucial in facilitating the completion of this book. Particularly, we would like to thank Sophia Trigg, who in her capacity as employee of the University and Center, gave us valuable design assistance. Eliza Giles assisted us with digital media aspects of our work and created podcasts derived from stories from Aiken's life and career.

Louis and I also want to thank the people responsible for the valuable advice I have received on early drafts of this book: two emeritus professors at UVM. Mark Stoler, who is an expert in diplomatic history, and who knew Senator Aiken, made important contributions on the Gulf of Tonkin section. Also, long-time UVM political science professor, Garrison Nelson, who has followed Vermont politics for at least 50 years and a friend, offered important content and structural changes. Professor Nelson, who wrote a definitive biography of former House Speaker John William McCormack, also provided ways the manuscript could be strengthened by the author if he wrote more about Aiken and his personality.

D. Gregory Sanford, who is now retired as the State of Vermont Archivist, also read the early drafts with a keen eye. Sanford and historian Charlie Morrissey completed in 1981 an oral history with Senator Aiken after he retired from the Senate and offered important advice and clarifications. The Aiken oral history project provided important insights into Aiken's long career in public service.

Jeff Danziger, the nationally syndicated cartoonist, who also lives part-time in Vermont, gave permission to use an essay he wrote about his Vietnam experience and Senator Aiken. We thank him for his recollections, which tells readers a lot about Aiken, the man.

A word about copy editing. All the advance readers offered valuable

Acknowledgments

advice, but the heavy lifting on copy editing was performed by Marjorie Ryerson of Randolph. She is a former Vermont journalist, state legislator, college teacher, and works in book publishing. Marjorie spent the month of June copy editing the manuscript and making suggestions for more information for readers. Louis and I are deeply grateful for Marjorie's important contribution and for her encouragement.

Jim Blair of Middlebury, a longtime photojournalist for National Geographic, offered invaluable assistance with his highly-trained eye and advice in reviewing the many Aiken photographs that are included in the Aiken Papers. Some of the selections were used and appear in this book. Additionally, Jim graciously made available a photograph he took while serving on the USNS Marine Adder, a troop ship which assisted in the evacuation of refugees from North Vietnam.

Thanks to Will Terry, who lives and works in Washington, D.C. and spends a lot of time on Capitol Hill, for his edits and observations.

Finally, I want to dedicate this book to my wife, Faith Terry, who not only read early drafts and made very valuable copy edit suggestions, but also encouraged me to keep writing and researching this book, which was all accomplished in a little outbuilding on our Middlebury property, which we call the "Chicken Coop". It was Faith who was the driving force for building this little structure as she knew it would help me keep my focus and attention.

She was so right.

Thank you, my loving wife.

Preface

Senator George D. Aiken was one of Vermont's most famous of the state's now deceased 42 U.S. Senators. Senator Aiken became part of a long history of prominent Vermonters serving in the halls of Congress, not only making a name for themselves in Vermont, but nationally as well. Justin S. Morrill served in the United States House of Representatives from 1855 to 1867, and in the U.S. Senate from 1867 to 1898, serving a total of 44 years in Congress. In his day, Morrill worked tirelessly to pass the Morrill Land-Grant Acts, which allowed for the creation of land-grant colleges and universities, using proceeds derived from the sale of federal lands. Morrill's efforts spanned nearly his entire career, from the 1860s to the 1890s, earning him a respected position in history as one of Vermont's most significant and well-known senators. Senator Warren R. Austin, who served in the U.S. Senate from Vermont from 1931 to 1946 before he was named the United States Ambassador to the United Nations by President Harry Truman, is arguably grouped with Aiken and Morrill as one of Vermont's most notable former senators. Aiken and Austin served together from 1941 to 1946 before Austin left the Senate for the U.N. Ambassadorship.

Aiken's portrait on the walls of the Vermont State House stands out as he is depicted during his later years in the Senate, already in his early 80s, rather than a more traditional portrait of him during his years as Governor of Vermont. The oil painting of Aiken by Thomas Clark of Perkinsville, Vt., was taken from a photograph of him in the early 1970's when he was the ranking Republican on the Senate Foreign Relations Committee. In the painting, Aiken is looking pensive while concentrating and listening intently to testimony brought before the committee. Aiken's portrait captures the essence of Aiken in his later life as a veteran senator in what has often been called the "World's Most Exclusive Club."

Aiken and the Presidents

The Vermont Senator frequently offered his advice to the six Presidents under which he served during his long career. While he did not have much interaction with President Franklin Roosevelt, Aiken was a close friend of Harry Truman's, who served as a Senator from Missouri before he became Vice President under Roosevelt. When Truman was notified of the death of FDR in 1945, a shaken Truman told Aiken that he was not sure he was up to the job of President. Aiken consoled his friend and offered him support.

Aiken worked closely with President Dwight Eisenhower during the two terms the former general served. Aiken advised the President on agriculture issues and served as his host when the President came to Rutland County for a fishing trip.

Aiken and Senator John F. Kennedy, D-Mass., worked together on New England issues such as the St. Lawrence Seaway legislation. After Kennedy became president, one of his first big mistakes was the bungled Bay of Pigs invasion, launched in an effort to remove the Castro Government in Cuba. The invasion was an embarrassing failure for Kennedy. One of the first people the new President reached out to after the Bay of Pigs fiasco was his New England friend, George Aiken, beckoning the Senator to the White House for a private meeting to seek his counsel.

Lyndon B. Johnson and Aiken were long time Senate colleagues before LBJ became President. While they sharply differed on Vietnam, they remained, for the most part, on friendly terms and worked together on issues to promote rural America.

Preface

President Richard Nixon's relationship with Aiken was mixed. The Vermont Senator was in early support of Nixon's policy to withdraw troops from Vietnam, and as long as Nixon continued to do that, Aiken was satisfied. But when Nixon invaded Cambodia, Aiken was shocked, and his shock turned to anger. And when it was revealed in 1974 that Nixon had tried to cover-up crimes surrounding the Watergate affair, involving a break-in of democratic headquarters at the Watergate hotel in 1972, Aiken joined others in urging Nixon to resign his office.

Overall, Aiken would always say he believed that each of the Presidents he served under tried their best, even if they made mistakes.

The Wise Owl

By the early 1970's, Aiken was one of the Senate's most senior and highly respected members. He was often referred to as neither "hawk nor dove" but "the wise owl." This characterization was first made by Senator Mike Mansfield, Aiken's long-time friend. The "wise owl" characterization came from Aiken's long interest in the policies surrounding the Vietnam War, as well as his thinking that often led him to propose common sense, middle ground, bi-partisan solutions to vexing national and foreign policy issues.

Aiken, although a life-long Republican, was never, however, a hard-bitten partisan nor an ideological party puritan. He was a supreme pragmatist who used his infectious warm and often humorous personality to attract support from fellow Senators. The issues he influenced ranged the gamut from Vietnam policies to finding an important historic compromise to pave the way for the passage of national civil rights legislation in 1964.

After Aiken's death, he was called the "balance-wheel of the Senate" by his former colleague, Sen. Abraham Ribicoff, D-Conn. Aiken always maintained the modest quality of a rural Vermonter who grew up on a flinty hillside farm. He was always quick to give others credit and he never tried to hog the political limelight.

The Vermont Character

Aiken became the personification of the Vermont character. His wispy shock of white hair and his compact five-foot eight-inch frame was the product of a man who spent his formative years working hard as a dirt farmer. Throughout his long career in politics, which included two-terms as Governor of Vermont during the Depression, and a long career in the Senate, Aiken's voice always had a whiff of the Vermont twang that could be heard in the hill country of the Green Mountain State.

At the end of the U.S. participation in the Vietnam War in April 1975, nobody was more conflicted than Senator Aiken. He had spent his last 20 years as Vermont's senior Senator looking for a pathway out of Vietnam. He was a product of his life's experience in politics. He kept looking for an answer that would maintain the nation's honor with a common sense solution.

As a farmer and horticulturalist, Aiken knew from experience that planting seeds for policy change almost always took a considerable amount of time to bear fruit.

Aiken's Life

To understand Aiken's Vietnam views a reader needs to have a footing of how Aiken lived his life. In order to help provide a complete picture of George Aiken, this volume is presented in two distinct parts.

Part One is about George D. Aiken and his role in this country's Vietnam War policy from 1954 to 1975. Part Two of this book is a short biography that highlights important milestones from the 92 years of Aiken's life, a life that stretched from 1892 to 1984. The author contends that Aiken's early rural life and his farming and small business efforts, combined with his state political experience helped shaped the man who would later become an influential national voice in the U. S. Senate on Vietnam War policy.

As formative as the issues of that time were, another valuable key is to understand how George Aiken, especially during his 34 years in the Senate, worked the political process during his career to achieve his desired policy goals.

One of his favorite sayings was that "You can catch more flies with honey than with vinegar." Aiken's political career was all about gaining support from wherever he could, regardless of the other's party or beliefs. Thus, as Vermont Governor, he rallied support from farmers and labor union members rather than from the captains of industry. Aiken's blue-collar supporters led him to promote public solutions for improving education, health care and social programs for children and low-income families in Vermont.

When it came to foreign policy, Aiken opposed efforts by the United States to dominate a country and thus prevent that country from developing self-government and self-sufficiency. In essence, this was his main objection to U.S. policy in Vietnam. Finding a balanced path was a task Senator Aiken thought a lot about. During the last 20 years of his 34 in the Senate, he worked toward finding a lasting solution.

As the ranking Republican on the Senate Foreign Relations Committee, and as Dean of the Senate from 1969 to 1975, he enjoyed some victories amidst many defeats and disappointments. The patient farmer who lived on a back road in Putney did not give up and continued to encourage the growth of his seeds for an eventual peace in Vietnam.

This is the story of George D. Aiken, the Vermonter, whose famous 1966 advice on Vietnam: Say We Won and Get Out, still resonates these many years later.

Part I

Vietnam: Substance and Shadow

Introduction

Aiken Gives His Advice

It was mid-morning on Oct. 19, 1966 when Vermont's Senior Senator, George D. Aiken, 74, entered the Senate Chamber. A hint of fall was in the air in Washington, while in Vermont, fall foliage was nearing its peak. On that day, Aiken had been in the office since 6:30 a.m., looking over mail and newspapers from Vermont before he and Lola Pierotti, then his Administrative Assistant, later his wife, left their office in the Old Senate Office Building at 7:50 to walk to the Senate cafeteria for their usual breakfast with Senator Mike Mansfield, the Majority Leader.

Over coffee and English muffins, the three would talk about the events of the day ahead. One highlight would be that later that morning, the venerable Vermont Senator would be delivering a prepared speech on Vietnam. Aiken provided Senator Mike Mansfield (D-Montana) with an advance copy of the speech as the Majority Leader wanted to be on the Senate floor to offer commentary after Aiken had delivered it.

The press in the Senate Press Gallery had also been alerted to the fact that Aiken would be speaking about the War. By that fall, the Vietnam War had already caused deep divisions in the country as well as in the Senate itself. President Lyndon B. Johnson was determined not to become the President that "lost Vietnam." In 1966, just under 400,000 American troops were actively stationed in Vietnam and no end was in sight for troop involvement or air bombing. At the peak of the war, there were 530,000

American soldiers stationed in Vietnam. The war was taking a bloody toll on both sides of the battle. The Draft had reached into every American home as 35,000 young men per month were being called up for service in the military. On Oct. 3, 1966, a few weeks before Aiken spoke, Russia had announced that it was providing military and economic aid to North Vietnam.

The White House had already announced that a week later, on Oct. 25, 1966, President Johnson would be going to Manila to meet with America's Vietnam allies: Australia, the Philippines, Thailand, New Zealand, South Korea and South Vietnam. It was Johnson's upcoming trip to Manila that convinced Aiken that it was time for him to speak out and to offer his advice on Vietnam. He wanted to provide a pathway for a way out of the war. The speech that he would deliver on Oct. 19 was one that he had been mulling over for months.

In February 1966, the Senate Foreign Relations Committee, on which Aiken was a senior member, had held televised hearings to examine U.S. policy in Vietnam. Along with the daily televised reports from the war zone that were beginning to lead the news broadcasts each night, these hearings were a catalyst for focusing the public's awareness on the war. In essence, unlike in any previous wars, the Vietnam War was becoming a living room war for American viewers.

When Aiken stood up to speak and adjusted the microphone on his desk, a buzz went through the Senate Press Gallery with the words, "Aiken is up!" In anticipation, the reporters covering the Senate moved to the front of the gallery that overlooked the ornate Senate Chamber below.

Aiken, with his craggy face and shock of white hair, physically embodied the Yankee image, and his austere and careful use of the spoken word personified the Yankee spirit. While he did not speak often on the Senate Floor, when he did, others listened. The 12-minute speech he gave, known formally as "Vietnam Analysis: Present and Future," quickly became known in the nation's political history and to journalists as the "Aiken Formula,"

In his talk, Aiken proposed that "The United States could well declare

Introduction

unilaterally that this stage of the Vietnam War is over [and] that we have 'won' in the sense that our Armed Forces are in control of most of the field and no potential enemy is in a position to establish its authority over South Vietnam."

Aiken said that with the declaration of winning, the United States could begin a gradual, phased withdrawal of U.S. troops from Vietnam. The U.S. could stop the bombing and could find a political solution to bring the fighting to an end. The next day, *The New York Times* ran a story by Richard Eder on the lower right-hand corner of page one, with this headline: "Aiken Suggests U.S. Say It Has Won War." The story also quoted the Senator saying that, "It may be a far-fetched proposal ... but nothing else has worked." The story also said that Aiken speculated that his suggestion might be adopted by Hanoi as well, with both sides declaring they had won.

Ironically, the lead story that day in *The New York Times* reported on a speech that President Johnson had made in Wellington, New Zealand on his way to Manila to meet with allies. The story, entitled "Johnson Appeals to Hanoi to End War It 'Can't Win,'" was in striking contrast to Aiken's suggestion.

The Aiken speech generated a lot of attention in national media on Oct. 20, 1966, as well as in Vermont. Yet the Aiken proposal seemed simplistic, and some thought it was a joke. It was not well received in the Johnson White House,

For more than 20 years, every morning the Senate was in session, Senator Aiken, a Republican, and Democratic Majority Leader Mansfield had breakfast. The only other person ever allowed at the table was Lola Aiken. It became a Washington institution. The discussions were always private. (U. S Senate Photo)

and it resulted in new tension between Aiken and Johnson, who had been friends with each other in the Senate before Johnson became President.

But Mike Mansfield, Aiken's long-time breakfast companion, praised the speech. "As usual," Mansfield said, "the distinguished senior Senator from Vermont has given us a great deal to consider and some additional food for thought."

The gestation for Aiken's speech had been a long one. It had started in late 1965 when Aiken joined Mansfield and three other Senators on a trip around the world to see if there was any prospect for peace in Vietnam. When the Mansfield-Aiken delegation returned, it was with a pessimistic message that they found no sign that Hanoi or the Viet Cong were going to quit the fight. In its public report to the Senate, called "The Vietnam Conflict: The Substance and the Shadow," the delegation reached the conclusion that, "There are no grounds for optimism that the end is likely to be reached within the confines of South Vietnam or within the very near future."

The report continued: "There are difficult and painful choices, and they are beset with many imponderables. The situation, as it now appears, offers only the very slim prospect of a settlement by negotiations or the alternative prospect of a continuance of the conflict in the direction of a general war on the Asian mainland."

If that public report was not pessimistic enough, the private report to President Johnson was even more bleak. Aiken and Mansfield told Johnson in mid-December 1965, upon their return, that the Vietnam War could not be won and that a negotiated settlement was the only possible way to stop the bloodshed.

This report may have led to a temporary Christmas 1965 bombing halt, but the cessation didn't last long. Neither the resumption of bombing nor the introduction of fresh ground troops improved the situation; instead they only further escalated the war.

Aiken's Oct. 19, 1966 12-minute speech was his best effort to try to stop Johnson's war policy, but it was one that Johnson rejected. The war would continue for another seven years. While Aiken did not succeed in altering war policy, his speech catapulted the Vermonter to national fame.

As Albin Krebs wrote in Aiken's obituary in the Nov. 24, 1984 issue of *The New York Times*: "Mr. Aiken, a vintage Yankee of the old school, earned a reputation as a maverick whose championship of liberal legislation often won him the enmity of members of his own party. He also had a reputation as a wary, commonsensical observer of the Washington scene who could pithily sum up a blunt solution to a complex dilemma."

"One of Mr. Aiken's most famous pronouncements came in 1966, when, after having supported Johnson Administration policy in the Vietnam War, he moved toward the position of Senate "doves." He said that if a face-saving device was needed to pull out of the fighting, President Johnson should simply "declare the United States the winner and begin de-escalation."

Krebs further wrote, "On its face, the suggestion seemed simplistic. But in 1973, after the Administration of Richard Nixon had negotiated a Vietnam pullout plan that would obviously lead to an eventual Communist takeover in South Vietnam, Mr. Aiken could say: "What we got was essentially what I recommended six years ago—we said we had won, and we got out."

The Famous Aiken Quote

More than 50 years have passed since the Vermont Senator made his famous speech on the Senate Floor that October day. If there is any lasting memory of George Aiken and Vietnam, most people who recall him will immediately blurt out, "Say we won and get out" or some variation of that theme.

Given journalistic shorthand, the "declare victory and get out" description was what stuck firmly in the public's mind. As a former reporter and editor, and a person who had worked for six years as an aide to Senator Aiken, I never heard him once claim that he had been misquoted on his famous speech. In fact, as his Senate term came to an end in 1975 and until his death in 1984, Aiken was quick to say that the popular version was the correct interpretation of his speech. In fact, in February of 1971, Senator

Aiken wrote to a friend in Massachusetts to say, "Although five years ago last fall I did ask the President [Johnson] to say we had won the war and to withdraw our troops, this was not done, as you well know."

Not only did Aiken never claim he was misquoted, but for many years after his famous speech, he would tell interviewers including, in 1981, Charlie Morrissey, the historian:

> ... In the fall of 1966, I suggested to President Johnson that we simply say we had won the war and to bring the troops home. I am sure, from what I've heard afterwards and since, that there would have been virtually no criticism from higher officials who have told me that that approach would have been entirely possible. President Johnson didn't like my suggestion at all. But after he finished his term he agreed then that it probably could have been done—that I was right about it.

It was unquestionably clear to me that, from 1966 on, Aiken firmly believed his speech was intended to send that very message.

This view was also confirmed for me after 1969 when the author of the first draft of Aiken's Oct. 19, 1966 speech—the late Nathaniel McKittrick of Arlington, VA, who was a consultant to Aiken on the Senate Foreign Relations Committee —said to me that Aiken's intention was to send a different message to Johnson so that the President could frame a U.S. troop withdrawal in a victory statement. As such, the "Aiken Formula" was enshrined in history.

A major challenge to that interpretation came in 1978 (after Aiken had left the Senate) from University of Vermont Professor Mark A. Stoler, now retired, who wrote an article in Vermont History entitled "What Did He Really Say? The 'Aiken Formula' for Vietnam Revisited."

Stoler wrote: "Unfortunately, there is a major problem with this now-accepted version (declaring victory and getting out) of the Aiken formula. Simply put, George D. Aiken never said that the United States should declare victory and get out of Vietnam. As with most 'legends' of American history, this one is a gross distortion of the facts."

But Aiken, himself, never disputed what his real intent was, which was to give Lyndon B. Johnson a policy reason for bringing the war to an end

Introduction

and bringing the American troops home. It was Aiken's genius and insight about human nature that if Lyndon Johnson could find an excuse to change his mind about the war, that the President could change his policy of escalation and negotiate a peace settlement. But as history has recorded, Johnson rejected that advice, even though in his gut he knew the Senator from Vermont was right.

Professor Stoler was correct, in my view, to the extent that Aiken's opposition "gave early anti-war sentiment a degree of respectability and bi-partisanship," which may have slowed down the Republican war hawks and may have put pressure on President Johnson to scale back troop increases sought by his military command.

As this book argues, Aiken's actual speech was more nuanced then the headlined version. What Aiken was proposing was that the United States declare that it had "won"—in the sense that the North Vietnamese and Vietcong couldn't achieve a military victory without a major escalation.

Aiken's plan recommended phased withdrawals to safer enclaves behind the front lines which would allow for the South Vietnamese Army to take control of combat operations while U.S. troops would be subsequently withdrawn.

So, how did a simple hillside farmer from Vermont become a national figure that is still remembered today? Why is the "Aiken Formula" still quoted as a novel way to find a solution to tough problems?

A continuous theme throughout Aiken's life was that the public, not the private, interest was his guiding principle, and that it was government's role to represent the public will and to put people first. This unshakable conviction led Aiken down a path from which he never wavered, whether it was foreign or domestic policy matters.

This book is about how that guiding set of principles led Aiken from his farm in Putney, Vermont to his role in defending the interests of the American people, and in bringing an end to the U.S. involvement in the Vietnam War.

Here is that story.

1

Aiken Joins Foreign Relations Committee

Aiken Begins to Wrestle with Foreign Policy

George Aiken was named to the Senate Foreign Relations Committee on Jan. 13, 1954, a year that turned out to be transformative in Southeast Asia. At the time, the French were engaged in their own long war in Vietnam. The Vietnamese had long resented the French colonization of their country, as well as Japan's brief domination of Vietnam, which continued until after Japan's surrender to the U.S. at end of World War II.

Ho Chi Minh, a nationalist and a Communist, created and led the League for Vietnamese Independence, also known as the Viet Minh. After World War II ended in 1945, he declared that Vietnam was independent. The French rejected the independent claim, which touched off a prolonged, bitter war for control between France and Vietnam.

A crucial moment in the French-Vietnam War took place during the spring of 1954. At that momentous time, Senator Aiken had just been named to the Senate Foreign Relations Committee. The United States was still recovering from the wounds of the Korean Conflict, a bloody war that finally had wound down when an Armistice was signed in 1953. At that time, the Cold War between the United States and the Soviet Union was very tense, especially after the Soviets exploded their first atom bomb in August of 1949. At the same time, Chinese Communist leader Mao Zedong was flexing his muscles after a civil war there had led to the creation of the

People's Republic of China.

In early 1950, China and the Soviet Union formally recognized the Communist Democratic Republic of Vietnam and began to supply economic and military aid to the Communist fighters who were seeking to exert political control over Vietnam. The immediate targets of the resistance in Vietnam were the French military outposts, since the French government still claimed Vietnam as one of its colonies.

During the same year, the United States targeted the Viet Minh as a Communist threat and began to supply military aid to help the French quell the Viet Minh guerrillas. By 1954, just before the French defeat at Dien Bien Phu, the U.S. Government was providing substantial support for the French effort.

Despite French requests, and although the U.S. was concerned about Communism spreading throughout Europe as well as Asia, President Eisenhower did not approve the use of ground troops as part of that support. However, the U.S. was so concerned that the then Secretary of State, John Foster Dulles suggested to France that the U.S. would consider supporting the French efforts to push back against the communist insurgency by the possible use of nuclear weapons.

1954: A Pivotal Year

Aiken's first year on the Senate Foreign Relations Committee did, indeed, prove to be a pivotal year, according to Committee records.

In a preface to the 1977 release of declassified records from 1954 Executive Sessions, Senator John Sparkman, committee chair in 1977, wrote:

> The year 1954 witnessed decisive events in the development of postwar U.S. diplomacy; it was a year in which the chickens came home to roost on more than one pressing and vital issue. Two surpassing problems confronted the country during this critical year: first building a tolerable solution to the war in Indochina, a French colonial war that had been transformed into a struggle to contain international Communism (and into an American war to boot in financial and material terms) and second, inducing recalcitrant French and Italians to ratify the European Defense

Aiken Joins Foreign Relations Committee

Community treaty, which would open the door to West German rearmament.

Aiken was in his 13th year as a member of the Senate, and by then his personal influence in the body had been slowly building. His maverick Republican reputation was already well-known, as he was one of the six moderate GOP Senators who had signed the Declaration of Conscience in June 1950. That declaration had been spearheaded by Aiken's close friend, Senator Margaret Chase Smith of Maine. It called on national leaders and the Republican Party to take a hard look at the activities of the House Un-American Activities Committee as well as at fellow GOP Senator Joseph McCarthy of Wisconsin, who months earlier had made a speech in Wheeling, West Virginia, alleging that known communists were infiltrating the U.S. Government. Senator Margaret Chase Smith's declaration represented growing frustration with Joseph McCarthy but had little impact on how McCarthy conducted himself.

Republican leaders in the U.S. Senate supported Aiken's request for appointment to the Senate Foreign Relations Committee in an effort to block McCarthy from gaining a coveted spot on the Committee. In order to do that, Aiken told me that he had to give up his senior status on the Senate Labor and Public Welfare Committee. But Aiken was ready to give up that post and get more deeply involved in foreign relations matters, particularly because of his interest in foreign policy that stemmed from his work on the Senate Agriculture Committee, which had helped to create the Food for Peace Program.

Joseph McCarthy's role as a Senator had already begun to decline by 1954 when Vermont Senator Ralph E. Flanders, a Republican from Springfield, introduced a resolution to formally charge McCarthy with "unbecoming conduct" and to remove him from his committee chairmanship. Writing in the Walloomsack Review, Anthony Marro of Bennington recounted Flanders' floor speech about McCarthy: "He dons his war paint. He goes into his war dance. He emits his war whoops. He goes forth to battle and proudly returns with the scalp of a pink Army dentist. We may assume that this presents the depth and seriousness of Communist penetration in this country at this time." By December 2, 1954, the Senate had voted, 65 to 22, to condemn McCarthy for "violating the dignity of the Senate," whereby any lingering and undue influence the disgraced Senator retained quickly dissipated.

Meanwhile, earlier that year, the French occupation of Vietnam had reached a critical juncture. In April, President Dwight D. Eisenhower warned that if the Communist forces took over in Vietnam, it would be the start of political disintegration in the region. This view, known as the "domino theory," would become a critical argument for future Presidents Kennedy, Johnson and Nixon, and a driver of American policy in Vietnam until 1975.

The French were dug in at Dien Bien Phu, a valley near the border with Laos. The French generals were convinced that the Viet Minh could not overwhelm the French forces. However, the chief military strategist for the Viet Minh, General Vo Nguyen Giap, had another plan. He decided that by controlling the mountains surrounding the valley, that the Viet Minh would have an advantage.

Starting in 1953, Giap moved his troops by night over steep hills and mountains so that they would not be seen by French bombers during the day. By early 1954, the Viet Minh controlled the mountains and held the "high ground" against the French forces in the valley below. The French were defeated by General Giap and surrendered to avoid a total massacre. This defeat caused the French to sue for peace.

Senator Aiken greets President Dwight D. Eisenhower. On the left is Senator Bourke B. Hickenlooper, R- Iowa. (Senate Photo)

Before the French surrender in 1954, President Eisenhower had been under heavy pressure to lend American military support to the French. But after weighing the opposition from his military leaders, Gen. Matthew Ridgway and Gen. James Gavin, and a lack of congressional support, President Eisenhower was unwilling to commit U.S. forces. When I served on Aiken's staff, starting in 1969, the Senator would recount for me the opposition of the U.S. generals to help the French continue its long war in Vietnam. This critical decision by Eisenhower to not give France the critical aid it needed at that time to defeat the Viet Minh was never lost on Aiken, and it provided the foundation for his famous advice to President Johnson in 1966, advice the President had summarily rejected.

Once France sued for peace, the negotiations on Vietnam's future were held in Geneva. The nations at the table, which included the United States, the Soviet Union, China, France and Great Britain, agreed to temporarily split Vietnam at the 17th parallel into two zones—the North and the South. Vietnam was then led by Chief of State and former Emperor of Vietnam, Bao Dai, who would later be ousted when Diem's forces overpowered South Vietnam. The United States, while present at the conference, did not sign the Accords. The Geneva Accords, as the agreement was called, were supposed to be temporary as internationally supervised elections were intended to reunify the country within two years by creating an independent country.

The elections never took place. North Vietnam was led by Ho Chi Minh, while the South was under the control of Ngo Dinh Diem who identified himself as anti-Communist. Diem, with the support of the United States, refused to abide by the terms of the Geneva Accords, thus setting the stage for continued warfare between North and South Vietnam.

While some skeptical voices were heard in the United States about the failure to hold the elections agreed-upon in the Geneva Accords, the opinion of the majority of the country aligned with the position of the Eisenhower administration, which held that the overriding U.S. national interest was to keep South Vietnam free from Communist control. As a result, the U.S. effectively undermined the electoral process.

The Geneva Accords had included a provision to allow people living in North Vietnam—or north of the 17th Parallel—to relocate to South

Vietnam. Likewise, people in the south were allowed to return to the north.

The window for leaving was temporary: from August 18, 1954 to May 20, 1955. During those nine months, some 310,000 civilians, 85,000 tons of cargo, and 8,100 vehicles were moved out of North Vietnam. Taking part in the large refugee resettlement, which the United States called Operation Passage to Freedom, were 109 ships and small crafts.

One of the participants in that sealift was former National Geographic staff photographer, James P. Blair of Middlebury, Vermont. At the time, Blair was a young Naval officer assigned to a troop ship, the USNS Marine Adder. His job was to help the refugees learn how to use the sanitary facilities on the ship.

As a young Navy man, Blair had a deep interest in photography and offered to take photographs of the refugees. This task proved to be life changing for him. Afterward, he embarked upon on a long career as staff photographer with National Geographic magazine, participating in many photoshoots and assignments throughout the world. Now living in retirement in Vermont, Blair recalls that at that time, the refugees were eager to flee the North because, as Catholics, they knew their days would be numbered when the Communist government took total control of North Vietnam, a possible development which greatly concerned George Aiken.

"They were happy to leave as they feared for their lives," Blair said 64 years later as he described the crowded conditions on his ship. Now in his late 80s, Blair said that based on his own personal observations, he believed that there was a solid basis for that fear.

Eisenhower and his allies would frequently cite the "domino theory," which postulated that if South Vietnam fell under communist control, the other countries in Southeast Asia would follow suit. This policy was expressed by Eisenhower in 1954 as the reason for coming to the aid of South Vietnam, which meant supporting Diem with military and economic assistance. For many years to come, this philosophy would serve as the bedrock of U.S. policy toward Vietnam.

A review of Executive Sessions of the Senate Foreign Relations Committee, made public in the late 1970s and early 1980s, provides an important

Aiken Joins Foreign Relations Committee

window into the thinking of the Committee from 1954 to 1960.

It shows that in 1954, during Aiken's first year on the committee, the public posture was that the U.S. was trying to keep France in the Vietnam

As a young man, James P. Blair captured this scene on the USNS Marine Adder in 1956. Blair went on to have a distinguished and long career as a photographer for National Geographic. He retired to Middlebury, Vt. (Photo courtesy James P. Blair)

War, but the U.S. out of it. In 1977, Committee Chair, Sen. John Sparkman, D-Alabama, would write in the preface to the release of the 1954 Executive Sessions that the U.S. was actually trying to avoid helping the French:

> The truth is that by any financial or material measure we were already into the struggle up to our necks. But, in the backwash of the Korean War, opposition on the home front to any U.S. troop commitment was strong and too much in evidence to be challenged lightly by any public official, presuming even that you find one who genuinely believed that it would be in the U.S. interest to become involved at this point in 'another Korea.'

Sparkman's observations made evident that, even in 1954, the United States could not incur a prolonged involvement in Vietnam unless it had the solid support of the home front, the Congress and the international community. Sparkman's views reinforced for Aiken his earlier thinking that wars could not be successfully fought on Executive power alone. War, Aiken believed, was a shared national responsibility. If it did not exist in that context, no war effort could be sustained.

Aiken Warns of the Growth of Executive Power

During the period from 1955 to 1959, the work of the Senate Foreign Relations Committee was primarily focused on issues surrounding the Middle East, Latin America, and the expanding influence of the Soviet Union. Tension had grown between the Executive Branch and the Senate. The debate over the President's responsibility as Commander in Chief, which was in opposition to Congress' constitutional power to declare war, was a frequent discussion point in the committee, with Aiken on the side of the role of Congress in the decision-making process.

The buildup of U.S. military support for South Vietnam began in 1959, after it was evident that the forces in North Vietnam were building a supply route through Laos and Cambodia to aid their guerrilla attacks against the Diem government in the South. That supply route became known as the Ho Chi Minh Trail. The trail provided support for the National Front for the Liberation of South Vietnam, or, as it was more popularly known, the Viet Cong.

The Ho Chi Minh Trail planners had the same strategy that the North Vietnamese forces had had in 1953 when, by night, those forces moved men and materiel to surround Dien Bien Phu, an action that led to the eventual French defeat.

Months before the November 1960 Presidential election in the U.S., Ho Chi Minh, in failing health, was replaced by Le Duan as head of North Vietnam's ruling Communist party, but Ho retained his influence in the

Aiken Joins Foreign Relations Committee

party until his death in 1969. Like Ho Chi Minh, Duan believed that the North had the stamina to fight and defeat the Americans, no matter how long it took. It took another 15 years.

In 1959, Senator Aiken was fourth in line in seniority on the Republican side of the 17-member Foreign Relations Committee. Senator Alexander Wiley of Wisconsin was the ranking Republican, followed by Bourke Hickenlooper of Iowa and then William Langer of North Dakota, who died in office Nov. 8, 1959. Aiken's fourth place ranking was followed by Homer Capehart of Indiana and then by Frank Carlson of Kansas.

Senate Democrats on the Foreign Relations Committee in 1959 were Senators Francis Green of Rhode Island; J.W. Fulbright of Arkansas; John Sparkman of Alabama; Hubert H. Humphrey of Minnesota; Mike Mansfield of Montana (Aiken's long-time breakfast companion); Wayne Morse of Oregon; Russell B. Long of Louisiana; John F. Kennedy of Massachusetts; Albert Gore, Sr. of Tennessee; Frank Lausche of Ohio; and Frank Church of Idaho.

A sea change occurred in early 1959 when the then Senate Majority Leader, Lyndon B. Johnson, engineered a committee leadership change by convincing 92-year-old Senator Francis Green of Rhode Island to resign as Chair. Green was replaced by J.W. Fulbright of Arkansas, who then served many years in that position. From 1969 to 1975, Fulbright and Aiken were the two committee leaders. Both were also Vietnam War critics.

In the early spring of 1959, Secretary of State John Foster Dulles became ill and, after a hospitalization, resigned his post. He died a short time later. In April of that same year, the Foreign Relations Committee and the full Senate considered and approved the nomination of Under-Secretary of State and former Massachusetts Governor Christian A. Herter as Dulles' successor.

Meanwhile, the Cold War was heating up with the tensions between the U.S. and the Soviet Union escalating over Berlin. A major event that year was the famous "kitchen debate" between Vice President Richard Nixon and Soviet Premier Nikita Khrushchev at the American Exposition in Moscow. Later that same year, Khrushchev toured the United States and demonstrated his gregarious nature as well as his belligerent personality, having been personally refused entry by Walt Disney to his California theme park for being an unabashed Communist.

As a senior in high school, I vividly remember Nikita Khrushchev's visit to the United States, which highlighted the intensity of the Cold War tensions between our country and the Soviet Union.

Concerns about Diem

Declassified in 1982, Senate Foreign Relations Committee records revealed that in 1959 Admiral Harry Felt, Naval Commander and Chief of Pacific Command, was raising doubts about South Vietnam President Ngo Dinh Diem's rosy assessment of the military situation in Vietnam and Cambodia.

The main issue that most captured the attention of the committee during this time was neither military nor diplomatic. Instead, it was the charges of corruption and mismanagement of the American aid program to Vietnam. This issue caused the committee to hold a series of investigative hearings of the U.S. aid programs.

Fox Butterfield of *The New York Times* wrote in a summary of the Pentagon Papers that from 1954 to 1959, the insurgency in Vietnam could be divided into three periods:

From 1954 to 1956, Vietnam enjoyed relative quiet as the Communist cadres in the South were engaged in their political work trying to build support. After Vietnam President Diem rejected the scheduled elections that had been called for in the Geneva Accords, dissident Communist cadres began to increase military sorties against the South Vietnamese communities.

1. From 1956 to 1958, after President Diem rejected scheduled elections in Vietnam, dissent forces began their insurgency. At the same time, there was evidence of corruption and mismanagement of the administration of American aid.

2. In 1959, Hanoi decided to take over the direction of the insurgency

activities in the South, and, as a result, the civil war in Vietnam moved to a full-scale conflict. U.S. financial and materiel support continued to assist the South, as arms and other weapons arrived on a regular basis. The CIA, according to the Pentagon Papers, gathered intelligence that indicated that, by 1959, the North was infiltrating the South on a large-scale.

3. The first American blood had been shed in 1959 when three U.S. soldiers were killed in a guerilla attack on their living quarters near Saigon. The Vietnam War was now a simmering pot ready to boil over.

It had already been boiling over in nearby Laos. Laos was a small, landlocked country in the middle of the Southeast Asian peninsula, which straddled Thailand and South Vietnam. In 1960, The Eisenhower Administration was focused on how to keep it an independent country, in an effort to prevent it from falling under Communist control.

The day before John F. Kennedy was inaugurated as President, outgoing President Eisenhower advised Kennedy that Laos was the key to all of Southeast Asia, John M. Newman wrote in his book *JFK and Vietnam*. If Laos fell, Newman predicted, communist-controlled governments would take over and the U.S. would have to write off the whole area.

2

Aiken During the Kennedy Presidency

Aiken Begins His Push Against the War

John F. Kennedy was inaugurated on January 20, 1961 as the 35th President of the United States. At age 43, Kennedy was the youngest man ever elected to the Presidency. His election had been hard-fought; Kennedy only narrowly defeated Richard Nixon. The containment of Communism around the world had played a major role in the election, with Vietnam and Laos an increasingly important issue in the United States.

After taking office, President Kennedy continued the Eisenhower policy of only taking a limited role in Vietnam, hoping to avoid a broader commitment. While the issue of Vietnam hung over all policy debates, Kennedy and his new administration's failed efforts to liberate Cuba through a military invasion at the Bay of Pigs in April 1961 was an even more immediate dark cloud on the United States. The CIA had trained Cuban dissidents and had funded the invasion to overthrow the Communist government of Fidel Castro. But Castro's forces handily defeated the American-led forces, giving the new U.S. President a black eye. Kennedy, hesitant to commit to serious military action in the weeks following the Bay of Pigs fiasco, sought to shore up the South Vietnam government using limited means.

U. S. Commitment Escalates Secretly

The Pentagon Papers show that in May of 1961, Kennedy increased U.S.

commitment to Vietnam by ordering 400 Special Forces and 100 other military advisers into the war zone. This force conducted secret operations against the Viet Cong. No public announcement was made about this Presidential decision. The military targets were the Communist infrastructure such as railroads, roads, bridges, trains, and trucks.

Another aggressive measure was taken by Kennedy in January 1962, with "Operation Ranch Hand." In that undertaking, U.S. planes sprayed Agent Orange and other lethal herbicides over rural areas of Vietnam to kill vegetation and food that was used for cover by the North Vietnamese troops as they moved South. In reality, the use of Agent Orange destroyed local civilian crop lands and induced serious health issues for those exposed and for generations thereafter, precipitating a humanitarian crisis alongside all of the other aspects of the war.

What started as a program to offer advisers to the South Vietnam Army grew to broadening the U.S. military commitment to buttress the Diem regime. The Pentagon urged Kennedy to send in more ground troops, but Kennedy was not eager to follow that recommendation. Yet, by October 1962, according to the Pentagon Papers, the U.S. had 16,732, troops stationed in Vietnam.

On the ground, the North and its Viet Cong allies were gathering momentum and becoming bolder in their attacks. Trouble was brewing with the people on the streets of South Vietnam. Since Diem was a Catholic, his favoritism toward the Catholic minority alienated him from the Buddhist majority. Diem was under political pressure at home and was also generally described as stubborn and unmovable by Buddhist protesters in the streets.

Senator Mike Mansfield, D-Montana, at President Kennedy's request, made a trip to Southeast Asia in late 1962. He returned with a warning that the United States could not win the war by just adding more U.S. troops to the forces on the ground. Instead, Mansfield recommended that the South Vietnamese should increase their own fighting commitment by adding more of their own troops to turn back the Viet Cong and the North Vietnamese forces invading the South.

Mansfield also recommended that, unless the U.S. wanted to repeat the experience of the French, the Kennedy Administration should begin to withdraw the 16,000 U.S. troops that were already in South Vietnam. Kennedy did not like that recommendation, which would have made it appear that he had "lost" Vietnam and rejected Mansfield's advice.

Kennedy later told Mansfield in private that he had reconsidered Mansfield's advice. Kennedy and Defense Secretary McNamara then initiated a secret plan to withdraw up to 1,000 troops before the 1964 elections. Only Kennedy, McNamara, and other very senior staffers were aware of the planned withdrawal, and Mansfield kept the secret.

Viet Cong Surprises South Vietnam Forces

By January 1963, the Viet Cong fighters were gaining ground. At Ap Bac, a village in the Mekong Delta southwest of Saigon, a small unit of Viet Cong were able to defeat the South Vietnamese Army, despite the South's four-to-one military advantage and its technical assistance from the U.S. This victory was a major morale booster for the Viet Cong and their allies in the North. It also called into question the capability of the South's army.

Diem, the South's leader, was pushing the U.S. to send in more troops, a request not appreciated by Kennedy, even though it appears that his Vice President Lyndon B. Johnson may have initiated the expansion idea during an earlier inspection trip to South Vietnam. The domestic political situation in Vietnam during 1963 was in a state of decay. Diem's unpopularity was increasingly on the rise as the Buddhist majority was expressing its displeasure with his Catholic government.

In May 1963, The Diem Government opened fire on a Buddhist protest march in the Central Vietnam city of Hue. Eight people were killed. The killing led to more anger and in June, 1963, the Buddhists determined to show America and the world their opposition in a dramatic way. With Western media tipped off and watching, the Buddhists crowded into the streets as a 73-year old monk immolated himself on a major Saigon thoroughfare. This shocking incident was seen worldwide and received major coverage by the U.S. news media.

Eroding Confidence in Diem

Confidence in Diem's leadership began to erode within the White House as well as with the American public. The U.S. urged Diem to soften his stance and to negotiate with the Buddhists. Instead, in August 1963, Diem struck back against them and ordered his Special Forces to raid Buddhist pagodas throughout the country, leading to many arrests and an estimated hundreds of deaths and injuries. This shocked Washington and even some officers in the South Vietnamese army, amongst whom coup plans were being hatched.

In early November, the political turmoil within the Diem government had reached its breaking point. Kennedy had already decided to replace Saigon Ambassador Frederick E. Nolting with Henry Cabot Lodge, Jr., the man Kennedy had defeated for the U.S. Senate in 1952, and again in 1960, when Lodge had been Richard M. Nixon's running mate. The United States, led by Ambassador Lodge, with Kennedy's approval, backed the South Vietnamese military coup against the very unpopular Diem and his brother, Ngo Dinh Nhu, who held no formal position in the government but wielded great de facto powers in the country. Diem and his brother were supposed to be arrested and sent out of the country but instead were brutally murdered by the South Vietnamese army. Their mangled bodies were photographed and shown throughout Vietnam and the world.

Senator Aiken looks over the shoulder of President John F. Kennedy as he signs the Partial Test Ban Treaty on Oct. 7, 1963 in The White House Treaty Room. Vice President Lyndon Johnson looks on with other members of the House and Senate. The Treaty banned nuclear weapons testing in the atmosphere, in outer space, and underwater. (White House Photo)

The Diem coup led to a series of unsuccessful attempts

to form a stable government in South Vietnam. Between 1963 and 1965, South Vietnam had 12 different governments, all replaced one after the other by military coups.

The Vietnam War took another major turn later in November 1963, when President Kennedy was assassinated in Dallas.

The night of the assassination, Senators Aiken and Mansfield rode together to Andrews Air Force Base to greet Air Force One, which was to carry the body of the fallen President. On board that same flight was the new President, Lyndon Baines Johnson, who had just been sworn in—aboard the aircraft.

While I do not know first-hand what the two Senators discussed on that trip to Andrews, I do know from my conversations with Aiken, years later, that both of them knew of Kennedy's secret plan to withdraw all U.S. troops from Vietnam after the 1964 elections. Aiken assured me that Kennedy himself had privately conveyed this information to the two Senators.

Kennedy to Quit Vietnam After 1964?

George Aiken and Mike Mansfield had been informed by Kennedy that he was secretly planning to withdraw from Vietnam after the 1964 elections. Their belief that the withdrawals would actually happen was firm, despite the fact that President Kennedy had been an early supporter of Diem in the late 1950s and early 1960s. After the Bay of Pigs disaster and the tension around the October 1962 Cuban missile crisis as well as civil rights confrontations on the home front, Kennedy appeared less willing to rely on his military advisers for advice on how to deal with South Vietnam. Instead, he started relying on his own gut instincts, informed by the experience of the French. He concluded that the United States could not suppress a nationalist uprising and impose colonial rule over Vietnam.

Kennedy was a canny politician who strongly believed that Democrats in 1964 did not want to be blamed for "losing" Vietnam, as they had been by Republicans for "losing" China in 1949. The Truman Administration had been heavily criticized by Republicans in 1949, when, following a civil war in China, the leader of the Chinese Communist Party, Mao Zedong, declared the creation of the People's Republic of China.

Kennedy was cautious about the use of American land forces in Vietnam. He did approve the use of Special Forces, but he did so under the guise of providing advisers for flood relief for South Vietnam.

The breaking point for Kennedy appeared to be on Nov. 2, 1963, when Diem was assassinated. Three months before that, Kennedy had approved the sending of a cable to Saigon Ambassador Henry Cabot Lodge, Jr., which, in effect, was a blank check on behalf of the U.S. to help the South Vietnamese Army overthrow Diem. Kennedy said later that he had not expected for Diem to be killed but instead had thought that Diem would be exiled from the country.

Political commentator Chris Matthews, in his book *Jack Kennedy: Elusive Hero*, wrote that Kennedy, on Nov. 4, had dictated a memo for his personal files in which he described the process leading up to the August cable in which he signed off on giving the green light for the coup. Kennedy wrote in that memo:

> I feel I must bear a good deal of responsibility for it, beginning with our cables of early August in which we suggested the coup. In my judgment, that wire was badly drafted; it should not have been sent on a Saturday. I should not have given my consent without a roundtable conference at which McNamara and Taylor could have presented their views.

Kennedy had stated in his memo that General Maxwell Taylor; Secretary McNamara; Jack's brother, Attorney General Robert Kennedy; and John McCone, the Director of Central Intelligence had opposed the coup. Supporting the coup, the President wrote, was the State Department, led by Averill Harriman, George Ball, and Roger Hilsman, and further supported by Michael Forrestal, one of the leading aides to McGeorge Bundy, the President's National Security Advisor.

The death of Diem and his brother shook the President and began his thinking that the U.S. had to find a way to get out of Vietnam. Matthews also reported in his book that White House staffer, Kenneth O'Donnell, said that Kennedy had told him that once the 1964 elections were over, he was determined to get out of Vietnam.

Withdrawal was also the consensus view of Senators Aiken and Mansfield. By November 1963, Aiken himself was convinced that the U.S. involvement in the Vietnam War would not lead to any successful end.

Chris Matthews wrote that Kennedy's speechwriter, Ted Sorensen, said he didn't know what the President would have done after the 1964 election. "I do not believe he knew in his last weeks what he was going to do," Matthews quotes Sorensen as saying.

Was Aiken right about Kennedy's resolve to get out of Vietnam after the 1964 elections? We will never emphatically know the answer. After many years, the question is still being debated by historians and Kennedy biographers.

It was clear, however, that Kennedy was beginning to act on his view that the U.S. should withdraw from Vietnam. He had ordered that, by the end of 1963, some 1,000 Americans should be withdrawn. Tragically, on Nov. 22 at 12:30 p.m. in Dallas, shots rang out on his presidential motorcade. And, with the death of the President, his Vietnam policy of disguising withdrawal died with him.

3

Aiken During the Johnson Presidency

The Wise Old Owl Makes His Stand

On Nov. 26, the day after the State funeral for assassinated President Kennedy, the nation was in a period of profound grief and sadness. On that same day, Lyndon Baines Johnson, the Vice President who on Nov. 22 had suddenly become President, held his first National Security Council meeting.

At this meeting, Johnson asked Kennedy's national security team to remain in place because Johnson said he needed them even more than Kennedy had. As a result of that meeting, National Security Action Memorandum 273 reaffirmed the U.S. policy toward Vietnam, which was the same as the policy of the Kennedy Administration. It described the purpose of the U.S. involvement as serving to "assist the people and the Government of that country to win their contest against the externally directed and supported Communist conspiracy."

President Johnson was quite resolute in his views about Vietnam. "I am not going to lose Vietnam. I am not going to be the President who saw Southeast Asia go the way China went," Johnson said, according to Tom Wicker, the respected New York Times reporter and columnist.

The 1964 campaign was a contest between President Johnson and Arizona GOP Senator, Barry M. Goldwater. Goldwater had been trying to make Vietnam an issue by saying that the fact the U.S. had not stopped the Communist invasion from North to South Vietnam showed a fundamental weakness. The Arizona Senator called for increased military commitment, while Johnson was cautioning patience, saying that he did not intend to send American boys to do what the South Vietnamese military should do for themselves.

The Vermont Senator and Senator Smith of Maine were close friends. Aiken placed Smith's name in nomination as President at the 1964 Republican Convention in San Francisco. (U. S. Senate Photo)

Senator Aiken was not a political fan of Goldwater's. In fact, at the 1964 Republican Convention in San Francisco, Aiken nominated his friend, Sen. Margaret Chase Smith of Maine for the GOP nomination. Goldwater won the nomination, though, and while Aiken gave Goldwater tepid support, Johnson won an overwhelming victory in the election with 61.1 percent of the popular vote.

Even Vermont, for the first time in its history, voted for a Democrat for President. The Johnson victory also helped to propel Vermont Democratic Governor Philip H. Hoff to a solid victory for a second term, and it also swept Democrats for lower state offices into those jobs. Vermont was now no longer safely Republican. The politics were rapidly changing in the Green Mountain State, which meant that, over a short period of time, public support for the war in Vietnam had diminished, thereby giving Aiken political room to express his growing opposition to it.

Johnson Escalates the Vietnam War

While the 1964 election season was well underway, Johnson's first big Vietnam test came on August 2, 1964 when the U.S. destroyer Maddox, on intelligence patrol duty in the Gulf of Tonkin, was reported attacked by two North Vietnamese Patrol Torpedo (PT) boats. Another report on August 4, which later proved to be false, said that the Maddox and the ship C. Turner Joy, which had joined forces with the Maddox after the initial incident, had both been attacked by North Vietnamese PT boats. Within 12 hours of that report, U.S. bombers were launched from carriers and sent to North Vietnam on reprisal raids.

The Johnson Administration was eager to authorize the raids and make them public because the raids showed military strength, and also had the added advantage of shutting down Goldwater's frequent campaign criticism that Johnson was not a strong leader. While the Johnson Administration was relying on its executive powers to order the bombers to North Vietnam, it wanted assurance support from Congress. The Gulf of Tonkin Resolution was drafted by the Administration and introduced to both Houses of Congress.

The Resolution stated, in part, that, "The Congress approves and supports the determination of the President, as Commander in Chief, to take all necessary measures to repel any armed attack against the forces of the United States and to prevent further aggression." Several years later, evidence would reveal that the U.S. ships, which were allegedly attacked by North Vietnamese PT boats in 1964, were trying to respond to secret U.S. naval operations against the North in the Tonkin Gulf. To this day, it is unclear exactly how these events transpired. The United States could have fallen victim to the North's attack, or it also might have been the United States itself that provoked the confrontation. Historians are still debating the sequence.

In August 1964, the message to the public and Congress from the Johnson Administration was that the two ships were the targets of an "unprovoked attack" by the North. As part of the effort to convince Congressional leaders that the war authorization resolution was needed, Johnson invited senior leaders to the White House for a briefing. Present at the meeting, among others, was Senator Aiken.

In 1982, University of Vermont Professor Emeritus of History, Mark A. Stoler, wrote in the spring issue of the journal Vermont History that Aiken and Mansfield had been skeptical of both the facts surrounding the attack as well as Johnson's solution. "Apparently," Stoler wrote, "all of them concluded by the end of the meeting that they could not stop the President from exercising his powers as Commander-in-Chief, and that the North

Vietnamese attacks, combined with presidential authority, left them with no choice save to back the course of action upon which Johnson had already decided. They would have to endorse a Congressional resolution of support."

"It remained for Aiken to summarize this sense of resignation, as well as his own anger and helplessness, with a bitter (and previously unpublished) final reply to Johnson at meeting's end: 'By the time you send it [the resolution] up [to Congress], there won't be anything for us to do but support you.'"

After the presentation about the alleged facts of the attacks, Senator Aiken asked: "Are you sure, Mr. President?"

"Yes," replied Johnson.

With that assurance, a skeptical Aiken joined Senators Fulbright, Mansfield, and others to tell the President they would support him. When the resolution came to a vote on the Senate floor, it was approved by an 88-2 vote. The Resolution was opposed by only two Senators: Wayne Morse, D-Oregon, and Ernest Gruening, D-Alaska. It passed the House by a 416-0 vote.

So Congress passed the Tonkin Gulf Resolution, and President Johnson's war policy received almost no domestic criticism.

Years later, in 1971, the Tonkin Gulf Resolution was repealed. Until that time, it was the main congressional authority used by President Johnson, and then—for a while—by President Nixon, for conducting the war in Vietnam.

The Pentagon Papers later revealed that six months before the Tonkin Gulf matter, the U.S. had, in actuality, been conducting secret military attacks against North Vietnam, all the while preparing a resolution to be used, in case needed, to authorize Presidential actions.

In November 1964, just after the United States elections, the Soviet Union and China began to increase their support of North Vietnam by sending aircraft, artillery, ammunition, small arms, radar and air defense systems, food, and medical supplies to that region. Additionally, China sent engineering support to help North Vietnam build needed defense infrastructure.

When President Lyndon B. Johnson took his oath of office on January 20, 1965, he made it clear that the United States could not stand aside and remain peaceful in isolation. "Terrific dangers and troubles that we once called foreign now constantly live among us." This was a strong signal that Johnson and his administration would remain a strong presence in world affairs, including in Vietnam.

In February 1965, President Johnson ordered the bombing of targets in North Vietnam in retaliation for a Viet Cong attack of a U.S. base in the city of Pleiku. This act signaled an escalation in the war effort to try to stop the supply lines from North Vietnam. In March 1965, Johnson ordered "Operation Rolling Thunder," resulting in a three-year campaign of sustained bombing in North Vietnam and along the Ho Chi Minh Trail.

March 1965 proved to be a pivotal month as U.S. Marine combat troops landed on the beaches of Da Nang, South Vietnam, unbeknownst to the American public. This addition of troops was the result of Johnson's decision to approve the deployment of 18,000-20,000 fresh troops to support South Vietnamese military forces, as well as American interests. Johnson still wanted the escalation to be kept secret, though it was clear that he was deepening the American commitment to the war.

Johnson Digs In

As President Johnson was opting for escalation of the war, other voices within the Johnson Administration were urging for a different course of action. The most vocal person against sending in more troops was Under Secretary of State, George W. Ball, who proposed in April 1965, that the U.S. "cut its losses" and withdraw. According to the Pentagon Papers, another voice of opposition came from CIA Director John A. McCone.

The Pentagon Papers revealed that in July 1965, Ball sent a memorandum to President Johnson that boldly stated that the war was being lost. Ball wrote: "The South Vietnamese are losing the war to the Viet Cong. No one can assure you that we can beat the Viet Cong or even force them to the conference table on our terms, no matter how many hundred thousand white, foreign (U.S.), troops we deploy." Ball seems to ignore the many people of races and creeds who fought for the United States in Vietnam.

Instead, Ball recommended that Johnson seek a compromise solution that would allow the U.S. to, over time, phase down its involvement in the war. Around the same time, Senator Mansfield was urging Johnson to consider a proposal made by France's President Charles de Gaulle for the U.S. to support a neutral Vietnam. Again, Johnson rejected that advice and returned to a pronouncement he had made on April 7, 1965 at Johns Hopkins University, in which he spelled out why the U.S. was involved in Vietnam.

In essence, the President said that the U.S. was in Vietnam, "because we have a promise to keep. Since 1954, every American President has offered support to the people of South Vietnam. We have helped to build, and we have helped to defend. Thus, over many years, we have made a national pledge to help South Vietnam defend its independence. And I intend to keep that promise."

As he ended his pronouncement at Johns Hopkins, Johnson offered up a massive New Deal-like program for the countries of Southeast Asia. "For our part, I will ask Congress to join in a billion-dollar American investment for this effort as soon as it is underway." History records tell us, however, that no actual U.S. investment of this kind was made for economic and/or humanitarian assistance to help bring the war to an end.

During the first six months of 1965, the Johnson Administration was dealing with escalating political turmoil in South Vietnam: the government was unstable, and the Viet Cong were hitting United States' installations, including the U.S. Embassy in Saigon, in terrorist attacks. By early April, Johnson was authorizing increases in troop strength and the American forces to scour the countryside in an attempt to root out the Viet Cong insurgents.

For two months, Johnson kept these decisions secret from the American press and public. His secret authorizations included the dropping of bombs on Viet Cong positions with U.S. and South Vietnam fighter jets. After Johnson delivered his Johns Hopkins speech, some 15,000 college students in Washington rallied to protest U.S. bombing in Vietnam, an early indication that opposition to the war was beginning to build.

In 1965, in an effort to determine whether North Vietnam would negotiate, the U.S. announced a temporary bombing halt. However, North Vietnam ignored the overtures and used the halt to repair air defenses and infrastructure and to send more supplies south down the Ho Chi Minh trail.

On June 18, 1965, Nguyen Cao Ky became the prime minister of South Vietnam, while Nguyen Van Thieu was named the official Chief of State. Their appointments were the tenth change in South Vietnam's government in the past 20 months.

More Troops and More Protests

During the Fall of 1965, demonstrations for and against the war in Vietnam were playing out in the United States and abroad.

As Marines struck against the Viet Cong in the first major ground offensive by U.S. Forces, public opposition against the war was building in the U.S. This opposition was fueled by reports from Vietnam that aired on American evening news broadcasts.

In November, two specific events captured the minds of many Americans.

A report revealed that nearly 300 American soldiers had been killed and hundreds more injured in the first major confrontation for the U.S., in an assault known as the Battle of Ia Drang Valley. Helicopters were called in to rescue the surviving Americans, a strategy that would often be used in the war. After the battle, both sides claimed a victory.

In that same month, a tragic scene, reminiscent of a similar occurrence on the streets of Saigon in the early 1960s, occurred in front of the Pentagon when a 31-year-old Quaker from Baltimore set himself on fire in protest against the war.

By the fall of 1965, Senator Aiken was urging the President to listen with care to the voices of the American people and not just to those of his Administration. In a wide-ranging Oct. 21, 1965 Senate speech on foreign policy, Aiken said he hoped that in the election year ahead, there would be no effort by either Republicans or Democrats to seek partisan advantages over foreign policy. "At the same time," Aiken said, "I urge the President to weigh with great care the criticism and comments from those outside his bureaucracy, regardless of party. The President knows ours is not a society in which the King can do no wrong."

Even though Johnson was approving more

Senators Aiken and Mansfield greet South Vietnam President Nguyen Van Thieu, left, during a visit to Washington. Thieu served as South Vietnam president from 1967 until 1975. He resigned just before the fall of Saigon to North Vietnam in April. (Senate Photo)

troops for the war, he kept looking for another strategy and pathway out of the mess that he felt he had inherited from the Kennedy Administration. As part of that effort, on Nov. 7, 1965, Johnson asked Senator Mansfield to select and then lead a delegation of U.S. Senators to "study" the situation in Europe and Asia, as well as in Vietnam.

"I anticipate that this mission would result in reports by yourself and your colleagues which would provide useful supplements to the flow of information which comes through the regular channels of the executive branch," Johnson wrote.

Senator Mansfield selected members for the mission from the Senate at large. The final delegation included Senators Mike Mansfield; George Aiken; Edmund Muskie, D-Maine; Caleb Boggs, R-Delaware; and Daniel Inouye, D-Hawaii. Assessing Aiken's involvement, Mansfield said: "He provided not only a bi-partisan strength to our purposes, but also provided his great wisdom and judgment and his knowledge based on a long Senate and committee [Foreign Relations] experience."

This trip proved to have one of the most significant impacts on Aiken's

Aiken during the Johnson Presidency

view of the Vietnam War.

At the end of 1965, U.S. troop levels in Vietnam reached 184,300, and, according to Gallup, some 60 percent of Americans approved of the U.S. war effort in Vietnam. Near the end of 1973, by contrast, 60 percent of the public thought it was a mistake to have sent American troops to Vietnam.

Senators Aiken and Mansfield were in Saigon in December 1965, when they got a first-hand, up-front taste of the war. The American Embassy had recently been bombed and much of it was unusable.

In 1981, Aiken later related to Charlie Morrissey, chronicler of the notable George D. Aiken Oral History Project:

> We could hear the bombs dropping on the highways around the city where they were trying to keep the enemy, the North Vietnamese or Viet Cong, from getting in. And then Mike and I stayed there with Ambassador [Henry] Cabot Lodge three days and nights. On the last morning we got a call about five o'clock in the morning that they had bombed the Metropol Hotel which was a billet for American troops. Of course, we went down there as soon as we could. They really had bombed it. They had about 125 casualties.

Aiken also recounted that when he visited the injured soldiers, "one boy looked up and said that his brother was from Barre, Vermont. Another one said he spent his honeymoon in Vermont. But it was a bloody mess all around."

After leaving the hospital, the senators went to the Tan Son Nhut Air Base for the trip back to Washington. As Aiken got on the plane, he noticed a lot of smoke at the end of the runway. He asked one of the officials why? He was told that the U.S. military had just dropped napalm at the end of the runway so the delegation airplane could leave South Vietnam. The army believed that Viet Cong soldiers were trying to shoot down planes.

Aiken and his colleagues left Vietnam and returned to Washington on Dec. 18, 1965 with the taste of the war in their mouths. Aiken, along with the other members of the delegation, had travelled 30,000 miles in 30 days, and they were all physically and emotionally drained. At 73, Aiken had held up well, but he was glad to get back to Washington. Soon he would return to his beloved Vermont where, over the Christmas break, there would be no bombs--only quiet woods and fields.

But before his return to Vermont, on Dec. 19, Aiken, joined by Mansfield, delivered a first-hand verbal report to President Johnson of their findings made during their trip. Aiken told me in 1969, after I had joined his staff, that their report to Johnson was very blunt: the U.S. was not winning the war, and unless it was willing to commit up to a one million troops, there was no prospect of defeating the North. In short, the U.S. should withdraw like the French had done in 1954.

The advice was similar to what Gen. Mathew Ridgway had told President Eisenhower in 1954, when Ridgway recommended that the U.S. not send in ground troops to aid the French. Eisenhower followed that advice, and very soon France withdrew from Vietnam and ended its decades of colonial rule. Aiken and Mansfield unequivocally urged Johnson to leave Vietnam and to bring an orderly close to America's involvement. Johnson rejected their advice.

By Christmas 1965, it was estimated that some 90,000 South Vietnamese soldiers had deserted while some 30,000 North Vietnam forces had infiltrated the South by way of the Ho Chi Minh Trail. U.S. casualties were mounting each week. The Vietnam War was becoming a television living-room war as daily news feeds from the war zone showed the bloody conflict in real time.

By early January 1966, the Mansfield-Aiken delegation had issued a public report called "The Vietnam Conflict: The Substance and the Shadow." The public report was highly pessimistic and said that the war was open-ended and that there was "only a very slim prospect" of a just settlement by negotiations. The report said the more likely outcome would be a continuance of the conflict, which would rapidly develop into a general war on the Asian mainland.

Johnson Intensifies the War

The non-classified portion of the Mansfield-Aiken report was made public on Jan. 8, 1966 with its submittal to the Senate Foreign Relations Committee. On Jan. 11, the Senate Foreign Relations Committee held a closed session on the report. Senator Mansfield asked Aiken to summarize the trip and the findings of the report. A declassified transcript of that Jan. 11, 1966 closed session was made public in February 1993.

Mansfield and Aiken's report said that the war was "being run from Washington by way of Honolulu," meaning that military orders were all issued through U.S. military command in Hawaii, and that it was unpopular with other nations, even in Southeast Asia. Importantly, Mansfield and Aiken reported that there was no indication that Hanoi or the Viet Cong would quit the fight. The war was an "open-ended" military situation, the men reported, with no alternatives other than escalation or withdrawal.

Sen. J. William Fulbright, D-Arkansas, the committee chair, asked what he could tell his constituents who were asking, "What the devil are we doing there?" Fulbright's questions were soon answered during a series of televised hearings that ran through May, 1966 with leading administration officials from the State Department and the Defense Department who testified on the Vietnam War and the situation amongst civilians and refugees in Vietnam.

The national televised hearings, especially those with Secretary of State Dean Rusk and former Chair of the Joint Chiefs of Staff, Gen. Maxwell Taylor, provided the American public a first look at the issues involving the Vietnam War. Some of the hearings in the Spring of 1966 were also held in closed sessions. The transcripts from those hearings were not made public until 1993. These public and closed sessions provided a real-time road map on how our leaders were thinking about the war.

The televised hearings included many witnesses: Secretary of State Dean Rusk; Under Secretary of State George Ball; Vice President Hubert H. Humphrey, and Defense Secretary Robert S. McNamara, among others. It represented the first time that the Senate Foreign Relations Committee began to dig deep into Vietnam policy. At the time, the Committee was deeply split between the hawks and the doves on the Vietnam issue. A majority of the American public was supportive of the U.S. policy in

Vietnam, even though opposition to the war was building on college campuses throughout the nation.

The Senate Foreign Relations Committee hearings on Vietnam called by Senator Fulbright increased the private tensions between the two Southerners, Fulbright and President Johnson. Fulbright, who had supported the Gulf of Tonkin Resolution, had, by 1966, become totally disillusioned with the war. He was determined to use Johnson's request for $275 million in supplemental foreign aid to focus public attention, and some anger, on the war effort.

The Fulbright hearings were held in the ornate Senate Caucus Room on the Third Floor of the then Old Senate Office Building, now the Russell Office Building. It was an historic room, the venue of many important moments in history. Senator John F. Kennedy had announced his 1960 presidential campaign there, as would his brother, Robert F. Kennedy, who announced his run for the presidency as an anti-war candidate on March 16, 1968.

During the hearings, Aiken would ask witnesses to explain their views on the current developments in Vietnam. As was his personality, Aiken was not combative toward a witness, but would ask incisive questions in an attempt to get some straight answers.

Aiken: "When do you stop chewing?"

During a televised hearing with General Taylor on Feb. 17, 1966, Aiken asked a series of questions about whether France and Japan were performing well, economically and socially, after they had withdrawn from Vietnam. Aiken commented that he thought nations could "bite off more than they can chew, and the question is when do you stop chewing?"

While some of his colleagues, who were very opposed to the war, like Senator Frank Church, D-Idaho, would try to reduce the amount of foreign aid assistance, Aiken, although a war opponent, would take an alternative point of view. Aiken felt that the more people that knew about the cost of war, the more they would be ready to lobby for it to be stopped.

Aiken's method of asking questions was often like offering up a fast pitch for the batter to swat at; the speaker would soon realize there was a hidden curve ball. For example, Aiken asked General Taylor if he was still giving advice to Johnson on troop levels, and also asked whether the President was listening. Before Taylor could answer, Aiken said, "Well that's probably an unfair question because if he wasn't, you wouldn't be here today." In this way, Aiken would get his point across without appearing to badger a witness, in contrast to the techniques often utilized by his colleagues, Chairman Fulbright and Senator Morse of Oregon.

The Fulbright hearings clearly enlarged anti-war sentiments. Protests were held at the end of March 1966 in New York, Washington, Chicago, Philadelphia, Boston, and San Francisco.

By early 1966, Johnson was so deeply involved in the Vietnam War that he would often lament how his efforts to implement many Great Society programs, and other items on his domestic agenda, were being neglected.

By April, the White House was closely supervising possible bombing targets in North Vietnam. The targets tended to be power facilities, war-support facilities, fuel storage tanks, transportation centers, and air-defense installations. The U.S. also started bombing oil facilities around Hanoi and Haiphong yet remained hesitant to carry out bombing runs on targets within the limits of the city of Hanoi, fearing that focusing on city targets would bring the Chinese into the war.

Anti-War Sentiment Begins to Build in Vermont.

Some Vermonters tended to follow Senator Aiken's thinking on the Vietnam War, but the state remained overall in support of U.S. policy in Vietnam. But by 1965, the average Vermonter was beginning to show more public signs of disagreement with President Johnson's Vietnam policies. By 1966, Aiken's growing opposition to the Johnson War policy was reflected in his comments on the Senate floor, in his letters to constituents in Vermont, and in what he said during the public hearings before the Senate Foreign Relations Committee. By the spring of 1966, some months before

Aiken's famous Oct. 19, 1966 speech, the anti-war movement in Vermont was picking up steam, led by religious leaders and peace activists.

In Vermont, most of the anti-Vietnam War opposition had been, for the most part, the focus of private conversations rather than large public meetings or protests. That changed on April 23, 1966, when a gathering at the Vermont State House called "The Vermont Community Meeting on Vietnam and Southeast Asia" was held on an early spring Saturday. The event was organized by Vermont religious and community leaders who were eager to hear the views of leading national figures. The format provided an opportunity for Senator Aiken to deliver a major speech on Vietnam after the 150-200 estimated attendees first heard from William Bundy, the Assistant Secretary of State for Far Eastern Affairs.

Following Aiken's address, a Vermont town meeting-like discussion was moderated by the state's top political journalist, Vic Maerki of the *Burlington Free Press*. According to the *Free Press* account of the event, published on Monday, April 25,1966, with no by-line but likely written by Maerki, Aiken was described as having "set aside some of his differences with President Johnson to give broad endorsement to the manner in which the President is conducting the war effort in Vietnam."

The *Free Press* story continued, "Aiken predicted that the United States will ultimately succeed in Vietnam, but he warned it will take a long time to bring about the desired results. Aiken also stressed that a military victory in Vietnam would prove too costly unless the United States continues to promote economic, social and political programs." Aiken was quoted as having said that he saw no easy way for the United States to get out the "ugly" predicament, but he offered the following suggestions, according to the *Free Press* account:

> I would not intensify the bombing of North Vietnam or extend the war beyond its present state. I would not withdraw from South Vietnam unless asked to do so by a responsible government of that country. With the protection which our bases can afford, we should continue to promote economic, social and political programs, without which a military victory could only be pyrrhic in nature.

Attending the event was the Rev. William Sloan Coffin, Jr., Yale Chaplain, and a leader of the national anti-war movement. The Coffin family also had a Vermont connection as it owned a home in Strafford. Coffin chided Aiken for not being tough enough in his opposition to the war. The *Free Press* story reported: "Aiken shot back that he had a duty to argue his point—and also a duty to support the President after a decision had been made."

This response by Aiken to Coffin's criticism captures the dilemma the Senator often confronted during the Vietnam War. While Aiken was a war critic, he would give the President deference when a Presidential decision was counter to his advice.

Nevertheless, after President Johnson rejected Aiken's advice following his Oct. 19, 1966 speech, Aiken started telling Vermonters and the media that there would be no change in U.S. policy as long as Johnson remained President. In a letter to a constituent from South Burlington, dated Nov. 13, 1967, Aiken lamented, "The President, however, is undoubtedly sincere in his belief that his present policies are correct, so I am not optimistic that there will be much change in our direction under this Administration." Aiken believed that a national political change was needed before the Vietnam War policy would be changed.

International opposition to U.S. involvement was also escalating. On Sept. 1, 1966, French President Charles de Gaulle, while in Cambodia, called for the withdrawal of American troops from Vietnam. By early October 1966, the Soviet Union announced its intention to provide

President Lyndon Johnson pats George Aiken on the shoulder during Aiken's 73rd birthday celebration held on Capitol Hill on Aug. 20, 1965. (Senate Photo)

military and economic assistance to North Vietnam.

Also, by October, Johnson announced he would conduct a war conference in Manila with American allies. He had been searching for the right time, and it was this announcement by President Johnson that prompted Aiken to finally deliver his major, now famous, speech on Vietnam, eventually called "Vietnam Analysis—Present and Future."

President Johnson signs into law the Aiken Rural Water Bill in October 1965. In the background is Senator Mike Mansfield and Vermont Gov. Philip H. Hoff. Standing in the far right is the author, Stephen C. Terry, then-reporter for the Rutland, Vt., Herald. (White House Photo)

On October 19, 1966, George Aiken went to the floor of the Senate and began to speak:

> The size of the U.S. commitment already clearly is suffocating any serious possibility of self-determination in South Vietnam, for the simple reason that the whole defense of that country is now totally dependent on the U.S. armed presence.
>
> Considering the fact that as every day goes by, the integrity and invincibility of the U.S. Armed Forces is further placed in question because there is no military objective, the United States faces only two choices: Either we can attempt to escape our predicament by escalating the war into a new dimension, where a new so-called aggressor is brought into play, or we can deescalate the war on the ground that the clear and present danger of a military defeat no longer exists and therefore de-escalation is necessary in order to avoid any danger of placing U.S. Armed Forces in a position of compromise.
>
> Faced with these alternatives, the United States could well declare unilaterally that this stage of the Vietnam war is over—that we have 'won'

in the sense that our Armed Forces are in control of most of the field and no potential enemy is in a position to establish its authority over South Vietnam.

Such a declaration should be accompanied, not by announcement of a phased withdrawal, but by the gradual redeployment of U.S. military forces around strategic centers and the substitution of intensive reconnaissance for bombing.

This unilateral declaration of military victory would herald the resumption of political warfare as the dominant theme in Vietnam.

This suggested strategy is not designed to solve the political problem of Vietnam.

It is simply designed to remove the credibility of U.S. military power—or more loosely the question of "face"—as the factor which precludes a political solution."

Aiken then concluded, "In all probability, our military strength would have to be deployed in that area for many years to come. We are a Pacific power, and no nation in southern Asia—possibly not even North Vietnam itself—would feel at ease were we to announce withdrawal from that responsibility."

The above speech has been called by historian Gregory Allen Olsen, Editor and Publisher at Texas A&M University, one of the "landmark speeches of the Vietnam War."

Lyndon Johnson and George Aiken were friends. In August 1965, Johnson had arrived at the U.S. Capitol to help celebrate Aiken's 73rd birthday. A year later, in August 1966, President Johnson came to Burlington to again join Aiken for his 74th birthday, which was also an opportunity for Aiken to show off the first Rural Water Project in Addison, Vermont. The grant money for the project had become available due to Johnson having signed into law the Aiken Rural Water and Sewer program in October 1965.

Then came Oct. 19, 1966, the day Aiken made his now famous Senate speech on Vietnam.

Aiken's timing on the speech was calculated to be delivered just before Johnson left Washington for his conference in Manila, where the President was to meet with American allies for an important war conference. The news that came out of that meeting in Manila was that the U.S. and its allies would withdraw from Vietnam within six months if North Vietnam would withdraw its troops from the South. This proposal went nowhere. Aiken was hoping for a lot more, and the lack of results from the conference left him dispirited.

On Oct. 26, 1966, President Johnson travelled to South Vietnam for the second time to visit the U.S. troops at Cam Ranh Bay. By this time, U.S. troop strength in Vietnam was 389,000, with 5,008 combat deaths and more than 30,000 soldiers wounded. During 1966, the American Allies fighting in Vietnam included 45,000 soldiers from South Korea and 7,000 Australians. Also, in 1966, an estimated 89,000 soldiers from North Vietnam intent on waging war infiltrated the South, via the Ho Chi Minh Trail.

Many years later, Dr. Patrick Stine, a Vermont physician who had served in the medical corps in South Vietnam, said about his Vietnam experience that the South Korean forces were the best trained and the most effective of all the allied forces in killing Viet Cong or North Vietnam regulars. "They were vicious fighters," Stine said. "If we wanted to win the war, we should have let them do it."

President Johnson had ignored Aiken's advice, and relations between the two old Senate friends cooled and social invitations to the White House abated. Still, Johnson sent Aiken a warm note after Aiken married his longtime assistant, Lola Pierotti, on June 30, 1967. Lola, Aiken's chief of staff, was a long-established figure on Capitol Hill. Her positive relations with Johnson's Capitol Hill Chief of Senate Liaison, Mike Manatos, ensured that political differences over Vietnam did not result in the White House freezing out Aiken's interest in projects that affected Vermont.

That same attitude did not extend from Johnson to Senator J. William Fulbright, D-Arkansas, the Chair of the Foreign Relations Committee. By then, Fulbright and Johnson were no longer speaking. In early January 1967, Fulbright had published the *The Arrogance of Power*, a book that was very critical of American war policy in Vietnam. Fulbright pushed for direct peace talks between the South Vietnamese government and the Viet Cong in his book, as he did in the Senate. Johnson was critical of Fulbright when talking to the media and to other opponents of the war. Johnson started calling them "Nervous Nellies and Sunshine Patriots."

Johnson Goes All-Out

When President Johnson delivered his State of the Union address before Congress on Jan. 10, 1967, he was resolute: "We will stand firm in Vietnam." On the same day that Johnson stood before the Congress, the U.N. Secretary-General, U Thant, expressed his doubt that Vietnam was essential to the security of the United States.

In early February, President Johnson acknowledged that there was no serious effort by North Vietnam to help to stop the war. At the same time, American religious groups were joining the nationwide anti-war movement, an escalating crusade to protest the war.

After a mid-February truce during Tet, the Vietnamese New Year Holiday, Johnson announced that the U.S. was resuming the bombing of North Vietnam. Senator Aiken was filled with despair. Despite his and others' warnings and advice, the war in Vietnam was expanding.

On March 1, 1967, Aiken delivered a speech on the Senate Floor entitled: "What Does the United States Seek in Vietnam?" The speech summarized Aiken's frustration:

> Mr. President, we have just concluded the second year of accelerated warfare in Vietnam. It was just two years ago in February 1965, that the Marines were dispatched to Danang to prevent what appeared to be a serious threat of military defeat to U.S. forces in Vietnam. Had our Marines at Danang been defeated at that time, the forces of South Vietnam itself would have been in very serious jeopardy. What happened in those two years?
>
> The only thing we can say definitely is that the threat of military defeat to our forces no longer exists; it has been removed. All else is as uncertain now as it was then.

> Meanwhile, 6,500 Americans have been killed and 45,000 wounded. Many times that number of Vietnamese soldiers and civilians from the factions on our side and the factions adhering to the Viet Cong have also been killed and wounded. We have spent at least $50 billion in military expenditures and another several in economic aid expenditures over the last two years. But this is not all the cost. At home the post war, bipartisan consensus, which since World War II supported the conduct of foreign policy in its important dimensions, has been fragmented. The conduct of foreign policy has become a major source of unrest and frustration all across our land.

Aiken reminded the Senate that the U.S. had said it was prepared to negotiate if it could get a positive signal from the other side, "but it is still unclear what it is we are prepared to negotiate about."

Aiken continued, "What is it that we have not won which we still seek to win? Surely, it is not a military victory beyond that which we have already achieved, for no military objective has ever been stated."

Aiken referred back to his October 19, 1966 Senate Floor speech:

> That is why I made so bold last fall to suggest that the President and our allies at the Manila Conference declare, militarily, the war had been won. I still believe that such a declaration would bring to the surface the essential political problems which beset the Vietnamese people and which only the Vietnamese people ultimately can resolve.

Finally, pronouncing what had been at the core of his issue with the U.S. war effort in Vietnam, Aiken concluded: "What makes the Vietnam War so incredible to so many here and abroad is the spectacle of the United States, largely through deployment of its matchless military power, attempting to reengineer the society of Vietnam."

Once again, Aiken's warnings went unheeded. One week after Aiken's floor speech, on March 8, 1967, Congress authorized an additional $4.5 billion to finance the war.

The cost of the war was rapidly escalating.

Aiken during the Johnson Presidency

The Tet Offensive, 1968

The entire nation was on edge as the calendar turned to 1968. The war in Vietnam was raging. Protesters were out in the streets. U.S. Sen. Eugene McCarthy, D-Minnesota, was challenging President Johnson in a primary for the 1968 democratic nomination.

Senator Aiken had wanted to retire from the Senate. He had been in politics since 1931. After two-terms as Governor, he had been in the U.S. Senate since 1941. At age 76, he was in good health, yet longed to come home to Vermont. That all changed when his close friend, Senator Mansfield, persuaded Aiken to promise that he would run again in 1968. Mansfield argued that, as a result of the escalating Vietnam War, the country needed Aiken's policy advice in the Senate.

The forthcoming year would prove a very important one in Aiken's political life. Aiken's decision to run again meant that he could become the ranking Republican on the Senate Foreign Relations Committee in January 1969. That is, if he was re-elected, which he easily was. Aiken received the nomination of both the Vermont Republican and Democratic Parties.

Aiken's Senate career would continue until Jan. 2, 1975.

Americans soon began to witness a dramatic change in the war in Vietnam. On Jan. 31, 1968—the beginning of Tet Offensive and the lunar New Year—nearly 70,000 soldiers from North Vietnam and their Viet Cong allies launched a surprise attack on U.S. and South Vietnamese installations throughout the South. The war shifted from its rural to its urban centers. More than 23 separate battles erupted throughout South Vietnam.

The Tet Offensive shocked Americans and further called into question the validity of U.S. policy in Vietnam. The Johnson Administration and its military tried to spin Tet as a U.S. military victory, but the critics of the war didn't buy it. In response to claims that the U.S. military had in fact "won" Tet by repelling North Vietnam and its Viet Cong allies, George Aiken wryly observed: "If this is a failure, I hope the Viet Cong never have a major success."

One of the most repellent photos of the war was taken on Feb. 1, 1968, at the start of Tet, when a Viet Cong guerrilla was shot in the head by South Vietnam's police chief, Gen. Nguyen Ngoc Loan, in full view of NBC news cameras and the Associated Press. The gruesome photograph appeared on the front pages of most American newspapers, and the taped footage aired on NBC-TV.

A despicable metaphor that became emblematic of America's conduct during the devastating conflict came from an American officer, who said of a village that had been leveled by American bombers, "We had to destroy it, in order to save it."

After Tet, the Johnson Administration was in turmoil over war strategy. Despite the public face that Tet was a U.S. victory, the military planners were urging for yet another big injection of American troops into South Vietnam. During the week of Feb. 11-17, 1968, 543 American soldiers were killed, the highest recorded number of American deaths during the war, and a constant and painful reminder of the war's bloody toll.

The Joint Chiefs of Staff had presented Johnson with an additional request to increase U.S. troop strength by another 206,000, a decision that Johnson agonized over. At the end of February, Johnson attended a meeting of the National Rural Electric Cooperative Association in Dallas, where he gave a speech about the war. Johnson told audience members that there would be more bloodshed and more voices of protest, but that he still vowed to continue the effort.

The public opinion body blow for Johnson came not from the battlefields in Vietnam but from Walter Cronkite, the CBS News anchor. At the time, Cronkite, the most admired and credible TV anchor, was watched nightly throughout the Nation. The former UPI newsman and World War II correspondent had recently returned from his own reporting trip to Vietnam. He regularly shared his views of the war on his nightly broadcast:

> "To say that we are closer to victory today," Cronkite said, "is to believe, in the face of evidence, the optimists who have been wrong in the past. To suggest we are on the edge of defeat is to yield to unreasonable pessimism. To say that we are mired in stalemate seems the only realistic, yet satisfactory conclusion.

Aiken during the Johnson Presidency

Johnson was reported, by his advisors, to believe that if he lost Cronkite that he had lost the support of "Middle America."

Meanwhile, Defense Secretary Robert S. McNamara continued to push for continued military support, despite the fact that, for at least two years, McNamara had been privately disillusioned with the war. At the end of February 1968, McNamara notably resigned and announced that he would become the President of the World Bank. There was much speculation, later, that Johnson had forced McNamara's resignation and had nominated him for the World Bank position as a way to get him out of Vietnam War policy formulation.

On Feb. 27, 1968, a farewell lunch for McNamara was held at Dean Rusk's office at the State Department. According to several historians, including Stanley Karnow in his book Vietnam a History (1983), the out-going Defense Secretary had expressed his deep reservation about the U.S. Vietnam War policy. Later, author Paul Hendrickson, in The Living and the Dead: Robert McNamara and Five Lives of a Lost War (1996), described a very distraught McNamara lamenting the mistakes of the U.S. military policy involving Vietnam and regretting his role in not stopping the war.

The decision to replace McNamara with Clark Clifford—a Washington insider, an establishment figure, and a former adviser to President Truman—triggered a new review of the Vietnam War strategy in early March 1968.

Meanwhile, Senator Aiken had been telling Vermonters in his constituent letters that no change would take place in U.S. war strategy until a change of administrations took place in Washington. For more than year, Aiken had, in essence, stopped believing that he or fellow antiwar Senators could convince the President to change course.

As a reporter for the Vermont Press Bureau in 1968, as I covered Aiken from my post in Vermont, it was very clear to me that, on the war issue, he had, indeed, given up on his long-time friend, Lyndon Johnson. Aiken's advice to Johnson was never taken while the man served was President. However, we do know that after Johnson left office, he told his friend Leonard

Marx, the former United States Information Agency (USIA) Director, that "Aiken was right" on his advice to get out of Vietnam.

After I joined the Senator's staff in 1969, I learned that Aiken knew then that even Johnson's mentor in the Senate, Sen. Richard B. Russell, D-Georgia, had long been privately urging Johnson to withdraw from Vietnam. Russell, a Southern conservative, was, for many years, the Chair of the Senate Armed Services Committee and was quite close to the President.

The March Bombshell

It did not take Clark Clifford long—once he started digging into the policy options for Vietnam—to conclude that no overall plans or strategy existed to allow for a military victory. Clifford told Johnson that the President should not continue to escalate the war and that the time was at hand to make decisions about the best future policy, with respect to the war.

This advice came at a time when Gen. William Westmoreland had placed before Johnson, yet again, a request to increase troop strength by 206,000, a request that was leaked to the press. The leak caused much consternation within the Administration, and as a result, Secretary of State Rusk was ordered to appear before the Senate Foreign Relations Committee for live testimony on the U.S. war policy.

A political bombshell exploded on March 12, 1968 when Johnson only won, by a narrow 300-vote victory, the New Hampshire first-in-the-Nation Presidential primary. That election result was universally viewed as a major political defeat for Johnson and proof that Johnson had lost support for his policies. Meanwhile, Sen. Robert F. Kennedy, D-New York who was on the edge of announcing his candidacy for President, offered Johnson a political deal. Kennedy would not run if Johnson would appoint a high-level commission, which included Kennedy, that would create a new policy course for the U.S. in Vietnam. Johnson, who did not like Kennedy, firmly rejected the offer.

On Saturday, March 16, Robert Kennedy went to the Senate Caucus Room and announced his candidacy for President. His platform was based on opposition to the war in Vietnam. At that point, anti-war protests were gaining supporters throughout the country, and Johnson now had two Democratic Senators running against him on the war issue, Kennedy and Minnesota Democrat Senator Eugene McCarthy.

In Vermont, Democrats were splitting off from Johnson. Most dramatically, on March 22, 1968, Vermont Gov. Philip H. Hoff became the first Democratic Governor to say he was supporting Senator Kennedy. Hoff's announcement brought to a head his own building opposition to the war.

In early December 1967, when Hoff was in Washington for the lighting of the national Christmas Tree on the Mall, he tried to engage Johnson on the war issue. President Johnson curtly cut him off. Johnson told Hoff to go home and run his business as governor and said that he, Johnson, would continue to run the country. Hoff was determined to continue his opposition, though, and he informed members of the Johnson Administration that he was going to endorse Kennedy. Johnson offered to send Secretary Rusk to Vermont to brief the Governor. Hoff declined.

Prior to his announcement of his endorsement of Kennedy, Hoff made one last call. He asked Senator Aiken if Aiken knew of anything that would cause Hoff to change his mind about the two candidates. Aiken said he knew of no reason Hoff should be dissuaded from his endorsement of Kennedy. Hoff then called a press conference for 4 p.m. on March 22, 1968, one day before the Vermont Legislature was scheduled to adjourn. State House reporters, of which I was one, knew that it would be a major announcement about the war.

While praising Johnson for acting "bravely and resolutely in the face of overwhelming adversity" Hoff said the time had come for a fresh approach to overcome what he called a "national sickness of spirit." Hoff went on to say that, "Senator Kennedy's candidacy offers the most realistic possibility for the people of America if we are to achieve the national regeneration of spirit that is so desperately needed."

The Hoff announcement made national news because the Vermont chief executive was the first to break from the ranks of Democratic governors. As it turned out very soon thereafter, Hoff's break was the first major crack before the political dam burst.

On March 26, Secretary of Defense Clark Clifford convened a meeting of a dozen of the so-called "Wise Men" to gather advice about the war. All but four of them advocated withdrawing from the war zone. Then, on Sunday, March 31st, during an address to the Nation, Johnson dropped a bombshell by announcing his unexpected decision to not seek re-election. He simultaneously urged Hanoi to begin peace talks. Johnson also proclaimed a partial bombing halt while stating that the U.S. would not bomb north of the DMZ, including Hanoi.

The Dark Spring of 1968

The anti-war effort picked up another powerful figure when civil rights leader, The Rev. Martin Luther King, Jr., joined those opposing President Johnson's war policies. Dr. King argued that the war was morally wrong and was draining away federal dollars that were needed to finance Johnson's Great Society programs. However, Dr. King's resounding voice was stilled on April 4, 1968 in Memphis when he was assassinated. His death sparked racial riots and unrest in more than 100 America cities, as fires broke out and smoke billowed through urban centers. A combination of racial unrest, demonstrations that turned into riots and destruction of property, and student protests erupted on campuses throughout the country. Students at Columbia University took over five buildings on the New York City campus. This protest touched off other student demonstrations across the country.

Meanwhile, the war in Vietnam was deteriorating. In April, the siege of Khe Sanh ended with the U.S. command quietly shutting down the Khe Sanh air base and withdrawing the marines who had been fighting there. On April 11, Defense Secretary Clifford announced that General Westmoreland's request for 206,000 more troops would not be approved.

The presidential primary continued with Democratic candidate, Vice President Hubert H. Humphrey, choosing not to contest in the states with elections, but, rather, to focus on gathering delegate support in those states with conventions. In the states with elections, Senators Kennedy and McCarthy slugged it out with one another. After Senator McCarthy won the Oregon primary, Robert Kennedy knew that he had to win the delegate-rich California primary to remain a viable candidate for the nomination.

Senator Kennedy did win the California contest and many Americans living on the East Coast went to bed after midnight thinking that he was on his way to the nomination. However, even after this victory, Kennedy was still short the required number of delegates needed for the nomination. That reality was further, and irrevocably, shattered when news came that Robert Kennedy had been killed by an assassin's bullet, shortly after giving a victory speech. America was overcome by grief due to the murder of a second prominent Kennedy family member.

The peace talks that began in Paris in early May became immediately bogged down. The U.S. demanded that the North Vietnamese troops withdraw from the South; the North insisted that the Viet Cong be at the peace table. The negotiation stalemate lasted five years before, finally, a resolution was reached in 1973. Meanwhile, the Vietnam War was hitting the United States' pocketbook hard. In July 1968, Congress approved a 10 percent income tax surcharge to help finance the War's ever-increasing costs.

At the same time, former Republican Vice President Richard M. Nixon was campaigning hard for the 1968 Republican nomination for President. As a reporter for the Vermont *Rutland Herald*, I was present at the Miami Beach convention hall in early August of that year and witnessed Nixon pledge, after he had won the nomination, that he would bring an "honorable end to the war in Vietnam." Nixon proclaimed that he had a "secret plan" to bring the war to an end.

Senator Aiken did not dispute Nixon's claim and was pleased to hear that the war in Vietnam would be an issue during the 1968 presidential campaign. As Aiken had been stating for more than a year, a change in administrations was necessary before the United States would enact a change in its Vietnam War policy.

The Presidential campaign of 1968 was bitter and controversial. Vice President Hubert Humphrey won the nomination after a raucous Democratic convention in Chicago, where more than 10,000 anti-war protesters were confronted by more than 26,000 Chicago police and National Guardsmen under the command of Mayor Richard J. Daley. The brutal and heavy-handed effort to control the protest was nationally televised, as were the many arrests accompanied by tear-gas that filled the area around Grant Park.

The Chicago Convention had a major impact in Vermont, too. Governor Hoff had considered becoming a protest candidate as Vice President but withdrew after more moderate Vermont Democrats talked him out of it. It had become clear that Hoff's friend, Sen. Edmund S. Muskie, D-Maine, would be tapped as Humphrey's Vice-Presidential running mate.

My Vermont Press Bureau colleague, reporter John Mahoney, was assigned to cover the Democratic convention. Once on the ground, John shed his reporter impartiality and joined the protest movement. Once he could no longer cover the Democratic convention, I took over for him. The contrast between the Miami and Chicago political events could not have been sharper.

John left journalism shortly thereafter and, in time, moved from Vermont to Canada, where he still lives with his wife, Jane, engaged in music and gardening. John had served in the Army in the past and wasn't one of those men facing service in Vietnam. Rather, like many thousands of others, the Vietnam War drove an American family out of the country.

The 1968 presidential campaign was waged against a backdrop of social unrest, with more than 220 student protests held at 101 colleges and universities around the country. The Republican Party was united as the party that would stop the war and restore "law and order," while Democrats were sharply divided and were pushing Senator Humphrey to make a break from Johnson on the war issue.

At the end of October, Johnson, once again, announced that he had stopped bombing in North Vietnam with the hope that the cessation would allow peace talks to restart in Paris.

As the 1968 Election Day drew near, the Johnson Administration declared that it was willing to entertain the possibility of a coalition government between the North and South with the Viet Cong to run South

Vietnam. This goal was an anathema for President Thieu. Thieu resisted the idea and became firmly opposed to it when he heard from a Nixon representative that he should hold out and expect a better deal if Nixon was elected President.

Nixon had sent that message through Anna Chennault, the China-born widow of Claire Chennault, the U.S. General who organized the Flying Tigers, a group of American pilots who had fought the Japanese in China during World War II. Anna Chennault was a noted socialite in Washington, D.C. She also was a fundraiser for Nixon's 1968 campaign.

Chennault's message to Thieu was meant to slow down any Thieu endorsement of a peace agreement with Johnson while he was still President. Johnson was furious when the FBI told him about the meddling by Nixon. Johnson called Nixon and confronted him about it, on Nov. 3, 1968, only a few days before the election. Nixon lied and denied it.

Johnson called Nixon's intervention "treason." Privately, GOP Senate leader, Everett Dirksen, agreed with the President. After a very close election, Nixon won by defeating Humphrey as well as third-party candidate, Alabama Gov. George Wallace.

By the end of 1968, U.S. troop levels in Vietnam had reached 495,000, with 30,000 deaths to date. By then, over 1,000 U.S. soldiers were dying per month in the war, and many more than that were injured each month. It was estimated by military historians that by 1968, 150,000 forces from North Vietnam had infiltrated the South. The North was still able to send soldiers and supplies, arms, munitions, and food, South via the Ho Chi Minh trail.

4

Aiken During the Nixon Presidency

Aiken's Crucial Last Term

In late April 1969, the Vermont Legislature was nearing adjournment when an end-of-the-session party was held in Montpelier. One of the attendees was then Republican Gov. Deane C. Davis, who had just completed his first legislative session. One of the most controversial bills which secured passage and became law was Vermont's first sales tax for which Davis had advocated.

I was Chief of the Vermont Press Bureau at the time, which was the news bureau that covered the State House for the *Rutland Herald* and the *Barre-Montpelier Times Argus*. As such, I had chosen to cover that debate in great detail throughout the session, much to the discomfort of the Davis Administration. Governor Davis made his unease quite evident when he told the crowd at the end-of-session party that he was glad that I going to Washington to join Sen. George D. Aiken's staff as an Aiken Fellow, and would be leaving reporting for a while. Aiken and Lola chose the fellows themselves, usually every other year; they were paid a stipend from the Senator's staff allowance.

After the session came to a close, it was with excitement and much anticipation that I loaded up my 1968 Volkswagen and said goodbye to my then wife, Sandy, and our one-year-old daughter, Megan as I left Waterbury to make the 10-hour trip to the Nation's capital. As I crossed from Maryland into the District of Columbia, I was listening to a local AM radio station and kept hearing an ad by an organization called Pride. It was urging residents to sign up for the "War on Rats" to help exterminate a rat infestation that had been prevalent in many neighborhoods local to Capitol Hill. For a Vermonter, whose familiarity and comfort level was more commonly with deer, woodchucks and squirrels, the notion of "rats on the loose" was a startling introduction to my new life.

Senator Aiken's staff had rented a place for me to stay at a hotel on Second and C Streets, Southeast, which was on the House side of the Capitol Complex. As a naive country boy, I was unaware that in the big city, you had to lock your car, even for a very few minutes, while you weren't in it. When I checked into the hotel, I was unable to carry all my belongings in on a single trip. When I returned to the car 20 minutes later for the rest of the luggage, it had all been stolen!

The Old Senate Office Building on Constitution Avenue, where Aiken's office was located, was just a short walk from my hotel. His office was Suite #358. I arrived early, as I knew Aiken and his wife, Lola, his Administrative Assistant, were usually in the office by 6:30 a.m.

Aiken had been in that office since he had first arrived in Washington, in 1941. Prior to that, Suite #358 had been the office of the late Vermont Senator Ernest W. Gibson, Sr., and then, for a short time, his son, Senator Ernest W. Gibson Jr., who was appointed to the job by Governor Aiken after the senior Gibson died in office in June, 1940. Aiken and the younger Gibson were long-time Windham County political allies and remained so for nearly 50 years.

My first day in the office, April 28, 1969, was eventful. Lola introduced me to the small staff of nine people, and set me up at a desk in a big room right next to Aiken's Office. Also working in the room were Lola and Elizabeth Quinn from Jeffersonville, who was Aiken's Executive Assistant. Aiken's office suite included five large rooms for the nine staffers. All but one of the staff were from Vermont.

Aiken did not have a Vermont office, believing that Vermonters could reach him easily at his Washington office. Aiken's office received constant phone calls and a high volume of mail each day from Vermonters and others, and the Senator did his best to faithfully act on the sentiments expressed by his constituents when he felt they were justified.

The first official business for me that day was to be taken to the Senate Disbursing Office in the Capitol and to get signed up for the Senate payroll. In those days, Senate staffers were paid in cash. Staffers needed to go to the payroll office each Friday and stand in line to get their brown pay envelopes. That practice continued for several more years until a direct-deposit system was introduced when the Senate started to modernize its functions with newer technologies.

My initial duties were to attend Aiken's Senate committee hearings and to take notes. Since I was known to most Vermont state officials because of my years as a State House reporter, I was soon assigned to projects that involved state agencies seeking federal help—usually federal money. I was also included in the Vermont constituent meetings with Senator Aiken, where I took notes and kept track of constituents' requests. Often, this part of my job included making appointments with federal agencies for those Vermonters.

The most important event of each day was to deal with the Vermont mail, delivered twice and sometimes three times a day. The mail would be opened by a staffer and placed in a box for the Senator to read. Once Aiken finished looking over the mail, Lola would then pull out the many social invitations and any other mail of a personal nature. The routine was then for Charlie Weaver, Aiken's long-time aide who had joined the Senator in 1954 after his work as editor of the Burlington Daily News, to look through the box to take out any letters involving agriculture and energy issues. Lastly, I would review the box and take out any letters involving State of Vermont issues and foreign policy matters, usually regarding Vietnam.

Vincent P. "Bill" Wilber, a retired official from the Agency of International Development and a former reporter at the *Rutland Herald* in the late 1930s, served for two years on Aiken's staff. He assisted the Senator with foreign policy issues. A month after I joined the staff, Wilber retired, and his foreign policy duties were turned over to me. I was ecstatic! I eagerly jumped into the task by spending as much time as I could with staffers on the Senate Foreign Relations Committee where Aiken was the ranking Republican at the time.

The protocol in Aiken's office was that any letter that arrived in the morning mail was to be answered and signed by Aiken by either the end of that same business day or, most certainly, by the next business day. If it took longer to research the problem and to provide the constituent with an answer, a letter would be sent to acknowledge receipt of the request with the status of the information being sought.

Before 8 a.m. each morning, I would also place a call to my friend, Norman James, the news director at WDEV at the time, to get a quick fill-in of the top Vermont news of the day. In 1969, no internet existed to bring us fast-breaking news. Those early morning calls provided substance for a short memo that I drafted for the Senator with the day's headlines. He often used this information to ask questions of Vermonters when they called or visited his office. At 76-years-old, the Senator, who did not have an office in Vermont, wanted to reassure his constituents that he was still very much on top of the issues at home.

At 8 a.m., during the days the Senate was in session, Senator Aiken, Lola, Betty Quinn and I would walk over to the Senate Dining Room. Lola and the Senator would sit at a separate table with Senator Mike Mansfield, and the three would engage in private conversations over coffee and English muffins. During the walk back to Aiken's office, the Senator would say nothing about the topics covered in the Aiken-Mansfield breakfast. He considered that information private.

Once back in the office, at 8:30 or so, the Senator would read over the morning papers—*The New York Times* and the *Washington Post*—that I would have picked up at about 6:40 a.m., on my way to work. The Aiken office subscribed to all the Vermont daily papers, as well as some of the weeklies. The papers would usually arrive by mail, two days later, and be perused by Aiken. The Senator would pay particular attention to *The Brattleboro Reformer*, the *Rutland Herald*, and the *Burlington Free Press*. He also reviewed the weekly, The Suburban List, published in Essex Junction. Many Senate offices had staffs located in both Washington and their home states. The Aiken office, based entirely in the Capitol, did not have a widely disbursed daily news summary. Instead, Aiken staffers were expected to be up to date about Vermont by reading one of the Vermont newspapers. Stories that included Senator Aiken were to be marked, later cut out and then saved for future reference or stored in the Aiken files.

About 9:30 a.m., the Senator would often punch one of the buzzers on his desk to call a staffer into his office for a piece of information or to discuss an issue. My call was a four-buzzer ring. When I heard that ring, I would jump up and enter his office. I would find him either at his desk, with a large photo of the Vermont State House behind it, or resting on a big leather couch. He usually had a question that pertained to an upcoming committee meeting he would be attending at 10 a.m. or to an issue to be voted on later in the day on the Senate Floor.

Since I was a former Vermont reporter, the Senator would often refer to me as his "newshound" and would begin our conversations by asking: "Anything new in Vermont?" In fact, Aiken had made it a practice to name "Aiken Fellows" from the Vermont press corps. The first one he named was Vic Maerki of the *Burlington Free Press* in 1965. Vic was followed by Tony Marro of the *Rutland Herald*, in 1967. I was named an Aiken Fellow in 1969. Unlike Maerki and Marro, who returned to journalism, I remained as a staff member, serving the Senator until Jan. 2, 1975.

The 1968 Presidential election, held on Nov. 5, was a nail-biter. The winner was not declared until the next morning, when television networks announced that Richard M. Nixon had won over Vice President Hubert H. Humphrey. Vermont followed the national voting trends and chose Nixon over Humphrey by more than a 15,000-vote margin. In state elections, Vermonters voted for Republican business leader Deane C. Davis for Governor over incumbent Democratic Lt. Gov. John J. Daley, a veteran who had seen serious combat in the South Pacific as a Marine in WWII. Senator George D. Aiken strolled back into office without any General Election opposition. To return to office, Aiken had spent a grand sum of $17.09.

Aiken's victory was momentous. With Nixon's election, a result that Aiken favored, the Vermonter's role in the Senate changed dramatically.

Aiken during the Nixon Presidency

In January 1969, Vermont's senior Senator returned to Washington to become the Dean of the Senate and the ranking Republican on the Senate Foreign Relations Committee. He served as the leader of that committee with veteran Democratic Chair, Sen. J. William Fulbright, D-Arkansas.

Aiken had been a long-time critic of the Vietnam War when Johnson was President. Now, he had to hope that Nixon would carry through on his "secret plan" to bring the war in Vietnam to an end.

As the GOP's chief contact on the dovish Senate Foreign Relations Committee, Aiken was expected to carry the new Administration's messages and strategy on the war issue into the Senate. While he was hopeful that Nixon would make good on his pledge, Aiken was prudently guided by a heavy dose of, "Let's see what happens."

Giving Aiken some confidence about what Nixon would do about the war was the new President's appointment of William P. Rogers as Secretary of State. Rogers had been Attorney General in the Eisenhower Administration. Before that, he had worked as a Senate staff lawyer, where he and Senator Aiken had become acquainted.

When I joined Aiken's staff, in April 1969, the U.S. troop levels had peaked at 543,000. By then, 33,641 Americans had been killed, a total that had exceeded the number of U.S. deaths in the entire Korean War.

The news cycle, dictated as it was by daily newspapers and a burgeoning television news scene, helped set the political agenda in Washington as it had earlier in the war. The critical influence of the news became evident when *The New York Times* reported in May that two months before, Nixon had ordered the secret bombing of Cambodia by U.S. B-52s, which targeted the supply lines along the Ho Chi Minh Trail where supplies were infiltrated from the North to the South.

As a result of the leak of the Pentagon Papers to the *Times*, Nixon ordered FBI wiretaps on four journalists and 13 government officials, including some on the staff of the National Security Council, in an effort to try to track down the "leakers." This action was the start of Nixon's war on the press, which he and his staff felt was the "enemy" of the administration.

Every night, on the evening news, the nation listened to and watched graphic and horrifying reminders of the deadly impacts of the Vietnam War.

A grizzly and futile combat engagement occurred during a 10-day period in May in which 46 men of the 101st Airborne died during the battle that became known as "Hamburger Hill," near Hue. Another 400 were reported wounded. U.S. troops eventually won the hill and were then ordered to abandon the ground. Once the Americans left, the North Vietnamese Army moved back in and re-took the hill unopposed.

The costly battle led to a political outcry in the United States. Critics of the war pointed to that battle as evidence that the war in Vietnam had resulted in the senseless loss of American lives. Nixon's Pentagon, now under the leadership of Defense Secretary Melvin Laird, a former Congressman, issued new field orders to Vietnam Commander Gen. Creighton Abrams. The order said that the United States would allow no future "Hamburger Hills" and that that fight would be the last search-and-destroy mission the U.S. conducted to try to eradicate North Vietnam and Viet Cong strongholds.

In the future, the administration communicated that only smaller military actions would be used to engage the enemy. When reviewed in hindsight, this newly announced military strategy indicated a major turning point in the war and came at an important time because morale among the U.S. draftees serving in the war was at a very low point. Drug usage was also becoming rampant among those serving in the combat zone.

On May 14, 1969, Nixon made his first national televised speech on Vietnam. He offered a peace plan in which America and North Vietnam would simultaneously withdraw from South Vietnam over the coming year. Hanoi rejected the offer.

"Vietnamization"

On June 8, Nixon met with South Vietnam President Nguyen Thieu at Midway Island, and Nixon told the South Vietnamese leader that U.S. troop levels would be reduced. At a press conference held at the end of the meeting, Nixon announced a U.S. troop withdrawal of 25,000 men. Senator Aiken was pleased by this development. When briefed privately before the announcement by the White House, Aiken publicly praised Nixon's actions as a positive development.

It was this war-policy change that caused Aiken to want to verify the weekly U.S. troop levels. At his instruction, I established a contact at the Pentagon whose job it was to keep a weekly head count. The result was that at 9 a.m. every Monday, I would call my contact and get the number of troops still in Vietnam.

I would write a very short memo to Aiken with the information that included the weekly totals and the amount of troop reduction from the previous week. If the number kept going down, then Nixon's war policy would continue to have the Vermonter's support.

Vietnamization was introduced by the Nixon administration during his first term as a framework for turning control of the war effort over to the government of South Vietnam, such that the United States could withdraw its troops in the field. The earned media attention that the plan enjoyed was short lived when the June 27, 1969 edition of Life magazine displayed the photos of all the 242 Americans killed in the previous week, including the 46 who had died on Hamburger Hill the previous week. The pictures of the Americans killed had a profound nationwide impact that resulted in an avalanche of anti-war mail to Aiken.

Looking through some old books and magazines some 48 years later in a musty attic in Corinth, Vermont, I was reminded, once again, of the emotional impact of this Life magazine issue, which had so vividly depicted the terrible cost of this seemingly endless war on an entire generation of young Americans—as well as on their families and communities.

In June, Senator Aiken was back in Vermont to deliver the graduation address for the 10 graduating seniors at Cabot High School. The 77-year-old Aiken had a special message about the war in Vietnam for the 18-year-old graduates in one of Vermont's most rural communities.

Aiken told the seniors that the war was having a distressing impact:

> Now we have something more serious than the historical impatience of youth.

> We are now seeing some of our young people radicalized because of world events — primarily the war in Vietnam.
>
> The values of American Life—equality, justice and liberty—have lost their meaning for many of them.
>
> Many of our young people are morally outraged by the great paradoxes of our time. They can't understand why young people have to fight wars which are promoted by those who would increase their own influence and power.
>
> They are unhappy, and frequently with justification, that our country has tried to force its ways upon other people.

Through his Cabot address, Aiken sent a message that he understood the protest against the war, which was once again ramping up across the country. Since I was one of his younger staff members, Aiken told me that he wanted to be sure that he was still connecting with young Vermonters.

Shortly thereafter, back in Washington, Nixon sent a secret message to Ho Chi Minh in July through a French emissary, urging Ho to agree to a war settlement. At the same time, Nixon said he would resume bombing if no agreement had been reached by Nov. 1, 1969. Hanoi responded by insisting that no peace talks could be held without the Viet Cong at the table.

In July 1969, Nixon began the gradual troop withdrawals; as troops returned home from Vietnam, others were sent into the warzone to maintain the stability of U.S. command in Vietnam, a process which continued into 1972. Each week, Aiken would monitor the withdrawals.

For the Senator, one of his happier moments of the Nixon Years came on July 25, 1969, when the President announced the Nixon Doctrine. The essence of the new Doctrine was that the U.S. would provide economic and military assistance to countries around the world fighting against Communism, but that no more American troops would be deployed on the ground in Vietnam or elsewhere.

In the place of American ground troops, the U.S. would rely on in-country South Vietnamese troops, but only when those soldiers were backed by

U.S. airpower and technical assistance. In effect, the U.S. would support local war efforts, but would no longer provide U.S. ground troops. For Aiken, the Nixon Doctrine represented a major policy shift. It had his full support.

Senator Aiken reaffirmed his support for the new Nixon policy during a speech on Oct. 11, 1969 at Norwich University. In it, he outlined why he had not supported the Johnson policy in Vietnam. Aiken said that Johnson's policy "in Vietnam was mighty unpopular, even with me, but he [Johnson] lay down his political career because of Vietnam and that was an honorable act."

Later in the speech, Aiken turned to the topic of Vietnam again:

I am here only going to repeat the heart of my objection—what I feel to be the heart of the Vietnam tragedy—because it is central to my thesis today.

The tragedy of Vietnam is that we have prevented self-determination through the weight of our intervention, even while proclaiming the preservation of self-determination as our goal.

It may or may not have been possible to reach this goal if we had acted more wisely; I gladly leave that kind of speculation to the historians and Monday-morning quarterbacks.

But ever since President Kennedy decided to intervene and consigned the first 35,000 troops to Vietnam, and President Johnson decided to intervene further with massive force after the attacks on our installations at Pleiku and elsewhere in February 1965, we have prevented self-determination in Vietnam just as surely as has the force that we have called the aggressor.

When the war became an American war and the government in Saigon came to exist only by Washington's consent, all hope for a settlement vanished—with the end not yet in sight.

I am afraid we have not even yet learned this lesson," Aiken observed.

Reflecting on Nixon's Vietnam War policy, Aiken remarked, "He is launching a new Asian policy which, in his words, will avoid commitments that could involve us in the internal struggles of nations there.

Say We Won and Get Out

> I, too, believe that the sooner we can reduce our presence in South Vietnam, whether or not the Paris peace talks make progress, the sooner we will escape from a predicament very largely of our own making.
>
> But we cannot achieve instant gratification through a precipitate withdrawal of our troops.
>
> The President needs time, and I for one, will do my best to see that he gets it.

In September 1969, Ho Chi Minh died and was replaced by Le Dann, who was much more militant than Ho. Dann said that Ho wanted his people to continue to fight "until the last Yankee is gone."

Another major event in September was the news that the Army would bring murder charges against Lt. William Calley over the massacre of Vietnamese civilians at My Lai in March 1968. The news of this massacre precipitated much larger-than-normal volumes of angry mail from Vermonters protesting the atrocity and demanding justice.

My Lai was very much on the minds of the "Moratorium" peace demonstrations in Washington that October, as well as at the "Mobilization" peace march on Nov. 15, 1969, which drew an estimated 500,000 to Washington for the largest anti-war protest in United States history. It was one of many major peace marches held that day across the country. Senator Aiken kept his office open on that frigid November Saturday for marching Vermonters who needed a respite.

A month earlier, public opinion polls showed that Nixon still had the support of 71 percent of the American public, including Aiken. On the day of the peace marches, Nixon reportedly spent the day inside the White House watching football.

The Silent Majority

The prospect of the peace marches did have an impact on the Nixon White House. Nixon was convinced that the North Vietnamese were bolstered by the growing war opposition in the United States. In fact, Henry Kissinger, the National Security Advisor, was urging that the U.S. troop withdrawals be slowed down, arguing that North Vietnam would have less incentive to negotiate at the peace table if it could wait out the domestic opposition in the United States to undermine support for Nixon in the next election.

The Vietnamization plan also appeared to employ massive airpower, with more South Vietnamese troops on the ground to leverage the North at the peace table. Politically, Nixon needed U.S. public opinion to support his policies as Democratic opposition was on the rise. On Nov. 3, 1969, Nixon addressed the nation and gave an update on the war in Vietnam.

Nixon began his national address, with this premise:

> I believe that one of the reasons for the deep division about Vietnam is that many Americans have lost confidence in what their government has told them about our policy. The American people cannot and should not be asked to support a policy that involves overriding issues of war and peace unless they know the truth about that policy.

Nixon said that by the time that he had become President in January, the war had been going on for four years and 31,000 Americans had already been killed in action. Nixon added that the training program for the South Vietnamese soldiers was behind schedule, and that 540,000 Americans were currently serviced in Vietnam, with no plan to reduce that number. Finally, Nixon said that no progress had been made at the peace table in Paris, and that the war was causing deep divisions at home.

Nixon said his strategy was to "win the peace" in Vietnam. To accomplish that, he asked for support from the "great silent majority of my fellow Americans." He added that "The more divided we are at home, the less likely the enemy is to negotiate at Paris…North Vietnam cannot defeat or humiliate the United States. Only Americans can do that."

Nixon's address drew support from many Republicans, Southern Senate Democrats, and national labor and veterans' organizations. Senator Mansfield expressed his disappointment in the talk, as did Senators Fulbright, McGovern, and Church. That address was the beginning of the end of goodwill from the doves on Vietnam. They figured that nine months had been enough time for Nixon to make a dramatic change from the policies of Johnson.

As this first year of the Nixon Administration came to an end, Nixon ordered another 50,000 troops to be withdrawn from Vietnam. Overall, the U.S. fighting forces in Vietnam had been reduced by 115,000 since Nixon took office. At the same time, the U.S. death toll had risen to 40,024, and the number of South Vietnamese forces on the ground was increasing.

While U.S. troops in Vietnam had declined in number, little progress had been made at the peace table in Paris. This failure in Paris led to the resignation of the chief U.S. negotiator, Henry Cabot Lodge, Jr., and the stalemate continued. At this point, Aiken was still supportive of President Nixon's policies when Aiken would speak from the Senate floor. He offered important political support to the media as long as the phased troop withdrawal continued.

Aiken Shocked by Cambodia Bombing

The year 1970 began with B-52 bombers striking the Ho Chi Minh Trail as the American Air Force tried to stem the tide of North Vietnam supplies being sent down the trail. Peace talks in Paris were still deadlocked. Henry Kissinger had begun a series of secret talks with North Vietnam's Le Duc Tho, a process that continued for the next two years. The political and military situation in Cambodia was very unstable when, in mid-March, the Cambodian leader, Prince Sihanouk, was deposed in a coup by General Lon Nol. Soon after, a Cambodian revolutionary named Pol Pot pushed out Lon Nol and launched a brutal regime. By the end of Pot's rule, an estimated one and a half to two million people had died due to starvation, executions, and forced labor.

In 1970, President Nixon, began his second year in office by focusing primarily on foreign policy. Besides Vietnam, he also had a big world-shaking event in mind. He had dispatched Henry Kissinger on a top-secret mission to determine a way to open diplomatic doors with Mainland China.

Nixon and Kissinger's diplomatic triumph eventually happened in early 1972.

In reality, Nixon, originally from the California political world, was a pragmatist. He made it clear that he was not going to engage in social issues that would water down his negotiating power. He had no interest in fighting with the Democratic Congress over most domestic legislation. Instead, he was content to let his moderate Republican Cabinet members work with Congressional Democrats on domestic legislation. Nixon kept most of his political capital for political showdowns on foreign policy matters.

On the home front, Nixon kept the anti-war movement and the country's allies off balance by continuing an aggressive policy of withdrawing U.S. troops. On April 20, 1970, Nixon announced the withdrawal of another 150,000 troops during the year ahead. Yet, during March and April, the secret U.S. bombing raids continued over Cambodia in an effort to shut off the supply lines from the North. The bombing raids were intended to keep the Viet Cong and the North Vietnamese Army from fighting a guerrilla war against the Americans and the South Vietnamese.

Nixon Stuns the Nation

Shortly before 9 p.m. on April 30, 1970, President Nixon sat alone in the Oval Office, watching the clock and waiting for the signal to begin his live television address to the Nation. His speech preparations had been completed, and he was ready. In fact, the military invasion he would announce had already begun; American combat troops were already moving across the Vietnam border into neutral Cambodia.

The speech marked another turning point for the Nation, but not for Nixon. He had decided, some time ago, to expand the Southeast Asia battlefront. For the President, the question had been when to make the move and how much force to use. In his mind, events in the war zone had made this the right time militarily, and Nixon himself had done all he could to make it the right time at home. He had prepared for the Cambodia announcement 10 days earlier by making another primetime television appearance to tell war-weary America that another 150,000 U.S. troops were coming home.

George Aiken, among others, had touted the April 20th troop withdrawal announcement as hard evidence that the so-called Vietnamization policy was not just a Nixon trick. The President clearly would keep his promise to end the war. The continuing troop reductions convinced Aiken that he was right when he urged fellow war critics to give Nixon more time.

Until the evening of April 30, when he made his address, Nixon had been the Peace President. Now he was prepared to show the world that as a hard-eyed commander, he would not be bullied by Communists nor by critics. The speech this night would be tough, threatening, and filled with righteous indignation.

In the final minutes before airtime, Nixon appeared as a passive participant while the television makeup crew attempted to smooth out the deep lines that accented his dark jowls and that gave him that sinister look, so beloved by two generations of cartoonists.

Several blocks away, in his fifth-floor apartment in the Methodist Building, Senator Aiken waited fretfully for the speech to begin. He was tired and was growing more depressed by the minute. Aiken had begun work, as usual, at 6:30 a.m., and most of the day had been spent in dealing, in one way or another, with the Vietnam/Cambodia situation. A series of telephone calls, committee hearings, and meetings, during the past 14 hours, had provided a prologue for Nixon's televised appearance.

Lola was in the apartment's kitchen hurrying to clean up the dishes in time for the speech. Earlier in the evening, she had driven Aiken to the White House for a congressional leadership meeting with the President, and they had only been home for a few minutes. As they waited, Aiken stood over his latest jigsaw puzzle, spread out on a card table in the living room. Normally, jigsaw and crossword puzzles were reliable pastimes for Aiken, but the leadership briefing had upset him beyond the ability of these distractions. He paced to the window and stood staring out at the East Front of the Capitol.

Lola reminded him to turn on the television set, which they were seated in front of when Nixon greeted millions of American viewers by restating his recent promises. "Ten days ago," he said, "in my report to the nation on

Vietnam, I announced a decision to withdraw an additional 150,000 Americans from Vietnam over the next year."

The Aikens had watched that earlier speech on the television in Lola's Montpelier house during a six-day visit to Vermont. They had spent three days in Montpelier and three days in Aiken's Putney home, so they had had plenty of time to get a reading on how the folks back home were feeling. They had returned to Washington convinced that the electorate was still with Nixon. Though the war remained on everyone's mind, for the most part Vermonters seemed to feel the same way Aiken did about Nixon's efforts, so far. Aiken repeatedly told Vermonters he talked with, "The President needs more time and I, for one, will give it to him," He assured them that Nixon, unlike Johnson, was keeping him and Congress informed.

In the spring of 1970, college campuses were quiet, constituent mail had dropped to a trickle, and, most importantly, the man in the White House was consulting with and evidently listening to the elected officials on Capitol Hill. For the first time in 10 years, Aiken's hope for peace seemed justified. At home, Aiken had found Vermonters preoccupied with state politics and local issues. Antiwar liberals were squared off against self-proclaimed conservatives in all the big races, with the conservatives holding front-runner status. Nixon had carried Vermont by a large margin in 1968 and was still in good favor.

Across the Nation, however, the draft had started to affect everyone, making the war a topic for debate in schools, churches, town halls, and around dinner tables.

Washington was tense with anticipation. Rumors were spreading that said a new crisis was building in Southeast Asia. Even in Vermont, the newspapers poured out wire-service stories quoting unidentified sources who warned of an imminent escalation of the conflict. Aiken did not put much faith in these unnamed officials' reports. In recent years, such anonymous sources usually turned out to be a Senator or Congressman who wanted to run for president.

Three decades in the Senate had reinforced Aiken's inclination to rely only on verifiable, and on his own, observations. When *The New York Times* reported on April 23, 1970 that the U.S. had agreed to sell arms to Cambodia, Aiken called officials in the State Department. They called him back at his home in Putney. They confirmed the *Times'* story but declared that these new arms sales did not appear to be cause for alarm. Despite widespread talk that Nixon intended to widen the war, the facts were that, for the first time since Kennedy was President, the number of troops in Vietnam had been reduced. Nixon had said all along that his plan was to turn the fighting over to the Vietnamese —basically the same position that Aiken had tried

From left to right, Senator Edward Brooke (R-MA), Senator Norris Cotton (R-NH), Senator Margaret Chase Smith (R-ME), Senator Aiken (R-VT), President Richard Nixon, Arthur Burns, Chairman of the Federal Reserve Bank, and an unidentified official. (White House Photo)

to get Lyndon Johnson to take several years earlier.

Johnson, of course, had rejected Aiken's advice and had instead tried to threaten and to beat the North Vietnamese into submission. He had failed, and consequently had been driven out of the office that he had spent his entire life trying to capture. It was, Aiken thought, a sad end for a man who otherwise might have been a great President. Nixon, the beneficiary of Johnson's great blunder, had privately assured Aiken that he would not make the same mistake. Three weeks after taking office, Nixon had described for Aiken how he planned to extract America from the Asian war.

Now, 15 months later, Nixon's phased withdrawal of troops was underway and, until March 1970, the number of GIs being killed had declined month by month.

As recently as March 31, Aiken had been involved in a long telephone conversation with Nixon, during which Aiken said he did not catch any hint from Nixon of a shift in war policy. The President had called him at home that night to talk about another matter. The talk was casual and friendly, and it ranged over a wide number of topics. There was no doubt in Nixon's mind, either before or after the call, that Aiken opposed any expansion of the war, as the old Vermonter has advised Nixon and the administrations prior. Right up until the evening of April 30, 1970, Aiken had believed the President was listening to him. More precisely, Aiken had believed that Nixon was a realist who knew that if he expanded the war, he would almost certainly become the third president whose legacy would be stained by it.

The pre-speech briefing at the White House, which began at 7 p.m., two hours before the speech commenced, had punctured Aiken's confidence in Nixon, a confidence that had been based on Aiken's faith in his own ability to judge people, a carefully tended skill that had nothing to do with whether he liked or disliked a person. Until the White House briefing, Aiken had been confident that Nixon was, above all else, a practical politician who had survived and prospered because he avoided the fatal traps of ideology, pride, and political principle. Aiken had believed that Nixon, the man who beat Hubert Humphrey with a "secret plan" to end Lyndon Johnson's war, would not, now—just two years later—turn Vietnam into "Richard Nixon's War."

Of course, everyone who had spent much time in Washington knew that what Nixon said and what he did were not always the same thing. But now that Nixon was President, Aiken felt that the Nation should give him the benefit of the doubt, at least until there was good reason not to.

Say We Won and Get Out

Nixon's Speech to the Nation

So at 7 o'clock on April 30, Aiken went to the White House expecting to meet with the man that the columnists had been calling the "New Nixon"— the President who wanted to work with, rather than fight against, the Congress; the leader who had the wisdom to put good men like Bill Rogers and Melvin Laird into key positions; the savvy politician who understood why Senators should have the right to choose federal judges for their own states. That night, Aiken found, instead, a belligerent, self-absorbed, and didactic man who wanted to lecture the congressional leadership, rather than consult with it.

Nixon clearly had called congressional leaders in as a perfunctory gesture, a last-minute detail that was merely part of his speech preparation. He quickly outlined what he was going to tell the Nation one hour later in a speech that was unmistakably in the manner and style of the Old Nixon, the testy hard-liner who had been rejected by the American voters in 1960. The 10-year metamorphosis was suddenly reversed, and his performance on the night of April 30th was, as Henry Kissinger described it much later, vintage Nixon.

Lola had waited outside in the car for Aiken while he was inside the White House. When he returned to the car, she said later, his disappointment was painfully obvious. The night was warm and sharply different from the raw weather they had found in Vermont a week earlier. The two of them drove quickly through the light, early evening traffic of downtown Washington and were back in the apartment in plenty of time to listen to the President's speech. Aiken took out one of the white legal pads he often used to take notes, knowing that the press would soon be telephoning for a response.

"The ranking Republican," the media would call Aiken in the reaction newspaper and television stories, and "the Dean of the Senate." As usual, most reporters would be looking for blood: a chance to use Aiken as a weapon against Nixon. The Washington press had never liked Nixon, and this speech exacerbated their anger towards Nixon as nothing ever had before, giving the press the excuse they wanted to use Aiken's own words against Nixon.

The President's face nearly filled the screen of the television "I warned," he said, referring to what he had told the nation ten days before, when announcing the withdrawal of 150,000 troops from Vietnam, "that if I concluded that increased enemy activity in any of these areas endangered the lives of Americans remaining in Vietnam, I would not hesitate to take strong and effective measures to deal with the situation."

Already, three sentences into the speech, Nixon looked as if he desperately needed to mop the sweat from his upper lip. He plunged ahead. "Despite the warning, North Vietnam has increased its military aggression in all these areas and particularly in Cambodia."

Thus, for the first time, the vast American public's focus was turned toward this tiny Asian country. Until now, Cambodia had only had a peripheral existence in American's awareness. Using carefully arranged props, Nixon brought the country's focus toward how closely Cambodia adjoined Vietnam. Using his pointer, he picked out the Parrot's Beak and Fish Hook sections of the jungle, areas where the Viet Cong was amassed and waiting to attack American soldiers who were trying to guard the autonomy of South Vietnam.

Aiken sat quietly on the sofa, his age-worn face sagging with fatigue and disapproval as Nixon described the Cambodian situation. The picture drawn by Nixon bore no resemblance to Aiken's own mental image of Cambodia, an image left over from his visit to Phnom Penh five years earlier with Mike Mansfield. Aiken remembered a busy country filled with cheerful, friendly people and governed by a monarch whose chief interests appeared to be having a good time and keeping his nation out of the Vietnam conflict. Aiken's most lasting memory was of Prince Sihanouk's insistence that his new American friends extend their trip so that they could see the ruler's young daughter dance in a ballet performance. The contrast between the Cambodians and the much more war-like Vietnamese was striking. The Phnom Penh palace, Aiken thought at the time, was a long way from the barricaded American embassy in Saigon.

But in his speech, Nixon took pains to show Americans how close Vietnam and Cambodia were geographically. Nixon illustrated the geographical landscape in one sentence: "To protect our men who are in Vietnam and to guarantee the continued success of our withdrawal and Vietnamization programs, I have concluded that the time has come for action."

Aiken swore at the television screen, Lola later recounted. "God damn," he muttered. "God damn it."

Lola, like millions of others watching the speech, was hanging on every word by that point and she said quickly, "Sssh, Guv, I can't hear the President." A Washington insider every bit as much as her husband, she was tuned in to the political nuances of this moment, as well as to the sense of historical drama that even casual viewers felt. More importantly, though, Lola Aiken couldn't afford to miss a single phrase. The unique merger of their professional and personal lives required that she be an extra set of eyes and ears for George Aiken. For three decades, she had helped guard him from blind-side attacks, and in recent years, she had become increasingly alert to the need to protect him from himself, especially when he was tired or angry and prone to make unintended comments.

Lola wanted to be prepared when the newspapers began to call. They watched Nixon in silence until he came to the punchline mid-way through the 32-minute address. He looked directly into the camera and said, "Tonight, American and South Vietnamese units will attack the headquarters for the entire Communist military operation in South Vietnam. This key control center has been occupied by the North Vietnamese and the Viet Cong for five years in blatant violation of Cambodia's neutrality."

Without blinking, Nixon added, "This is not an invasion of Cambodia."

Transfixed by the video image in front of him, Aiken shook his head and said quietly, "No. No, no, no."

For the Aikens, the worst was yet to come. After warning other nations not to misinterpret his actions in Cambodia and then after justifying the attack as the will of America's silent majority, the President suddenly brought into range a new target. He and the American people, Nixon said, were being "assailed by counsels of doubt and defeat from some of the most widely known opinion leaders of the Nation." He identified one of these troublemakers as "a Republican senator [who] has said that this action I have taken means that my party has lost all chance of winning the November elections."

It was not a strictly precise quotation. What Aiken had previously said to the President was that if Nixon expanded the war, "This fall the Republicans won't be able to elect a dogcatcher in Vermont." Aiken had made the comment in March when Secretary Rogers was testifying before the Foreign Relations Committee, in what was supposed to be an executive session. During that same session, Aiken also had asserted that if Nixon enlarged the war, he would be a one-term President. The comments were pure Aiken, and they were promptly leaked to gleeful reporters working for columnist, Jack Anderson, and U.S. News & World Report. Aiken confirmed the story, after grumbling, as he told me, that if reports from executive sessions were leaked, at least they ought to be accurate.

Nixon's paraphrase may not have been entirely accurate, but his aim was. He hit the Senator squarely below the belt, and he did it on prime-time nationwide television. The reference to Aiken was bracketed by Nixonian rhetoric that harkened back to the days when he verbally horsewhipped Helen Gahagan Douglas, who had run against him. Douglas, who had been called by Nixon "the Pink Lady," retaliated in turn, branding Nixon with the infamous nickname, "Tricky Dick" —a name that stuck. By association, Nixon put Aiken into the "anarchy" camp, in league with those who make "mindless attacks on all the great institutions," and those who, when the chips are down, would have "the world's most powerful nation, the United States of America, act like a pitiful, helpless giant." Those people, Nixon said, would "take the easy political path" and "bring all of our men home immediately ... even though that would mean defeat for the United States." Those who put political considerations first, he said, would "desert 18 million South Vietnamese people who have put their trust in us."

Nixon said he would not buy a few Congressional seats for the Republicans if the price had to be paid for by "400,000 brave Americans fighting for our country." He would rather be a one-term president than secure re-election by "humiliating the United States." He did not shy away from humiliating George Aiken, though.

The speech was, indeed, vintage Nixon, a form of political terrorism in which one victim is mauled in public and others of the same stripe are cowed.

Aiken Reacts with Anger

"I didn't think the President would do it. I was wrong. It's all-out war now, short of atomic bombs," Aiken first said privately about Nixon's speech in his office before later repeating the line to U.S. News & World Report. A furious Aiken, feeling as if he had been misled by the President, said of Nixon, "He couldn't be elected dogcatcher now." Aiken also used the same line with members of the media in Washington and in Vermont.

I had never seen Senator Aiken so angry. Only days before April 30, Secretary of State Rogers, before the Senate Foreign Relations Committee, had given no hints of a major new war strategy. While Aiken had been told privately that some troops might be sent to Cambodia, he had not believed it.

Aiken was quoted on the front page of the May 1, 1970 edition of the *Burlington Free Press*, that he was "surprised." He said that this shift in policy would make it harder for the South Vietnamese to take over the primary ground-fighting role of the war. In speaking about his disappointment with the Administration to media outlets, Aiken was unable to stay silent after Cambodia had been bombed, and he took his first steps to publicly criticize Nixon on the war.

Aiken's animus towards the President's actions was shared by many in the Senate and in the Nation. The blowback was immediate. Protests erupted throughout the country on college campuses and in major cities. The press coverage proved mainly unfavorable for Nixon. Large elements of the religious community--those who favored peace—condemned the invasion.

The eruption of protests on college campuses soon turned deadly. On

May 2, in a protest against the war, the ROTC building at Kent State University was set on fire by an unknown party. On May 4, Kent State students gathered in protest on the central campus and would not leave when ordered to by the Ohio National Guard troops, who had been called to the campus to maintain order. The National Guard members fired at the unarmed students and within 13 seconds, four students were dead, and nine others were injured. In response to these deaths, students in more than 400 colleges and universities across the country protested and refused to attend classes for days or even weeks in response to the shootings.

Campus demonstrations were held across the entire country. Students went on strike, shutting down their campuses. Ten days after the Kent State shootings, a major uprising occurred at Jackson State College, an historically black college in Jackson, Mississippi. Two students were killed, another 12 injured in that protest. This tragedy had as much to do with racial issues on campus as it did with negative sentiments towards the war.

In Vermont, the killings caused a deep political rift between the incumbent Vermont Governor, Republican Deane C. Davis, and his fellow Republican Lt. Gov. Thomas L. Hayes. Davis was a strong backer of Nixon, while Hayes strongly supported Aiken's opposition to the war. While Davis was out of state, Hayes ordered state flags lowered to half-staff in a tribute to the students who had been killed as they protested the war in Vietnam. In response, Gov. Davis cut his out-of-state meetings short and flew back to Vermont to countermand Hayes. The Governor immediately rescinded the order to lower the flags.

The Vermont media was also split, with the *Free Press* supporting Nixon and the state's other large daily, The *Rutland Herald*, supporting Aiken's anti-war sentiments and criticism of President Nixon's actions.

President Nixon's decision to invade Cambodia was clearly a major change in the Administration's war tactics. It called into question Nixon's long-touted "plan" to end American involvement in the war. Many, like Senator Aiken, had taken comfort in Nixon's planned phased withdrawal of U.S. combat troops from Vietnam. As noted, at the beginning of each week, Aiken had kept a keen eye on the troop levels in Vietnam. As long as the trajectory continued downwards, Aiken was convinced that Nixon would keep his promise to bring the war to an end.

While Aiken accepted the continuation of air bombing over Cambodia and Laos in support of the South Vietnamese Army, Nixon's decision to expand the war by sending American ground troops into Cambodia was the final straw for Aiken. His support for Nixon evaporated.

Aiken had noted that Nixon had promised to have all the U.S. troops in Cambodia withdrawn by June 30, 1970. This was a pivotal date for Senator Aiken. Up until that time he had been opposed to any legislation that would have used the Congressional power of the purse to force the Executive Branch to alter its foreign policy. In other words, Aiken now favored placing restraints on the President's power to conduct war without Congressional approval.

For more than a year, Senators George McGovern, D-South Dakota and Mark Hatfield, R-Oregon, had been pushing the Hatfield-McGovern Amendment to end the war. The amendment was strongly opposed by the Nixon Administration and its allies as a usurpation of executive war powers. Aiken was opposed to the proposal, arguing that a "precipitous" action like that would cause instability and would not bring the war to an end any time soon.

Yet Nixon's pledge that he would withdraw the troops by June 30 provided an important plank upon which the Senate doves could build support for legislation that would cut off funding for the troops in Cambodia after that date.

Senator John Sherman Cooper, R-Kentucky, a former U.S. Ambassador to India, was a fellow member of the Senate Foreign Relations Committee and an opponent of the war, and was Aiken's seatmate on the Republican side in the Senate with whom Aiken would often confer. Senators Cooper and Aiken had worked together in 1969 when the Senate debated the Anti-Ballistic Missile Treaty. Aiken joined Cooper in voting against that treaty.

Senator Cooper was approached by Sen. Frank Church, D-Idaho, also a member of the Senate Foreign Relations Committee, and asked to sponsor an amendment to the House-passed Foreign Military Sales Act, an amendment that was designed to stop the funding for any American troops stationed in Cambodia or Laos after June 30, 1970.

Cooper agreed to join Church in supporting the amendment, but only if Aiken and Mansfield would sign on as co-sponsors. Aiken agreed. He and Mansfield argued that it was a way to help Nixon keep his word to the American public. While that argument persuaded Aiken and Mansfield to support the amendment to cut-off funding for the first time, it outraged the President and his Administration. The President considered the amendment an intrusion on his war powers.

The bill, the Cooper-Church-Aiken-Mansfield Amendment, or just the Cooper-Church Amendment as it was later known, consumed the Senate in a bitter and emotional debate for more than two months.

As with any high-profile legislation, much of the behind-the-scenes work involved work by the staff aides of the sponsoring Senators. As the Aiken staffer assigned to Foreign Relations Committee matters, I had a front row seat to this high-stakes negotiation.

Many hours of staff strategy sessions took place to ensure that enough committee votes existed to allow the amendment to pass. Each Senator was asked if a convincing counter-argument might sway their vote. For those Senators who were on the record as being firmly against the war, the task was easier. For those Senators backing Nixon, the job was more difficult, and in many cases, impossible.

The first key vote took place May 11, when the Senate Foreign Relations Committee, in a 9-to-5 vote, adopted the amendment. Nixon was livid. He saw the legislation as a direct challenge to his role as President. He instructed his aides to fight back hard, and he accused Senators who favored the amendment of stabbing American soldiers in the back.

The Senate commenced debate on the Cooper-Church Amendment on May 13. Senator John Stennis, D-Mississippi, argued that the amendment was a "grave mistake" and said that it would undermine the President "while the battle is still going on." According to Robert Mann, in his seminal book, *A Grand Delusion*, America's Descent into Vietnam, Senator Church responded to Stennis, claiming that approving the amendment would present Congress with an "historic opportunity to draw the limits on American intervention in Indochina,"

As a result of Nixon's actions in Cambodia, the country was raw with emotion and deeply divided by the protests and the tragic deaths on two college campuses. From my vantage point, The White House was quite nervous about the changing dynamics within the Senate, since the debate surrounding the amendment was being closely followed by the national media. The Nixon Administration responded by ginning up opposition to the amendment through intensive lobbying. Lobbyists focused on Senators with ties to the American Legion and to the Veterans of Foreign Wars, urging members of each organization to contact their Senators and to ask them to oppose the legislation.

In Vermont, Aiken was criticized on the editorial pages of the *Burlington Free Press* for his support of the amendment. Student protests were conducted at the University of Vermont, Middlebury College, and Goddard College. Prominent religious leaders in the state condemned Nixon for his excessive use of force in Vietnam and Cambodia, which had long been claiming the lives of innocent civilians caught in the crossfire.

Vermont Democrats were actively seeking nominations for Governor and for the U.S. Senate in anticipation of the elections to be held in the fall of 1970.

The political split over the war impacted the state's three-person Congressional Delegation. Aiken supported the Cooper-Church Amendment, while the state's junior Republican, Senator Winston L. Prouty, opposed it. The most surprising shift came from U.S. Rep. Robert T. Stafford, R-Vt., a veteran member of the House Armed Services Committee. Until the Cambodian invasion, Stafford, a Navy veteran, had been supportive of U.S. war policies. But Cambodia pushed him over the edge. He joined the Doves on the war. Many years later, Stafford told me that his four daughters, in opposition to the war, had influenced him to change his opinion.

The *Burlington Free Press* gave prominent play to the Senate debate on its news pages. The editor of the editorial page, Franklin B. Smith, continued to criticize Aiken for his support of the Cooper-Church Amendment.

Cartoons on the *Free Press* editorial page depicted Aiken as trying to stop a bulldozer labeled "Cambodia." One of the toughest anti-Aiken *Free Press* editorials appeared on May 15, 1970, when Smith recalled that in 1941 Aiken had voted against the Franklin Delano Roosevelt Lend-Lease legislation. Under the headline of "Sen. Aiken Retreats Again," Smith wrote: "Aiken didn't want to help Britain to defeat Hitler in 1941, so nobody should be surprised that the venerable Vermonter doesn't want to help the small nations of Southeast Asia."

President Nixon rebuked Aiken on the Cambodia issue, without making direct reference to him regarding his comment that Nixon could not get elected "dog-catcher" if he was on the ballot in 1970, a midterm election year. Aiken said that didn't bother him. He observed that, "Even if you support a person 98 percent of the time, and disagree two percent, that there will still be criticism, but it doesn't matter."

By June 30, 1970, the full Senate voted 58-37 to adopt the Cooper-Church-Aiken-Mansfield Amendment. The vote was a turning point in the U.S. Senate. A solid majority of the body was ready to challenge the President and his war-making policies. It was the beginning of the end of the Vietnam War. While Nixon still had narrow public support for the war, his "Silent Majority" was losing ground.

On June 1, 1970, Senator Aiken delivered the Commencement Address at Middlebury College. He told the graduates that if they wanted to have their voices heard, they needed to get involved in elective politics and local matters. More importantly, they needed to be sure to cast their votes.

Aiken under Pressure on Vietnam

The President withdrew U.S. troops from Cambodia by July 1st. Senator Aiken came under political pressure from some Vermonters to cease his opposition to President Nixon on the Cambodia issue along with Nixon's handling of the war. One meeting Aiken attended in 1970 involved a delegation of some prominent business leaders including former Rep. Luther F. Hackett, R-South Burlington, and Joe Jones, a Rutland Republican and insurance executive.

The business leaders met with Aiken in his Senate office at the Russell Building. They tried, without success, to convince Aiken that he should support Nixon on the war despite the Cambodian invasion. I was at the meeting and observed the veteran Vermont Senator reminding them, without rancor, that he had been a supporter of Nixon's war strategy as long as the President continued to withdraw troops. Aiken said that the Cambodia invasion was a dramatic change in policy and that it was not likely to succeed. He explained that he feared a continuation of U.S.-led fighting by ground troops in Cambodia and a slowing down of the South Vietnamese assuming more of that role.

The fact that 350 Americans soldiers died during the two-month invasion was not lost on Aiken, either.

The 1970 meeting came at a time of great political turmoil in Vermont over the war. The Vermont supporters of President Nixon intended this meeting as an unwritten threat to Aiken. Unless he continued to support the President, he would not get their support should he run for re-election in four years.

Lt. John F. Kerry, then member of Vietnam Veterans Against the War, testified April 22, 1971 before an emotional jam-packed Senate Foreign Relations Committee. During his testimony Senator Aiken and Kerry discussed how the North Vietnamese would help the U. S. leave South Vietnam. (Photo courtesy HENRY GRIFFIN/AP)

Of course, none of them knew at the time that Aiken had no intention of running again, a decision that he and Lola had made privately after his 1968 re-election. (Aiken did not formally announce his decision until Feb. 14, 1974.)

Aiken shook off the pressure and told me later that the political threat was mild considering what he had faced in Vermont during the late 1930s from the "Old Guard" business interests who had lined up in opposition to him—all without success.

In the mid-term elections in 1970, Nixon and his Vice President, Spiro Agnew, urged voters to turn out and show their opposition to the violent protesters against the war. Despite Nixon and Agnew's efforts, Democrats retained their majority in the U.S. Senate and increased their majority in the U.S. House. Yet, apart from Jim Jeffords' victory in the race for Attorney General of Vermont, the 1970 election results in Vermont still were pro-Nixon. Sen. Winston L. Prouty, R-Vermont, was elected over anti-war candidate, former Democratic Gov. Philip H. Hoff. And another prominent Nixon supporter, Republican Gov. Deane C. Davis, was easily reelected. Only Senator Aiken remained a major political voice in Vermont in opposition to Nixon, based upon the Cambodian invasion.

By the end of 1970, despite continued opposition from the Nixon Administration, Congress had completed action on a watered-down version of the Cooper-Church Amendment.

When the year ended, troop levels in Vietnam had declined to about 280,000. The deaths were continuing, though, as was racial unrest within the U.S. military command. Causing yet more discontent among U.S. troops were increasing incidents of "fragging," in which unpopular officers were attacked by members of their own forces.

During 1970 and 1971, running simultaneously to the debacles of the Vietnam War, Senator Aiken spent much time on legislation that would give electric co-ops and publicly owned utilities the same opportunities to invest in civilian nuclear power plants as the investor-owned utility companies. Aiken successfully argued that not permitting public power systems to participate in nuclear ownership was an antitrust violation.

In 1971, the Vietnam War was raging, and controversy over President Nixon's war policies emerged as an irrefutable issue in Vermont's political climate. While the state had supported the war and stood behind its Congressional delegation in previous months, the events of 1970 had caused a decline in public support for the war. By March 1971, Nixon's overall national job approval rating was hovering at 50 percent, while approval of his Vietnam strategy had slipped to 34 percent. Nearly half of Americans polled felt that the Vietnam War was morally wrong.

Early in the morning of March 1, 1971 a bomb went off in the U.S. Capitol, apparently planted by a protester opposed to the extension of the war into Laos. Senator Aiken, Lola, and I walked over to the Capitol to be shown the damage by Capitol Police. It was a seminal moment for the Vermont Senator. He was witnessing, firsthand, the deep divisions that were forming in the country over the war, and the domestic terrorism that was emerging as a result.

I recall being stunned that a bombing had occurred within the very heart of the government and that such intense emotions regarding the war had turned the country into a powder keg.

In the United States, the ravages of the war were made even more brutally evident when on March 29, 1971, Lt. William Calley was found guilty for the murders of 22 civilians in My Lai and was sentenced to life imprisonment. Senator Aiken received a mountain of mail from Vermonters critical of both Calley as well as Nixon who then had ordered Calley released from Leavenworth Prison and returned to house arrest at Fort Benning, pending appeal. Calley's house arrest lasted for three and one-half years. In 1974, Calley was released from federal custody. His sentence had been reduced to house arrest by President Nixon.

The war, and opposition to it, was front and center in the nation's capital during mid-April 1974. The Vietnam Veterans Against the War began a week-long protest that culminated in a dramatic two-hour scene when, in a profound and moving statement, 1,000 or more veterans mounted the steps of the East Front of the U.S. Capitol, took off their service medals and decorations, and threw them over the Capitol fence while calling out their names, hometowns, and branches of service.

At the time, the Senate Foreign Relations Committee was holding hearings on legislative proposals to end the war. The most powerful moment of that April week came as Navy Lt., John F. Kerry—future Massachusetts Senator and Secretary of State, then the principal spokesperson for the Vietnam Veterans Against the War—appeared before the Senate Foreign Relations Committee on April 22, 1971.

Aiken during the Nixon Presidency

The hearing room in the Dirksen Building was standing room only, with a long line in the hallway trying to get in to hear Kerry's testimony. As an aide to Senator Aiken, I was allowed in. I sat, as I usually did, at the hearing room's press table to the side of the witness table. Lt. Kerry's presentation was one of the most dramatic moments that I experienced during my six years in Washington working for the Senator.

From my perspective, and still resonating 47 years later, was Lt. Kerry's most riveting statement, when he insisted that someone has to die every day in Vietnam so that "President Nixon won't be the first President to lose a war." I am still haunted these many years later by his query, "We are asking Americans to think about that, because how do you ask a man to be the last man to die in Vietnam? How do you ask a man to be the last man to die for a mistake?"

As Kerry finished his prepared statement, the room burst into a sustained applause. Even some reporters at the press table, with whom I was sitting, stood up and clapped. It was a highly unusual event, as the press rarely showed an outward demonstration of emotion or support. The Senators in attendance, including Aiken, were clearly moved.

Chairman J. William Fulbright, D-Arkansas., was first to respond: "Mr. Kerry, it is quite evident from that demonstration that you are speaking not only for yourself, but for all your associates, as you properly said in the beginning. You said you wished to communicate. I can't imagine anyone communicating more eloquently than you did. I think it is extremely helpful and beneficial to the committee and the country to have you make such a statement."

Kerry had declared that if the Congress would set a date to end the war, the President should declare a ceasefire, stop his blind commitment to the Thieu-Ky regime, and accept a coalition government that would represent all the political forces in the country.

When it came to Senator Aiken's turn, the following dialogue occurred:

> Senator Aiken: "Mr. Kerry, the Defense Department seems to feel that if we set a definite date for withdrawal when our forces get down to a certain level, they would be seriously in danger by the North Vietnamese and the

Vietcong. Do you believe that the North Vietnamese would undertake to prevent our withdrawal from the country and attack the troops remaining there?"

Mr. Kerry: "Well, Senator, if I may answer you directly, I believe we are running that danger with the present course of withdrawal because the President has neglected to state to this country exactly what his response will be when we have reached the point that we do have let us say, 50,000 support troops in Vietnam.

Senator Aiken: "I am not telling you what I think; I am telling you what the Department says."

Mr. Kerry: "Yes sir, I understand that."

Senator Aiken: "Do you believe the North Vietnamese would seriously undertake to impede our complete withdrawal?"

Mr. Kerry: "No, I do not believe that the North Vietnamese would, and it has been clearly indicated at the Paris peace talks they would not."

Senator Aiken: "Do you think they might help carry the bags for us?" (Laughter.)

Mr. Kerry: "I would say they would be more prone to do that than the Army of the South Vietnamese." (Laughter and Applause.)

President Nixon was increasingly under fire for his Vietnam policies. On April 24, 1971, just two days after Kerry's testimony, another mass demonstration in Washington attracted almost 175,000 people who marched on the Capitol demanding an end to the Vietnam War.

By this time, the number of Vietnam deaths had surpassed 45,000. Despite the troop withdrawals, an end of the war was not in sight. During a college speech in early June 1971, Senator Aiken's close friend, Majority leader Mike Mansfield, called the war in Vietnam a "tragic mistake." Aiken agreed.

The Pentagon Papers

On June 13, 1971, all hell broke loose in Washington and beyond when *The New York Times* published a first installment of the "Pentagon Papers": a secret Defense Department study of the decisions made during the Kennedy and Johnson Administrations concerning the Vietnam War. The study had originally been ordered by Defense Secretary Robert S. McNamara as a guide for future generations.

Upon reading the *Times* headline, I said to my friends, "This must be it!" The "it" I referred to was the Pentagon Papers, a secret study of the war that had only been hinted at by Senators during meetings of the Senate Foreign Relations Committee, which I had attended as Aiken's staffer. It turned out that the committee had secretly received a copy almost a year earlier from Daniel Ellsberg, who had been involved in the study as a contractor for the Rand Corporation. The committee had kept the study under heavy security and only a few staffers and Senators were aware of its existence. Aiken knew about the Pentagon Papers, but he had never revealed their contents or whether he had even read the Papers.

The highly classified study was leaked by Ellsberg to *The New York Times*, and later to the *Washington Post* and the Boston Globe. The Nixon Administration was livid. The *Times* published the second installment the following day, Monday, June 14. Attorney General John Mitchell demanded that the *Times* stop publishing that material. The paper refused. On June 15, the *Times* ran the third installment, and the Nixon Administration went to court to stop the paper from further release of that material. Federal Judge Murray Gurfein slapped a gag order on the *Times*, stopping any further publication of the Papers altogether.

The gag order included the *Washington Post*, which by this time, had its own copy of the classified papers by way of Ellsberg. The government argued that publication of the papers would hurt national security. On June 25 and June 26, 1971, the Supreme Court heard arguments in the case with the *Times* arguing press freedom based on the First Amendment. The government argued that further publication would cause "irreparable harm to the United States' national interests." On June 30, 1971, in a landmark decision by a vote of six to three, the Supreme Court upheld the right of the newspapers to publish. The newspapers immediately went to press with the rest of the Pentagon Papers.

The Pentagon Papers, which had taken more than 18 months to compile, were nearly 3,000 pages of narrative history. They revealed that the Defense Department had bungled Vietnam War policy, with much of the blame directed towards President Johnson's wavering strategy on how to deal with and run the war.

The release of the Pentagon Papers stirred the Nation and increased the pressure on the Nixon Administration to find an expeditious solution to end the war. By June 22, 1971, the Senate passed a non-binding resolution expressing its desire for the removal of all of the American troops by the end of the year. Whether by design or coincidence, some 6,100 U.S. troops were withdrawn during one record week in early July.

Nothing in Washington serves an administration better than a change of subject. President Nixon did just that on July 15, 1971, when he announced that in early 1972, he would be visiting Mainland China. This visit represented a major diplomatic breakthrough and an opportunity to explore an alternative pathway out of Vietnam.

The leak of the Pentagon Papers, however, had created a sense of paranoia inside the Nixon Administration. As a result, the Plumbers Unit, as it was called then, was deployed by Nixon aides John Ehrlichman and Charles Colson to investigate the leaks. Colson took the effort one step farther and compiled an "enemies list" that included some 200 names of journalists, politicians, activists, and others who were considered "anti-Nixon."

The atmosphere in Washington, from my vantage point as an Aiken staffer, was extremely tense. An unpredictable President lashed out at critics while the anti-war movement continued to spread.

In Vermont, as in other places throughout the country, the central question of the time was: "Are you for the war or against it?" Those Vermonters opposed to the Vietnam War painted anti-war slogans on their barns and outbuildings.

Those who favored Nixon asked for support from the "Silent Majority."

By mid-August 1971, two of the staunchest United States' allies, New Zealand and Australia, announced that they were going to withdraw their support troops from Vietnam. Members of the U.S. 1st Air Cavalry refused orders to go out on patrol. In time, more units would engage in refusing to obey combat orders.

By the end of 1971, U.S. troop levels had been reduced to about 157,000, yet the bombing continued over North Vietnam military installations as the Nixon Administration argued it was trying to encourage progress at the Peace Talks in Paris.

Aiken and his Senate Diary

Writing in his Senate diary, his weekly recounting of events from January 1972 to January 1975, Senator Aiken provided, in his own words, a running commentary of this momentous period of time. The diary included events in Vietnam as well as other significant activities in the Senate. The diary is an important first-hand source of Aiken's thinking in 1972, an election year. The diary also covered the period of the Watergate break-in, the firing of special counsel Archibald Cox, the start of impeachment proceedings in the U.S. House, and the resignation of President Nixon. It concluded with his last day in the Senate, Jan. 2, 1975.

The diary consisted of over 400,000 words contained in 27 loose-leaf notebooks. Senator Aiken would dictate his thoughts for the week on Saturday mornings to one his key staffers, Ellen Jones of Poultney. She would take his dictation in shorthand and then would type up the material.

Lola Aiken would often read the manuscript Ellen Jones had typed up and only make changes for accuracy. She made no attempt to change or delete any of Aiken's observations or conclusions or to soften his sometimes-barbed comments about his colleagues or members of the Nixon Administration.

The Senator took his diary with him upon leaving the Senate in January 1975, when he returned to his hometown of Putney. Aiken then struck a deal with the Stephen Greene Press in Brattleboro to publish the diary, formally titled, *Aiken: Senate Diary* January 1972-January 1975. For assistance, the Senator turned to his long-time friend, Vermont author and historian, Ralph Nading Hill of Burlington, to edit the 400,000 words into a 370-page book. The book was published on Jan. 1, 1976, almost a year to the day after Aiken retired from the Senate.

These many decades later, that book remains one of the most important documents for revealing Senator Aiken's perspectives. His thinking on Vietnam during the Nixon Administration, for example, is especially important as it captured the ups and downs of Aiken's relationship with the President over the many issues of the war. From the diary, it is clear that Aiken wanted to give Nixon the benefit of the doubt much of the time, but in other instances, Aiken's frustrations with Nixon's war policy were articulated thoroughly and in stark tones.

While focusing primarily on Aiken's Vietnam thinking, the Senate Diary is also valuable for its portrayal of his other policy considerations during his time as ranking Republican on the Senate Foreign Relations Committee. Additionally, Aiken spent much time in his last term (1969-1975) dealing with non-Vietnam issues, such as agriculture, food stamps, national school lunch programs, atomic energy, and the protection of Eastern Wilderness Areas. As Dean of the Senate, Aiken also served as the primary contact for Vermont officials who were dealing with issues involving state relations with the federal bureaucracy.

The diary, as well as my own memory and notes from that time, offer an intimate perspective into the thoughts and thinking of the venerable Vermonter during that critical period.

A war-weary nation heralded the upcoming presidential election in November 1972 as a referendum, a time when the war would be the major influential issue at the ballot box. Nobody understood the ramifications of the war better than Nixon. As a result, he began the year with the announcement of an eight-point peace plan for ending the Vietnam War, a plan that Henry Kissinger had been negotiating in secret for more than a year with the North Vietnamese. Nixon's proposed peace plan was a futile gesture, though. It went nowhere as Hanoi firmly rejected the proposal.

For a short while in February, the war in Vietnam became a noisy footnote as all the world's media attention was diverted to the historic trip Nixon and his entourage undertook to China, from Feb. 21-Feb. 28. The press and Nixon aides were flown by Pan American to Beijing. A long-time Vermont friend of mine, Karen Meyer of Colchester, was a young stewardess on the Pan Am flight at the time. She recalled, many years later, her excitement, and that of the media on her airplane who covered the events. She also recalled her trepidation as Chinese authorities demanded all their passports when the crew landed in China, only to be returned when all passengers were accounted for on their departure.

The trip was a huge media success for Nixon and a major, historic, diplomatic accomplishment for the United States. The trip was also of great concern for the North Vietnamese, as they feared that China, the North's wartime ally, would agree to peace terms that would undermine their position at the Paris Peace Table.

North Vietnam's concern had been rooted in its planning for a major military invasion. The North's strategy had been to capture ground in the South. This strategy was based upon the withdrawal of U.S. troops and the growing strength of the anti-war movement in the United States, which left the South Vietnamese military in a weakened position.

The so-called Eastertide Offensive by the North was, in hindsight, an attempt to conduct another Tet Offensive like the North had launched in 1968 across South Vietnam. While in 1968 Tet had been a major surprise for the United States, it had not resulted in the goals sought by the North. Our military commanders even argued at the time that the new Tet was in fact an American military victory, although this claim was met with significant skepticism in the United States. U.S. troop strength had dropped to 69,000 by 1972, a fact that gave the North Vietnam military command encouragement that this time its invasion in the South would succeed. When Tet came to pass, however, the anticipated invasion by the North did not occur.

The Nixon Administration reacted aggressively to the anticipated

North Vietnamese offensive with heavy bombing strikes targeting artillery positions which the North had been using to shoot down U.S. planes. Nixon also ordered the mining of harbors and oil depots in the North.

As a result of heavy bombing strikes by the U.S. and South Vietnam, a napalm bomb was mistakenly dropped on civilians, including children. Footage of a badly burned young girl running, fleeing the bombs, became one of the most memorable scenes of the long war. This one photo resulted in international condemnation and a new round of anti-war protests in the United States.

It was later revealed that North Vietnam had struggled with the impact of the U.S. heavy bombing. The North, having not even attempted its planned offensive, was hit hard by U.S. air power and South Vietnamese troops on the 1972 Tet holiday.

In early July 1972, the peace talks resumed in Paris. By mid-August, the last U.S. ground combat troops left South Vietnam, turning the combat role over to the South Vietnam military, although U.S. airpower continued to support the South's ground troops. On Oct. 8, a diplomatic breakthrough between Kissinger and Le Duc Tho resulted in major concessions on both sides. The U.S. agreed to allow North Vietnamese troops stationed in the South to remain there fighting, while North Vietnam agreed to end its demands that South Vietnam President Thieu resign and his government dissolve.

The heaviest fighting of the war ended in 1972 with the North having suffered nearly 100,000 military casualties and with an estimated 40,000 South Vietnam soldiers having been killed. On Nov. 7, 1972, President Nixon won the Presidential Election in a national landslide, after he declared before the voting that "Peace is at hand in Vietnam."

Senator Aiken viewed the 1972 General Election with mixed feelings. Nixon had won 49 of the 50 states. Only Massachusetts voted for Senator George McGovern. While Aiken was satisfied with Nixon's landslide as it meant a continuance of Republican leadership, he was very unhappy that his close friend, Sen. Margaret Chase Smith, R-Maine, had gone down in defeat. Aiken and Smith were close friends and colleagues. In 1964, Aiken had nominated her at the Republican National Convention in San Francisco as a candidate for the Presidency. At that time, however, Smith had been defeated for the nomination by fellow Senator, Barry Goldwater.

In his diary, Aiken wrote for the week ending, Nov. 11, 1972:

> I never expected the Republicans to take over the Senate, but the losses of Maine, Iowa, and Colorado came as a real shock to me in those states. The loss of Margaret Chase Smith in Maine was the sharpest blow to the Republicans and was undoubtedly due to the fact that her re-election was generally taken for granted, and so she stayed in Washington attending to the nation's business at a time when many others were out on the campaign trail.

On election night, Aiken told mt that he had privately feared that the Republicans might take control of the Senate. This would have elevated him to Chair of the Senate Foreign Relations Committee, a job he said he "was not thirsting for."

If Aiken had become chair, he would have been under considerably more pressure from the Nixon Administration to provide stronger support for the Administration's Vietnam policies. As was his style, Aiken wanted to be independent and free to voice his concerns without towing the party line.

The Democrats ended up retaining control of the Senate and the House. Aiken was privately relieved.

Prophetically, after his massive re-election, Nixon ordered a resumption of the bombings of Hanoi and Haiphong Harbor. Shortly before Christmas, on Dec. 18, 1972, Aiken declared that the bombing had "horrified millions of Americans who had voted for Richard Nixon on Nov. 7."

Aiken wrote in his diary: "The question asked over and over: what has happened to the man we elected President? Why did he lead us to believe that a peace settlement was at most only a few weeks away? Is he now determined to win a military victory to show the world that we are the strongest nation on Earth?

"As one who supported President Nixon for a second term in the White

House, and as one who had freely predicted that our military involvement in Indochina would be over before Christmas, I find these questions to be extremely embarrassing," wrote a despondent Aiken.

On Dec. 29, 1972, Hanoi agreed to come back to the Paris Peace negotiations. On Jan. 8, 1973, Henry Kissinger and Le Doc Tho were back at the peace table, a move that Aiken called a "ray of hope."

Aiken was still deeply concerned with Vietnam as the new Congress was about to convene following President Nixon's Second Inauguration set for early January 1973.

At that point, Aiken wrote in his diary:

> The Vietnam situation is still unsettled, although, there are rumors to the effect that an agreement with North Vietnam is near. I hope the rumors are true but having heard similar rumors and outright predictions on the part of the Executive officials for the last several months now, I am rather skeptical. The responsibility for bringing the war to an end clearly rests with the President, and I hope that the Congress does not relieve him of this responsibility by taking it upon its own shoulders.
>
> We should insist upon his carrying out the will of the American people as expressed by their duly elected Representatives. Early in the week (Jan. 13, 1973), General Secretary Leonid Brezhnev of the Communist Party of the Soviet Union, indicated that he thought the Vietnam War was about over. I interpreted this statement to represent pressure on Hanoi to agree to a settlement without further delay.

Aiken, Lola, and several staff members, including myself, watched the inaugural events from the Aikens' fourth floor apartment in the Methodist Building, which overlooked the entire East Front of the Capitol. It was a cold, raw, and windy day. Aiken was pleased when the President told those present, and the world, that an agreement would soon be reached. We all watched the ceremonies with the television on so we could hear the events live as they were underway.

Senator Aiken toasted Nixon's second term with his favorite drink, a Brandy Alexander.

The 1972 elections were not yet impacted by news of the break-in at the Watergate Hotel and Office Building on June 17, 1972. Events would later unfold as a result of the formation of the Senate Watergate Committee on Feb. 7. 1973, and its lengthy investigation that continued until June 27, 1974, when it issued its final report.

In early 1973, Aiken was still fixated on Vietnam, not Watergate.

"I hope that the President's feeling that peace in Indochina is near is well founded, and I believe, it is. We have carried on this face-saving war for at least six years now, and if Dr. Kissinger can arrive at any arrangement which gets us out of this mess and saves faces of the parties involved, I will have to back away from my previous opinions."

It was the first time that I recalled Aiken wondering out loud if he was being too critical of Nixon's war policy. While Aiken strongly opposed the resumption of the Christmas 1972 bombing, he was hoping that, despite the heavy damage and increased deaths, it really had resulted in forcing Hanoi to get serious about peace negotiations.

An irony of the Vietnam War was highlighted by the death of former President Johnson on Jan. 22, 1973. The very next day, Nixon chose to proclaim that a peace agreement had been reached which "will end the war and bring peace with honor."

On Jan. 27, 1973, the Paris Peace Accords were signed by the United States, North Vietnam, South Vietnam and the Viet Cong. The terms called for the halt of all military activities and the withdrawal of all remaining military personnel within 60 days. The Accords provided that an estimated 150,000 North Vietnamese troops could remain in South Vietnam. The North Vietnamese agreed to a cease-fire and to the release of American POWS within 60 days. Vietnam would remain a divided country, one half led by President Thieu, the other half by the Viet Cong.

Writing in his diary that day, Aiken expressed hope that the Peace Accords would result in a "new era, an era of peace and improved welfare and economic conditions throughout the world."

His life-long hatred of war was reflected in his January 27, 1973 diary entry in which he commented that if a more peaceful world should evolve, "then I shall feel that the years I have put into the Senate have not been in vain, and that, after all, life is worth living." While only known to Aiken and Lola at the time, this self-reflection of his was, in retrospect, a clear signal that Aiken was proud of his accomplishments in the Senate, ready to return to civilian life, and would not be a candidate for re-election in 1974.

Troops Withdrawn

By March 29, 1973, the last of the American troops were withdrawn from Vietnam as President Nixon declared that, "The day we have all worked for and prayed for has finally come."

The withdrawal of the last U.S. troops inspired historians to reflect upon the country's longest war. They tabulated that during the 15 years of warfare, over two million Americans had served, and more than 500,000 had seen actual combat. According to the National Archives, 58,209 Americans were killed in action in those 15 years, including just over 8,000 pilots and women. One hundred of those who died were Vermonters. The war also caused more than 10,000 non-combat deaths and 153,239 seriously wounded victims, which included many amputees.

As 1973 began, an estimated 2,400 American POWs/MIAs were still unaccounted for, soldiers who needed to be found and returned. Meanwhile, the long war had resulted in a death toll in the millions for the people of South Vietnam, Laos, Cambodia, and Thailand.

Captain Robert White, the last known American POW, was released in April 1973.

The announcement of the Paris Peace Accords in early January was not a satisfying event for the government of South Vietnam as Northern troops remained in the South. To placate South Vietnam, Nixon made a secret agreement with President Thieu that the United States would use full military force against North Vietnam if it violated the agreement.

As American participation in the Vietnam War was winding down, political wars in Washington, D.C. were heating up. In the U.S. the draft ended since American troops were no longer needed to send troops into battle

Aiken during the Nixon Presidency

in Vietnam. In the near future, an all-volunteer military system would take its place.

For Senator Aiken, the growing controversy over Watergate and the turmoil inside the Nixon Administration was deeply troubling. The Senator was bothered most by the continued political attacks on Nixon and the controversy surrounding the Watergate break-in. The political sparring was viewed by Aiken as the cause of serious wounds to the Presidency and those attacks were driven, Aiken believed, by the ambitions of some Democratic Senate colleagues who were trying to make Nixon look bad.

As a result, Aiken focused his thinking and thoughts during the Spring of 1973 on domestic issues. It was the first time since I had joined his staff in May of 1969 that I saw his attention shift away from Vietnam. Instead, Aiken appeared to adopt a more partisan edge regarding domestic issues.

His diary entry in the end of March 1973 exemplified his thoughts of the time. Aiken wrote, "Another matter of partisan interest has been the Democrats continuing to make hay with the Watergate episode. Apparently, the Republican bigwigs never heard of a counter attack. Otherwise they could certainly come back and accuse Democrats, some of them pretty well known, of breaking into Republican offices previous to the election of last fall." Aiken would often privately refer to the Senate Watergate hearings as a "circus with too many clowns."

John A. Farrell, in his seminal 2017 book *Richard Nixon: The Life*, wrote that Nixon was, by mid-1973, consumed by Watergate more than he had been by Vietnam. While the Watergate scandal dominated the political climate in Washington at the end of April 1973, Nixon fired his two top aides, H. R. Haldeman and John Ehrlichman.

In Senator Aiken's office, the mail on the war slowed to a trickle while a torrent of mail on Watergate poured in. Opinions were split, urging Aiken to either support Nixon or to bring about his impeachment. Meanwhile, Congress reached a bi-partisan consensus to pass legislation to forbid any further military actions in Southeast Asia by the President without specifically getting Congressional approval after Aug. 15, 1973. The vote turned out to be veto-proof because the Senate approved the legislation 64-26 and the House voted 278-124 to support the measure.

The Nixon Administration did not have enough support in Congress to fight the legislation any longer, or even to argue that his Executive Branch constitutional war powers gave him authority to ignore Congress.

Farrell wrote in his book, "Nixon could have vetoed the legislation and taken his case to the American people. Instead he signed it." Thus, the long battle for the U.S. Congress to use its power of the purse to shape war policy, a battle that started with the Cooper-Church-Aiken-Mansfield Amendment in 1970 regarding troops in Cambodia, had now become a total prohibition for all U.S. military activities in Southeast Asia.

The new law meant that there would be no more U.S. bombing in either North or South Vietnam. This law resulted, by spring 1974, in the North building up its troop strength in South Vietnam.

Meanwhile, Henry Kissinger became the new Secretary of State with the resignation of Aiken's long-time ally, William P. Rogers. Aiken never warmed up to Kissinger. The Senator would often say in private that Kissinger "oozed with conceit." But, given Aiken's position as Ranking Republican on the Senate Foreign Relations Committee, once Kissinger had been nominated for the position, Aiken took on the responsibility of shepherding Kissinger's nomination through the Senate. In that task, Aiken often spent time with Kissinger, advising him on confirmation strategies. On Sept. 21, 1973, the Senate voted 78-7 to confirm Kissinger for the job. His nomination process had taken almost a month, as there was controversy over Kissinger's major role in the wire-tapping of Nixon critics. Some of those who were wire-tapped were members of the National Security Council staff.

Senator Aiken asked me to join him on Sept. 22, 1973 at the White House when Nixon issued the oath of office to Kissinger. It was an impressive ceremony. Kissinger was not only the first foreign-born person to assume the post of the nation's top diplomat, but also he been raised in a middle-class Jewish household by parents who had fled Nazi Germany during World War II. Kissinger's parents were in the East Room of the White House when he was sworn in.

To this day, I am honored to have been a witness to such an important historical event.

Years later, I recalled that powerful Saturday morning in 1973 when on Sept. 1, 2018, Kissinger delivered one of the eulogies for the late Sen. John McCain, R-Arizona. He had been released on March 14, 1973, from a POW camp in Hanoi as part of the Paris Peace Accords negotiated by Kissinger. McCain had been imprisoned for five and one-half years after he had been shot down in a bombing raid over North Vietnam.

Saturday Night Massacre

By late fall 1973, the scent of scandal was heavy in the air over the Nation's Capital. On Oct. 10, 1973, Vice President Spiro Agnew resigned his office after being implicated in a scandal that involved the trading of campaign donations for kickbacks during his time as Governor of Maryland. Agnew was then replaced by Congressman Gerald R. Ford of Michigan. Aiken was supportive of Ford and felt that his appointment would help Nixon in his frayed Congressional relations.

The Agnew resignation was soon overshadowed by the events of Saturday, Oct. 20, 1973 that quickly became known as the Saturday Night Massacre. On that day, President Nixon ordered Attorney General Elliot Richardson to fire Independent Special Prosecutor Archibald Cox. Richardson refused and resigned on the spot. Nixon then ordered Deputy Attorney General William Ruckelshaus to fire Cox. He also refused and then resigned. Nixon then ordered the third in command, Solicitor General Robert Bork to fire Cox. Bork did as ordered.

I vividly recalled that day when, 45 years earlier, I had been on a weekend vacation with my young family observing the wild ponies on the Assateague Island National Seashore. Even in that remote place in Virginia, the local news had been dominated by the events in Washington. I remember having the feeling that the national government was becoming unglued.

The political reaction to the firing of Cox had been swift and very negative for Nixon's reputation.

"Either Impeach Him or Get Off His Back"

Aiken's continued support of Nixon and the firing of Cox was beginning to have some adverse political consequences for the Vermonter back home, as well. Much of the growing agitation came from Vermont Democrats, led by Former Gov. Philip H. Hoff, who was asking if Aiken, then 81, was too old to run for another term. If he ran in 1974 and was elected, Aiken would have been 89 at the end of his term in 1981.

While occasional news stories in the *Rutland Herald* and a United Press International (UPI) political column from Vermont raised the age issue, Aiken did not back away from his continued support for the President. Rather, Aiken made a speech in the Senate on Nov. 7, 1973 titled "Watergate and the Presidency," which ran as a Page One story in the Nov. 8, 1973 issue of *The New York Times*. In it, Aiken was critical of Nixon, saying that the President's "public explanations of the Watergate mess have been astonishingly inept." Yet Watergate was not a reason for impeachment, Aiken insisted, despite the controversy involved. Additionally, Aiken said, Nixon should not resign. Aiken was convinced that Nixon's resignation would cause problems throughout the world.

"Those who call for the President's resignation on the ground that he has lost their confidence risk poisoning the wells of politics for years to come," Aiken had told the Senate. Aiken said that it was "the President's duty to his country to not resign. That which the American voter has done, let no man undo except through due process."

Aiken said that the U.S. House had a clear duty to "frame a charge of impeachment and to set itself a deadline for the task." If no agreement could be reached by that deadline, Aiken said, "the leaders of the House should tell the American people that no agreed charge could be found."

It was clear from Aiken's speech that he had little confidence that a special prosecutor outside of the Congress itself could determine the President's ability or worthiness to govern. Aiken said that only Congress could make that significant judgment.

Aiken then said as a potential juror in an impeachment trial, he would "not have anything to say about guilt or innocence. If the President is convicted, so be it."

Aiken then issued this advice for future politicians:

> None of us was elected to be a megaphone for the loudest voices in our constituencies. We were elected to legislate and to hold the President and his administration accountable for their actions. We cannot afford at this critical time to practice the politics of outraged emotions in carrying out these vital tasks. Confidence will only be restored by a determination on our part to follow procedures laid down in the Constitution.

Ever the canny politician, Aiken ended his speech with this headline-grabbing quote: "May I now pass on to this Congress advice that I received recently from a fellow Vermonter, "Either impeach him or get off his back"?

The advice came from Rep. Peter Giuliani, R-Montpelier, a well-known lawmaker in Vermont. Giuliani was a friend of Aiken's, and a moderate Republican who expressed the views of many Vermont Republicans in saying that the Watergate Affair should not dominate the national government and the events in Washington, D.C. Aiken held similar sentiments, yet his refusal to call out Nixon in 1973 was beginning to undermine his long-held progressive brand in the Republican Party amongst some Vermonters.

Aiken changed his mind on this matter in August 1974 when he concluded that Nixon had no choice but to resign.

Was Aiken becoming more partisan in his last Senate term? He had yet to make the announcement that he would cease running for Congress. But he seemed to be losing patience with the Senate process. While Congress was still a place for bipartisanship, the ideological cracks were beginning to show in many members of that body, Aiken included. In retrospect, the growing political divisions in the Senate in 1973 were a symptom of the ravages of the Vietnam War.

Aiken during Nixon's Last Year in Office

Say We Won and Get Out

The war in Vietnam was fading into unsettling memories by 1974, as Washington was becoming consumed by Watergate and its impacts on the Nixon Administration.

During the first week of the new year, Senator Aiken received a "Happy New Year" call from President Nixon. Aiken told Nixon that he hoped the year ahead would be happier than 1973 had been. Aiken and Nixon discussed the foreign policy achievements of the Nixon Administration but had little discussion about the domestic troubles currently surrounding the President.

At this time, based on my observation as a staff member, Aiken was still personally supporting Nixon, despite the growing chorus of Vermonters who were calling on Aiken to abandon his pro-Nixon stance. Vermonters began to question whether or not Aiken was becoming overly-partisan. Was he forgetting that his progressive, independent approach had been the basis for his enduring strong political support in Vermont?

In addition, the Vermont media and political operatives were raising Aiken's age as an issue. In late January, the *Rutland Herald* ran a story by Howard Coffin, in which Coffin suggested that during a speech Aiken had delivered in Vermont, he had seemed fuzzy and rambling in his delivery. Coffin's message was clear that Aiken, then 82, was too old to serve another term. A day after the story ran, Robert W. Mitchell, publisher of the *Rutland Herald* and former reporter who had covered Aiken in the late 1930s when he was Governor, defended Aiken, saying, "He was always fuzzy."

Writing about the incident in his diary, Aiken said in his own defense:

> L.P.A. (Lola Pierotti Aiken) says I ramble. Of course, I ramble. It is my nature to ramble when I get speaking, but it isn't always a question of fuzziness or uncertainty, because sometimes a speaker can fend off a more difficult situation by diverging from the subject.

While many had assumed Aiken would run again, only the Senator and Lola knew that Aiken would not. Lola's task here, as his wife and chief political adviser, was to help Aiken keep his cool and not tip his hand, yet, on his political intentions for the future. She and Aiken had a reason for this strategy: Aiken wanted to be sure to preserve, for as long as possible, his influence over the Nixon Administration and his status as the respected Dean of the Senate, with his long-held reputation for speaking with common sense.

Aiken knew that after he announced his political plans, that his political and personal influence on the "World's Greatest Deliberative Body," as it is often called, would start to wane. Yet, Aiken knew that to be fair to Vermonters and potential candidates for his seat, he could not wait too far into the year before making his big announcement. Clearly, many Vermonters were wondering if Aiken would run again.

President Gerald Ford, right, with Lola and George Aiken at a Vermont testimonial dinner in honor of Senator Aiken. On the far left is Senator Robert T. Stafford. (Aiken Family Photo)

Aiken noted in his diary for the week of Feb. 9, 1974:

> Governor Tom Salmon of Vermont dropped in Wednesday afternoon. He didn't have any special issue on his mind, and folks in my outer office said he was dropping in to look me over to see if I might be healthy enough to run for re-election. Tom is having trouble enough with his legislature in the state, and while he undoubtedly has further political ambition, he seems uncertain about what to do about it at this time.

Chittenden County State's Attorney Patrick J. Leahy had already announced his intention to run for the Democratic nomination for Aiken's U.S. Senate seat before Salmon was able to express his interest in doing the same.

Senator Aiken Announces He Will Not Run

Senator Aiken rocked the state on Thursday, Feb. 14, 1974, when he announced that it was time for him to come home and that he would not be a candidate for re-election later that year.

Writing in his diary, Aiken said:

> On Thursday morning, I gave out the only news that had not come out of Washington without being leaked. I announced that I would not be a candidate for re-election next fall. This happened about 10:30 in the forenoon and the rest of the day was spent answering the telephone and sitting in the office in the glare of TV lights and cameras.

When Senator Aiken announced, on Feb. 14, that he was not going to seek another term, Anthony Marro of the Washington Bureau of Newsday wrote a story the next day about Aiken's decision to go home. Marro, a former reporter for the *Rutland Herald*, wrote that, "In the 1930s, during his rapid six-year climb up the Vermont political ladder, Aiken cleared the way for electrical cooperatives to be established in Vermont. This broke the power the private companies had held over the state's economy and earned him the lasting enmity of the conservative wing of the state's Republican Party."

"When I first went up to Montpelier," Aiken liked to say, "they put me on the Conservation Committee. They did that because I like wild flowers. But that committee also handled the power bills." Pause. "And that's where they made their mistake."

The Newsday story also carried a photo of Aiken with this 1967 quote from him as the caption: "If [the power companies] had gotten their way, I'd never have become a Senator. I'd have stayed home at Putney and been stung to death by the bees."

The Senator had been thinking of making the announcement for several months but had waited until he felt it was the optimal time. In answering the media, Aiken said it was time to go home to complete a lot of unfinished business. "A few will claim that they scared me out, but I understand confidential polls taken by both parties in Vermont indicate that I might have had about 70 percent of the vote, had I chosen to continue in the field of public service."

Aiken during the Nixon Presidency

As a Vermonter, then in my 30s, I had already had enough political experience in Vermont to conclude that if Aiken ran, he would have been re-elected, even in face of the strong anti-Watergate mood in the country, a mood that permeated the 1974 election. Personally, I was happy that Aiken decided to not run, and I was not totally surprised.

During the time I spent on his staff from April 1969 to January 1975, Aiken, more often than not, would generally remark, "Quit while you are ahead." I knew, privately, that this aphorism was a message for his future, although I never asked for confirmation.

Aiken, at 82, was becoming more fragile, though he rarely missed a day of work. His schedule was punishing. He started work at 6:45 a.m., and often, during the week, didn't end his work day until 11 p.m., given the very busy social schedule he kept as a sought-after dinner guest. Also, during his last year in office, the Senate often met well into the evening hours. While other staff members ended their days at about 5:30, my task, when the Senate was in session, was to remain with the Senator as long as he needed me after 6 p.m. Often, the sessions would run until 10 p.m.

Our routine was predictable. Around 5:30 p.m., we would retire from the Senate Floor to his private office, which was adjacent to the Senate Floor, overlooking the West Front of the Capitol with a view of the Washington Monument. In the office was a bank of telephones, a television, and a small, privately-stocked bar. A couch, a desk, and two easy chairs filled the small room. These discreet offices were prized possessions and were reserved for the most senior members of the Senate. At first, Aiken did not want one, but he was prevailed upon to take the office because, if he hadn't, it would have touched off wrangling among his colleagues.

While awaiting session responsibilities in the evening, I would mix Aiken a Brandy Alexander, while I had a Scotch or Bourbon with water. If press calls needed to be returned, Aiken would do that. If not, we would often talk about Vermont in an earlier time when Aiken was in the State Legislature or serving as Governor. I was an eager listener since all of these conversations were history lessons for this much younger Vermonter.

Senator George D. Aiken was a favorite of the press corps because he was usually available and quotable. While he would rarely duck media questions, he was not a usual "media source," in that he could not be counted on to leak sensitive information to favored members of the media.

In fact, he despised leakers and would often tell me that leakers sought to make themselves important, especially those members of Congress and their staffs who had political ambitions. Aiken practiced what he preached. He had a rule that no staff member could leak to the press. For the most part, that rule was adhered to.

At times though, Aiken himself would be a source of inside Senate information, though not national-security-related, for the press. His favorite outlet was the U.S. News & World Report magazine that used to have a "Washington Whispers" column in which unattributed Senate gossip was printed. Aiken also told me that he used to have background conversations with Drew Pearson, and later, Jack Anderson, for their famous "Washington Merry Ground" syndicated column.

About 6:00 p.m., Aiken and I would leave his small Capitol Office and walk one floor down to the Senators' Dining Room, where he would order a cheeseburger and a dish of chocolate ice cream. After our quick bite, we would return to the Senate floor for the evening session.

I would sit on the big leather couches on the Republican side, in the back of the Chamber. Since Senator Aiken had an aisle seat, I could easily observe him. If a contentious debate on an issue took place —though not one dealing with Vietnam—I would see Aiken getting ready to speak. By then, I had a pretty good idea what might get him stirred up. If I thought he might respond in agitation, I would quietly slink down by his aisle seat, and say: "Governor, count to 20." If this failed, I would have the opportunity to edit his remarks in the Congressional Record, a practice that has long since been curtailed under Senate rules.

One week before Aiken announced that he would not seek re-election, on Feb. 6, 1974, the House Judiciary Committee voted to begin investigating a possible impeachment of President Nixon. This vote followed revelations in late 1973 that an 18½ minute gap was present in the subpoenaed Nixon tapes. On March 1, 1974, the Watergate scandal drum roll continued to beat as indictments were handed down for seven former Nixon's aides and campaign staff members. Another hammer blow came on April 16, 1974 when Leon Jaworski, the Special Prosecutor who had replaced Archibald Cox, issued subpoenas for 64 more of Nixon's tapes.

The Watergate news was all-consuming, as was the mail to Senator Aiken about the subject. On May 9, the House Judiciary Committee began impeachment hearings. Nixon had attempted to hide some of the requested tapes he had been ordered to submit. This choice of his resulted in a legal case that went before the United States Supreme Court. On July 24, the Capital and the world shook when the U.S. Supreme Court, in a unanimous decision in the case United States v. Nixon, ordered that the President had to turn over those tapes to investigators.

Nixon reluctantly complied. On July 27 and July 30, the House Judiciary Committee approved three articles of impeachment. The tapes had confirmed that President Nixon had ordered a cover-up and had tried to obstruct justice. These revelations were the death knell for the Nixon Presidency. It became evident that if the House formally voted for articles of impeachment, enough votes—including Aiken's—were present in the Senate to convict the President..

When Senators Hugh Scott and Barry Goldwater told Nixon that he did not have Senate support, Nixon decided to resign.

On August 8, Aiken was one of the 15 members of the House and Senate invited to the White House before the 9:00 p.m. address to the nation, in which Nixon would announce his resignation. The Vermont Senator said that the meeting was very emotional, with many tears in the room, including those of the President's. Aiken agreed that Nixon should resign because, once it was revealed that he was complicit in the cover-up, Nixon would have lost his credibility and ability to govern.

In his diary for the week ending Aug. 10, 1974, Aiken wrote:

> Of course, the big news of the week—the big sensation—was the resignation of Richard M. Nixon as President of the United States. Although, I had constantly opposed resignation on the President's part, preferring the impeachment process if he were found guilty of the charges made

against him, my position collapsed on Monday when it came out that the statements he had been making for the last two years were not true, and that he was aware of the Watergate break-in scandal soon after it occurred.

Aiken then said, when this admission was made, that Nixon had lost the support of Congress as well as most of the American people. While Aiken knew that, down deep, Nixon still wanted to fight the charges, Aiken agreed with Nixon that resignation was now the best course of action. Aiken communicated his opinion to Nixon directly.

While some Vermonters were urging strong punishment for Nixon, Aiken said that most people and the Congress were "relieved that this crisis in American history has been met. What they want now is for our government—all three branches—to perform honestly and successfully the responsibilities placed upon them by our own Constitution."

When Vice-President Gerald Ford became President, he announced that the nation's long national nightmare was over. Shortly thereafter, he issued a complete pardon for Nixon for his crimes. When Ford assumed office, he became the sixth U.S. President to deal with Vietnam. On Sept. 16, 1974, Ford announced a clemency program for deserters and draft evaders if they returned, took an oath of allegiance, and did two years of community service. Historians report that about 22,500 individuals, of the 124,000 eligible, took advantage of the program.

President Ford resisted all pleas by South Vietnam to come to its assistance as the North Vietnamese were building up its troop strength for what would become the ultimate defeat of the United States in Vietnam on April 30, 1975.

By then George Aiken was retired from the Senate and was back home in Vermont. United States involvement in the Vietnam War was over. Until his death on Nov. 19, 1984, Aiken firmly believed that if Lyndon Johnson had listened to his advice on Oct. 19, 1966 and had announced that the U.S. had won, that our country could have withdrawn from Vietnam. Instead, the war dragged on for another nine years.

5

Conclusions on Vietnam

Senator Aiken's Impact

What impact did Vermonter George D. Aiken have on the long, emotional debate over Vietnam War policy? Are there lessons to be learned from his opposition to the war? How does history judge his involvement? How was it that this farmer and horticulturist from Putney, who grew up with his hands in the soil and never went beyond high school, emerged as one of the most respected and influential voices in the Senate on U.S. foreign policy?

The simplest answer is that he was a man of honesty, decency, and independence of thought and action. Aiken knew how to listen and how to talk with people. He was never a "high-hat" nor a stuffed shirt. Aiken was a common man with a common touch. He lived his whole life with his hands and feet deeply rooted in the soil. When Aiken left the Senate, he wanted to do nothing more than go back to his garden, get his hands dirty, and make his garden even bigger.

On the anniversary of Aiken's 90th birthday, on Aug. 20, 1982, David Remnick, then having just started a job at the *Washington Post*, wrote a very revealing piece about Aiken titled, "George Aiken at 90." Remnick is now editor for The New Yorker, a position he has held since 1998. *The Post* story was based on a Remnick interview with the aging Vermont Senator at his home in Putney.

Aiken's character and his affection for Vermont is succinctly described by Remnick in this way: "Aiken retired in 1974, and unlike Senate colleagues such as Hugh Scott, J. William Fulbright, Gaylord Nelson, and John Sherman Cooper, he left Washington for good and came home."

"I am a Vermonter," Aiken said. "I was in prison for 34 years, and it was time to go free."

Ethel Page, who was two months older than Aiken and was his classmate at the little red school house that still stands on West Hill, said, "George is one of us. Always has been one of us."

Aiken was not a perfect human being. He often said that any person in political life is as "honest as any person you might find listed in the telephone book." In short, all humans have their strengths and weaknesses. He would ascribe that description to himself, too.

It was this insight about himself and his fellow citizens in Vermont and the nation that gave him standing when he spoke in the U.S. Senate. During his 34 years in the Senate, Aiken was one of the "poorer" members, as far as monetary resources. Even then, the Senate was becoming populated by Senators with financial resources and high social standing. Only a few, like Aiken, still called themselves farmers, an occupation that he always ascribed to himself. This status gave him special standing and influence.

His long-time friend, Senator Mike Mansfield, observed, "When George Aiken takes a position, it becomes respectable." Mansfield also said that his friend, Aiken, was "neither hawk nor dove, but a wise owl." Mansfield was the Democratic Senate Majority Leader while Republican Aiken advocated moderate and, in many cases, progressive positions on world and domestic issues.

Aiken was not by nature a sharply partisan person, even though during his last term he stood by President Nixon longer than some had expected. The venerable Vermonter supported Democratic-sponsored programs in the Senate as long as it helped people. He would tell me that he wouldn't vote against legislation when it benefitted his constituents, no matter who sponsored it: "Why would I say no to a bill when it would help my people?"

Aiken was also a supporter of federal government spending programs, especially in the health, education and welfare areas. This belief is why

Conclusions on Vietnam

he supported, as Governor of Vermont, some of the New Deal social programs, such as rural electrification and the Civilian Conservation Corps, while he opposed others that he argued would deprive people of their land or take over their water and natural resources for private interests.

Aiken was also a strong supporter of the legislative powers conferred by Article One of the U.S. Constitution. He opposed the usurpation of those powers by the Executive Branch of government. This approach could be seen in his first vote in the U.S. Senate, in March 1941, in opposition to President Franklin D. Roosevelt's Lend-Lease legislation, as well as in his support for using the Legislative branch's power of the purse to curtail Executive powers to wage war without congressional consent. With these strong principles embedded in Aiken's thinking, it was not surprising, when looking back at Aiken's long Senate career, that he was always skeptical of U.S. involvement in a land war in Southeast Asia.

As seen in earlier chapters, as far back as 1954, when Aiken first joined the Senate Foreign Relations Committee, the Vermonter had learned from the lessons of the French experience in Vietnam. The French had found that they could not spend enough resources nor sacrifice enough lives to "win" the war in Vietnam. The most important lesson for Aiken was that neither France, nor any other country, could defeat a nation that did not want to be colonized by a foreign power. It was not until 21 years later, in 1975, that the United States itself lost the war in Vietnam, a defeat that still lingers and haunts our national conscience 44 years after our defeat.

Reflecting on my up-front-and-personal experience with George Aiken, many years after his death, I have concluded that his influence came from his ability to forge bipartisan solutions for thorny legislative issues. He did this work through the power of his engaging personality and wisdom that came from his deep rural roots and small-town experience. Aiken knew that people don't like to be told what to do, especially when something is forced upon them by governmental decree.

An example of his personal philosophy occurred in 1964 when Aiken helped forge a compromise on an important civil rights bill by proposing what became known as the "Mrs. Murphy Clause." This bill allowed a person, with fewer than five rooms for rent, to not be subject to housing discrimination policies in the public accommodations section of the new civil rights bill. This important compromise helped gain passage of the legislation that President Johnson signed into law on July 2, 1964, with Aiken in attendance.

While not a scholar, Aiken seemed to have a penchant for finding the right word at the right time. Staffers of the Senate Foreign Relations Committee have told me that, during the mark-up of bills, the committee would get stuck on the right way to describe the bill's intentions. It would be Aiken, a lover of *The New York Times* crossword puzzle, who would be able to provide the answer.

Aiken's real influence came with his bipartisanship and his willingness to buck his party if he thought it was warranted. It was this trait that he brought with him to the Senate in 1941, since his experience as Governor was one of having won political battles by appealing to farmers, blue collar Vermonters and labor unions. Often, he took positions that pitted him against the Republican establishment, or the Old Guard.

When Republicans took control of the Senate in 1952, the Senate Republican leadership tried to convince Aiken to become a party leader. Aiken declined because he did not want to feel restrained by party politics and thus lose his growing influence as an independent Republican. The Vermonter did yield to GOP leadership, though, in its desire to use him to block Sen. Joe McCarthy, R-Wisconsin, from joining the Senate Foreign Relations Committee. The committee position launched Aiken towards his critical future role on Vietnam policy.

Aiken's personality and natural openness was his main character trait that served him well in the U.S. Senate. He got along with his fellow Senators, whether they were Republicans or Democrats.

For most of his 34-year career in the Senate, Aiken was in the minority, since Democrats controlled the committees. The result is that he put into practice early on his favorite old Vermont saying: "You catch more flies with honey than with vinegar." This philosophy was what allowed the Yankee farmer from Vermont to get along so well with his fellow Senators

Conclusions on Vietnam

from the South, while Democrats were, in Aiken's early years, hard line segregationists.

While Aiken did not always agree with the political philosophy of his Southern Democratic colleagues, he would not let that get in the way of making progress on those issues that they did agree on. An example would be Aiken's relationship with Sen. Richard B. Russell, D-Georgia., who was the long-time powerful Chair of the Senate Armed Services Committee. Russell was, for decades, the leader of the opposition to the Civil Rights Movement; Aiken was a Republican supporter of civil rights legislation. Despite that sharp difference, the two men were friends and remained in constant communication on the Vietnam War issue.

Russell was the political mentor for Lyndon B. Johnson when the Texan was in the Senate, serving as Majority leader. In private, Russell would counsel Johnson after he became President, telling Johnson to be very wary of sending U.S. troops to Vietnam. Johnson knew that Russell could be trusted to keep his cautious opinions on the war between them and never leak anything to the press.

Two Senators, however, who knew Russell's views on Vietnam were Aiken and Mansfield. Both Senators were opponents of President Johnson's escalation policy on the war. Aiken was more public about his opposition to expanding the war than Mansfield was, since the Montana Senator was also the Democratic Majority Leader. As a result, Mansfield was somewhat more constrained about how much he could criticize his party's Democratic President. It was often felt in Washington that, because of Aiken and Mansfield's close friendship, Aiken would express publicly what Mansfield was thinking privately.

The deep and lasting trust Aiken enjoyed with his Senate colleagues was the main source of his bi-partisan influence in the Senate. Even when Republican Richard Nixon became President, Aiken did not hesitate to provide criticism when the Vermonter felt that Nixon was headed down the wrong track in Vietnam. Aiken's constant challenge was that he favored Nixon's troop withdrawal policy but was skeptical and often openly critical of Nixon's use of air power and bombing to keep constant pressure on North Vietnam.

Aiken's internal conflict over Nixon's war policy, though, had the benefit of increasing his influence on the Vietnam question with his fellow Senators and the news media.

In this way, Aiken's influence on Vietnam was important as it helped him to keep his bi-partisan stance. The other important factor in what made Aiken special in the world of American politics, and in the Senate particularly was his enduring friendship and collaboration with Senator Mansfield, an alliance unheard of in today's Washington. Aiken's ability to reach across the aisle and make lasting alliances and friendships with his political opponents extended beyond Mansfield, and helped Aiken accomplish much where he would have been unable to otherwise.

By contrast to the Washington of today, and despite the bitter policy dispute that Aiken had with President Johnson over the Vietnam War, the two men still maintained a cordial relationship. This was evident in a letter from outgoing President Johnson, dated January 17, 1969, that I discovered at the Johnson Presidential Library in Austin, Texas. In the letter, Johnson wrote:

> Dear George,
>
> Thank you for your wonderful words. You may refer to yourself as a farmer, but to me, you will always be a statesman, and one of the best. You have brought honor to the institution that I love deeply. You have brought friendship to an institution that I love dearly. You have brought friendship to my family and me. For that, I salute you.

In another letter, also dated January 17, Johnson wrote to Aiken, requesting to have one final word as President with the Vermonter, a man he considered both an "adversary" and a "supporter," but "always respectful."

Johnson left Aiken with this final thought: "I know you will continue to provide a strong and clear voice in the halls of Congress. You have my very best wishes. LBJ."

Aiken's ability to reach a bipartisan consensus on vexing issues extended past the Vietnam War. For example, his persistence in working with

Conclusions on Vietnam

Republicans and Democrats enabled Aiken to gain passage of the Eastern Wilderness Act. Aiken was also able to secure funds for creation of a federal fish hatchery on the White River in Bethel. He won that accomplishment by bringing the then-chair of the Senate Appropriations Interior Subcommittee, Alan Bible of Nevada, a gallon of Vermont maple syrup.

Senator Aiken in retirement at his Putney home. (Aiken Family Photo)

For the remaining 10 years of his life, Aiken remained a revered figure in Vermont. He was a sought-after speaker. The media kept asking to interview him.

Before Aiken moved to the Heaton Woods Residence, Aiken and his wife, Lola, divided their time between Aiken's home in Putney and Lola's home in Montpelier. During his retirement, he and Lola travelled to Italy to visit Lola's ancestral home. This trip was the only time the former Senator left his home state during his final years.

The Senator became a Scholar in Residence at the University of Vermont. He would spend several days a month on the UVM campus, meeting with students and engaging with academicians Charlie Morrissey and Gregory Sanford as they conducted an important oral history project based on the complete collection of Aiken Papers that were housed at UVM.

In early 1976, Aiken's Senate Diary—January 1972 to January 1975 was published by the Stephen Greene Press in Brattleboro. The book consisted of the Senator's personal thoughts during the last three years of his time in Washington. The thoughts expressed in the book were pure Aiken. The book was his running commentary on the people and the politics of Washington during those critical years, words that still provide a window into Aiken's wisdom and his thinking.

George D. Aiken died at age 92 on Nov. 19, 1984 at the Heaton Woods Residence in Montpelier.

Aiken's death, his very simple family-only funeral on Thanksgiving Day, 1984, at the Putney Federated Church, and his burial under a clump of evergreen trees at the Mount Pleasant Cemetery in Putney, brought to conclusion a public life lived with humility and deeply-held principles.

Vermont is a state that has been in the past, and will continue to be in the future, a wellspring of democratic ideals and values that are pervasive throughout the state. Only from a small, rural state like Vermont could a Senator like George D. Aiken rise to such national prominence and remain true to himself.

The late Vermont Gov. Richard A. Snelling said it best on the day of Aiken's death in November 1984: "George Aiken was Vermont."

Part II

George D. Aiken's Life and Legacy

6

Who was George Aiken?

George David Aiken was born Aug. 20, 1892 in Dummerston, VT, the fourth of five children, to a vegetable and dairy farmer father and a homemaker mother. George had two sisters, Annie (nicknamed Maud) and Ethel, and two brothers, Roger and Ralph. The youngest brother, Ralph, died at a young age in 1918, a victim of the Spanish Flu that took more lives in America than did WWI. Aiken's parents, Edward Webster Aiken and Myra Cook Aiken, both natives of Windham County, married each other at ages 19 and 18, respectively.

Aiken's place of birth was known as the Corser Farm, located just south of the Putney town line, a demarcation that no longer exists since it was torn down to make way for Interstate 91. Aiken used to say that the highway was a $7 million monument to the place of his birth. In 1893, the Aiken family moved to a 50-acre farm on West Hill Putney, where young George was raised and lived for the next 20 years.

Aiken's ancestors came from Londonderry, Ireland. They were Scots, whom George Aiken said did not get along with the Irish. They left Ireland for America in 1718 and settled in Londonderry, NH. Branches of the Aiken family migrated West and South. Some of Aiken's forebears settled in Aiken, SC, named for the family. Meanwhile, a Col. Edward Aiken became an early settler in Londonderry, Vermont, and another Edward Aiken (a different Aiken than George's father) later moved to Windham, Vermont.

Edward Aiken, George's father, was raised in the Houghtonville district of Grafton, VT and his mother, Myra, was born and raised in the Pettengill district of Andover, VT. Aiken's father, Edward, was a farmer who raised vegetables and tobacco for sale from a cart in the Putney Village. He also cut and sold wood for a living, plus kept a few dairy cows. George often remarked that one of the worst days of his life was when his father found out that he could milk cows by hand.

George Aiken's parents were born and raised in Windham County. (Aiken Family Photo)

In 1981, at age 88, some three years before his death, George Aiken wrote a long letter to his family called "The Way it Was and Is." In it, he wrote about what it was like growing up between ages 10 and 15. When he was not in school, he did chores around the farm such as "pulling weeds at age 12, peddling vegetables, going to school, cleaning stables, helping to cut wood and limbed-out trees while my father brought wood to Putney Village for $4.50 per cord. Edward Aiken sometimes drove logs all the way to Brattleboro and received $20 per 1,000 feet for pine."

Aiken's senior portrait from Brattleboro High School (Aiken Family Photo)

George Aiken also wrote that, as a child, he had "racked hay and helped put it in the barn," and he noted that "at 15, he could hand mow and cradle oats, and pick potato bugs." Aiken recalled "on rainy days I might go trout fishing, and occasionally fish for hornpout [bullhead] after dark."

At age 14, George Aiken joined the Putney Grange, where he said he learned public speaking. This skill proved to be an important addition to his

Early Life: Who was George Aiken?

life because it was here, in the Grange, that Aiken learned that his ability to talk would "have a favorable affect" and would provide him with some early political training.

Aiken's recollection of his school days provides a portrait of education in small-town Vermont. Initially, the elementary school had one teacher for nine grades, but the school was later reduced to eight grades. At that point, grade 9 was moved to the Putney Town Hall. Later, in 1905, a new school building with four classrooms was opened in Putney. It had one teacher, who was paid $12 a week. The high school classes she taught were English, algebra, geometry, history, Latin and German. For the entirety of his fourth year of high school, Aiken walked five miles to the train station, then took the train for nine miles to Brattleboro, and then walked another half a mile to the high school. Aiken graduated in 1909 at age 16, the youngest member of the class. He was also a member of the high school track team. It was as a student that Aiken first visited Washington, DC when his senior class trip was to the White House. There, the students all shook hands with President William Howard Taft.

George Aiken spent his last year of high school commuting by rail from Putney to Brattleboro. He also was a member of the high school track team in the second row, upper right. (Aiken Family Photo)

Growing up on a hillside farm in Vermont at the turn of the 19th Century had its high and low moments. Some of the high moments involved George Aiken's love of wildflowers, of birds of all kinds, of sheep and lambs, and of his black Morgan Horse. He also liked to visit the big oak tree on his property, which he always said was the largest tree in Vermont.

He also like to reminisce about catching bullheads, going to corn husking parties, where he met his first wife, Beatrice Howard, and tapping the big maple trees near the family home for maple syrup. One other aspect of his early life that he loved was the family dog, Shep, who herded the cows every afternoon "and who was more scared of thunderstorms than I was."

Some of the low moments of his childhood included minor ailments such as a toothache and Aiken's concerns that a family medical emergency and grocery bills would put a serious strain on family finances. But nothing was more "hated as a kid" than when the family pig was slaughtered. "When my father killed the pig in November, I hid under the bed so I couldn't hear him squeal. My mother would eat no part of the pig she had raised all summer. When the pig was stuck and hung up in the maple tree, I got his bladder which made a fairly good football." The internal conflict between Aiken's sensitivity regarding the pig being slaughtered and his enjoyment of the "bladder football" is best explained by the youngster's familiarity with the realities of farm life.

George Aiken's father, Edward, was a member of the Vermont House for three terms. He as a life-long farmer who sold vegetables to customers from a one-horse wagon in Putney. George Aiken followed his father in the Vermont House when he was first elected in 1930 to represent Putney. (Aiken Family Photo)

Aiken's Hillside Mentality

George Aiken's political philosophy was deeply rooted in the hillside mentality that formed his life. In 1938, in his book *Speaking from Vermont*, Aiken wrote that people like to live in the mountains "where freedom of thought and action is logical and inherent."

Vermont has long been a state where preservation of individual liberties is a cherished value. Vermont is

Early Life: Who was George Aiken?

also a state where public service is viewed as an essential ingredient for vital and strong communities. The Aiken family had many generations that served in elected and appointed positions in their communities. As a young man, George Aiken learned from the example of his father , who served four terms in the Vermont House, from 1913 to 1920. Before that, Aiken's grandfather and great-grandfather also served in the Vermont House. It was a family tradition.

Allen R. Foley, President of the Vermont Historical Society from 1970 to 1974 and Professor Emeritus of History at Dartmouth College, wrote an essay about an episode during Edward Aiken's tenure in the Vermont House that gives us a window into the elder Aiken's personality:

> At the time the Vermont legislature was discussing adoption of the 19th amendment to the Constitution of the United States," **Foley wrote,** "which gave women the right to vote. Senator George Aiken's father happened to be a member of the House. Mr. Aiken, who favored the extension of suffrage to women, was being interrogated by a member who opposed this move. The colloquy went something like this:
>
> "Mr. Aiken, you say you favor this amendment."
> "Yes, I do."
> "You realize, Mr. Aiken, that this will include jury duty."
> "Yes, I do."
> "Well, Mr. Aiken, suppose in a criminal case that runs on for four, five or six days, your wife was the only woman on the jury and had to be closely confined with those men during all this period. How would you like that, Mr. Aiken?"
> "Well," said Mr. Aiken after carefully studying the big chandelier in the center of the hall, "I think it would all depend on who we had hired for a girl at the time."

In 1920, Edward Aiken decided to not seek re-election to the Vermont House; instead he opted to launch a bid for the Vermont State Senate from Windham County. In announcing his candidacy for the Vermont Senate in *The Brattleboro Reformer*, Aiken joked that he "waited until after the Chicago convention to see if I might not get the nomination for president, but, alas! I did not." An advertisement for Edward Aiken's election campaign appeared in *The Brattleboro Reformer* on September 13, 1920, which urged voters to "send Aiken back to Montpelier," if they believed "that a record is better than a promise; and if you believe that fifty years of farming and eight years in the Vermont House of Representatives qualify a man to go to Montpelier as your senator." Evidently, as Edward Aiken did not assume that position the following year, he must have been unsuccessful in his Senate campaign, likely failing to make it through the primary election.

Edward Aiken was a "Bull Moose" progressive Republican who supported Teddy Roosevelt in 1912 when Roosevelt ran against President William Howard Taft. Later, George Aiken described his father in an oral history interview with Charles Morrissey as an "anti-conservative." "Teddy Roosevelt was a rebel and I think my father had it in his blood somewhat. And it had come down from generation to generation. And he was a progressive in a way. He never had any money."

Aiken was not old enough in 1912 to vote, as did his father, for Teddy Roosevelt for President. The younger Aiken did accompany his father to Brattleboro in 1912, however, to witness Teddy Roosevelt campaigning from the back of his train car. Many years later, Aiken would recount the scene to me and to many others. Aiken's lasting memory was of Roosevelt proclaiming to the crowd in a high-pitched voice: "I took the Canal Zone and let Congress debate; and while the debate goes on, the canal does also." This statement was a reference to Roosevelt's leadership in the construction of the Panama Canal.

George Aiken was born on a farm. He was known for his cultivation of fruits, berries and wildflowers. While he once owned a small herd of Jersey cows, he freely admitted that he never enjoyed milking them. As Governor, though, he did like being photographed with one. (George Aiken Papers)

Charles Morrissey's significant oral history revealed that in

Early Life: Who was George Aiken?

1981, Aiken had written a letter to Theodore Roosevelt III in 1939, in which Aiken said: "I only wish your father was here in Vermont fighting with us today. One of the great regrets in my life is that I was not old enough to vote for him in 1912, but how I did holler."

George Aiken had said that he always wanted to be a farmer, "ever since I was two years old."

After high school he had returned to his father's farm to peddle vegetables downtown or milk cows. But he wanted something more. So he blazed his own path forward and chose to run a nursery that specialized in fruits and wildflowers.

Aiken as an apple grower in Putney in the 1920s. (Aiken Family Photo)

In 1912, at age 19, he and business associate, George Darrow, bought a 40-acre field near the Aiken homestead on which, in summer, they planted apples and wildflowers and, in winter, cut blocks of ice from a small ice pond. The ice was harvested and stored in sawdust until it was needed in the summer for people who had icebox refrigerators.

Aiken took a $100 loan from a local bank to pay for his share in the partnership. The business was called Darrow & Aiken. Later, Darrow's name was dropped from the business after Aiken bought out Darrow's share.

In 1914, Aiken married Beatrice Howard, who could be described as a person of strong country stock. In a 1974 senior thesis on Aiken, Princeton history major, Arthur Walter Schmidt, Jr., wrote about Mrs. Aiken: "Undoubtedly Beatrice Aiken's fortitude was tried early, when the young couple spent their honeymoon at a state grange meeting. It was clear that George's public instincts would supersede personal considerations." Many years later when Aiken recounted the story to me about going to the state grange meeting in Montpelier after his wedding, he said with a smile: "I wouldn't do that again." Obviously, his wife had not been pleased.

The first Presidential vote Aiken cast was in 1916. Aiken's political maverick history had an early start when he cast his first Presidential vote at age 24 for Democrat Woodrow Wilson, who was elected to his second term over the GOP candidate, Charles Hughes. Vermont supported Hughes with 62 percent of the vote.

During that 1916 Presidential Election, Wilson ran on a platform of promoting world peace, while his opponent, then U.S. Supreme Court Associate Justice Charles Evan Hughes (Hughes' career would span from Governor of New York to Chief Justice of the Supreme Court), would involve the United States in the ongoing war in Europe. Wilson won reelection on this platform of peace but was unable to prevent the United States from becoming involved in World War I, which had been raging in Europe since 1914.

By 1917, Aiken Nursery was doing well. Aiken also was an active member of the Grange in Putney. That same year, at age 25, Aiken was elected President of the Vermont Horticultural Society as well as leader of the local Boy Scout troop. In 1920, Aiken then became a member of the Putney School Board (or "school director" as it was then called), an office he held for nearly 18 years.

7

Vermont Political Career

In 1922, two years after his father had retired from the State Legislature, the younger Aiken stepped up to run. His opposition was Fred Leach, whom Aiken described as an old-fashioned Democrat. Aiken later told Morrissey: "Somebody spread the story that if I went to the Legislature, I'd vote to close all district schools and centralize them. That's the last thing I would have done. I was so darn mad I wouldn't deny it, and I lost by a few votes. So, then I laid low until 1930."

The way he described the 1922 defeat to me was that he never had learned who had started the rumor about the schools closing, but that he also felt he didn't need to respond to the accusation. After that first and only election defeat in his long political career, Aiken said his political ambitions "subsided for a while."

Between 1922 and 1930, Aiken spent time further building up his nursery business and continuing to be active on a statewide basis as a leading horticulturist. One of his accomplishments was to become the first person to raise trailing arbutus commercially. He learned to cultivate arbutus when he observed the plants being plowed under in a field. He saved some of the plants and began to perfect their propagation. He also patented the ever-bearing strawberry plant.

By the mid-1920s, Aiken and his wife Beatrice were the parents of four children, three daughters and one son. In a 2004 newspaper column, George

Aiken's grandson, Burr Morse of East Montpelier, shared some valuable insights into his grandmother, whom he called "fast paced with a purpose." Burr wrote of his grandmother: "Always a champion of the underdog, she could smell out folks in need almost before they knew themselves. Her generosity knew no bounds. She was forever dropping off furniture and canned goods for families in need and usually did it incognito.

"One time she took in two brothers, 15 and 17, who had fled Hungary. She taught them English and raised them as her sons until both were off [as] American citizens to American colleges." Burr Morse said that his grandmother always supported her husband. "If it weren't for her, he [Aiken] would never have gone to Washington and done all those great things for mankind, which included his thriving nursery business, an apple orchard, even when it meant going to Washington for bill signings and the White House events. She knew the way there; she also knew the way home."

Morse also recounted that his aunt Barbara, the youngest of the Aikens' four children, told him that before George Aiken entered politics, he would go to the Aiken Nursery on Putney Road, Route 5, "every day in a shirt and tie. He would get up, dress, and come to the kitchen table, where Ma would tie his tie and wash his glasses."

Aiken vs. "The Old Guard"

The late University of Vermont Historian, Professor Sam Hand, wrote the seminal book on the Vermont Republican Party, *The Star That Set*. Hand was also a follower of George Aiken and his political career. In his book, Hand documented how Aiken, as a Progressive Republican, took on what was often called the "Old Guard" of the Vermont Republican Party, which never supported Aiken since he was the voice of farmers and the labor movement in Vermont. The Old Guard members in Vermont were supporters of the banks, utilities, and big business, such as the Proctor Family and Vermont Marble as well as National Life Insurance Co. Try as they might, however, the Old Guard faction could never dislodge Aiken from public life.

Vermont Political Career

George Aiken's political career, which began in 1930 with his election to the Vermont House and ran until his 1975 retirement from the U.S. Senate, often followed his philosophic "North Star," which was rooted in progressive and liberal thinking. Consistent themes for Aiken were his loyalty to the common folk of Vermont, and his suspicion of big money and big business—like the utilities, banks, and insurance companies. Wherever possible, Aiken favored co-operatives, whether it was for milk processing or for providing electric power to the people who lived off the main roads. He consistently advocated that the natural resources of the state, such as water and land, belonged to the people and should not be used by big corporations to increase their profits.

It is evident, when you examine Aiken's speeches, papers, and actions at the Vermont State House from 1930 to 1941, and throughout his entire political career, that these beliefs were the bedrock tenets upon which he built his political philosophy. I joined his staff during the last term of his Senate career in May 1969 and worked beside him until his retirement in 1975. There would hardly be a day that he wouldn't rail against the Old Guard that had tried to derail him many times—without success—even when he was in his late 70s and early 80s.

Following the Great Flood of 1927, which claimed the life of Lieutenant Governor Hollister Jackson in Barre, and which caused the loss of life of numbers of other Vermonters as well as millions of dollars of destruction, the state of Vermont made a determined effort, as did the rest of New England, to improve flood control with new dams and impoundment structures. As a result, Aiken's first political victory over the big utilities came during his freshman year in the Vermont House in 1931.

Professor H. K. Barrows of the Massachusetts Institute of Technology proposed and designed a flood control system that he suggested be built throughout New England. Barrows' plan envisioned that the private utilities would build the dams to help defray the costs to Vermont citizens, and he determined that the dams should also be used to generate electric power.

Aiken was strongly opposed to the plan because, as he would often recall, it would have meant that some 80 Vermont rivers and streams would be dammed up, with the power generated going out of state. The Barrows' Plan in Vermont was sponsored by then Republican House Speaker Edward Deavitt. The legislation was assigned to the House Conservation and Development Committee, of which Aiken was a member.

As a freshman member of the Vermont House, Aiken bided his time on the committee until the time was right. When he noticed on March 3, 1931 that not all the supporters of the Barrows Plan were in the committee room, with nine of the 15 members in the room, Aiken moved that bill be reported adversely. His motion carried with six votes for and three opposed. Aiken, ever the person wanting to give an opponent an opportunity to save face, then asked that Speaker Deavitt be given the opportunity to withdraw the bill, which he did.

Years later, during the Aiken Oral History project, Aiken had this exchange with his interviewer, Gregory Sanford, who later became the longtime state archivist and lifelong Aiken admirer:

Sanford: "Who was supporting that bill? The power companies?"

Aiken: "Oh, the power companies, the railroads, and even the granite industry and the marble industry—even the insurance—the big boys."

Sanford: "So it brought you in conflict with the Old Guard?"

That successful Aiken political strategy to kill the Barrows Plan propelled Aiken's career and inspired him to consider running for a State Senate seat from Windham County during the 1932 elections. However, his political friend and ally, Ernest W. Gibson Jr., the son of the incumbent Vermont Senator and a lawyer who had helped Aiken earlier to collect on bad business debts, was then Assistant Secretary for the Vermont Senate. Gibson, according to Prof. Sam Hand, had a better idea, which would be a "dramatic shortcut to higher office."

Gibson recommended that his friend run for another term in the Vermont House and then run for Speaker in 1933. As a result, Aiken ran against Barre banker, Charles Wishart, the candidate of the Republican establishment. Aiken quietly campaigned across Vermont, meeting House members, seeking support for his Speakership candidacy. He won, and, as Gibson had predicted, that win took Aiken a leap up the Vermont political ladder.

The year 1933 was an important year in Aiken's political life. It was the first year of the New Deal following the inauguration of Franklin Delano Roosevelt as President. In Vermont, and throughout the nation, bankruptcies were occurring, and banks were either closing or foreclosing on many businesses. The common man was particularly hard hit.

The Worthy-Debtor Law

As Aiken told it to me, he stopped Walter Fenton, the lobbyist for the Central Vermont Public Service Corporation of Rutland, Vermont, in the State House one day and asked him, "Why don't you do something useful?" Fenton asked Aiken what he had in mind. Aiken said he wanted the "little fellows" to have the same protections that big business had when it declared bankruptcy. Fenton then drafted legislation for Aiken that did just that. The bill, known as the "Worthy-Debtor Law," passed the Legislature. While other states attempted to pass similar laws, only Wisconsin was successful.

Aiken was proud of this effort. Over the years, he loved recounting the story. He would point to this achievement as an example of his commitment to the average Vermonter, rather than to corporations or big business.

Rural Electrification Act in Vermont

In 1935, Aiken became Vermont's Lieutenant Governor, the last farmer elected to the post until David Zuckerman was elected in 2016. In Vermont at that time, the private power companies would serve only those customers close to the main roads. Those living on backroads, mostly farmers, had no access to electricity.

During his time in office, Aiken made his mark on the state by delaying the adjournment of the Legislature in order to get enabling legislation

George Aiken as Lt. Governor enjoying a cake at a Vermont county fair. (Aiken Family Photo)

overnighted by train from Washington that authorized the creation of rural electric cooperatives. Aiken had convinced a teetotaling State Senator from Lamoille County to move for an overnight adjournment after the dinner hour, because senators returning from dinner had imbibed. As the proposed motion to adjourn was non-debatable, Aiken, the presiding officer, called the question. The Senate adjourned for the night, giving Aiken time to pass the Rural Electrification Act legislation the next day. This made it possible for the formation of electric cooperatives to get power to people living on the hillsides. Thanks to the rural electric co-ops. you can still see evidence of power lines strung across fields and forest land in order to serve a few isolated customers.

While Aiken was critical of some FDR New Deal programs, he was not of all of them. He favored those programs that helped to promote health, education, and public welfare. Where he would draw the line were those New Deal programs that sought to move people off or to take away their land, or to impose federal flood control projects on Vermont waterways, as he feared they were exercising federal power over state's rights.

The Green Mountain Parkway

The proposed Green Mountain Parkway would have created a 260-mile scenic highway from the Massachusetts border to the Canadian border, along what is now basically Vermont Route 100. The idea was to create a national park of some 50,000 acres. Despite the fact that the project was designed to support tourism and provide construction jobs for some 16,000 unemployed Vermonters, it rubbed Aiken the wrong way.

Vermont Political Career

The parkway was a very controversial highway that had its powerful citizen supporters, mostly in central and northern Vermont, with opposition based in southern Vermont. The Vermont Chamber of Commerce and Gov. Stanley Wilson supported the project when it was first talked about in 1934. Then in 1935 and 1936, surprise opposition came from the Green Mountain Club, the caretakers of the Vermont Long Trail, and from Mortimer Proctor, a backer who later became Governor of Vermont.

Governor Aiken, on the far left, is at a National Governors Association lunch with President Franklin D. Roosevelt standing in the middle. (White House Photo)

In 1935, the Vermont Senate approved the plan by a narrow margin. However, it was then rejected by the Vermont House in a close vote. The supporters had been promoting the project as a way to keep youth in the state and to give a big push to the emerging tourism economy. Opponents said the project would spoil Vermont and require $500,000 in state bonding to purchase the rights-of-way for the parkway. Additionally, just as the New York parkways had brought Jewish tourists to the Catskills, opponents of the Green Mountain Parkway feared the same would happen in Vermont. Aiken told me flatly that anti-Semitism was involved in the decision, but most anti-Semites found other reasons to voice their opposition.

Gov. Charles Smith, who had decided not to seek another term, called a special session in December 1935 to deal with the contentious parkway issue. As a result, a statewide referendum on the issue was scheduled for Town Meeting Day in March 1936. For Aiken, the referendum became a dilemma since he had recently entered the primary for the Republican nomination for Governor. Although he privately opposed the parkway, Aiken refused to take a firm position before the March vote. In a February 1936 letter, he wrote that he could not "get excited enough about the Parkway to let either side use my name in any propaganda. I am sure it would not do the harm its opponents claim it would, nor would it do as much good as its proponents claim."

When Vermonters voted on the issue in their Town Meeting referendum, 42,873 Vermonters had voted against the project, and 30,795 had voted in support. Aiken told me some 33 years after that 1936 vote that he thought some Vermonters had opposed the project because it would open the way for more persons of the Jewish faith to migrate to Vermont. Prof. Sam Hand said that most historians viewed the results of the vote as "partisan politics, a view supported by evidence that most Republicans voted against, and most Democrats voted for the parkway."

Years later, Aiken would tell me that Vermonters "knew where I stood [on the issue]." As his aide, it was never clear to me.

Opposition to the New Deal Resettlement Administration

As House Speaker, and then later as Lieutenant Governor, Aiken launched a full-scale assault on the New Deal with his opposition to a plan by the Resettlement Administration to move Vermonters whom they called "poor" off the "sub marginal" hillsides to more prosperous valley towns and land. The idea was that the federal government would purchase the land and then lease it back to the state as long as it remained unoccupied. The catch was that the federal government would retain all mineral and oil rights.

Aiken objected to the entire plan, and, in time, the FDR program lost support in Vermont as it was deemed to undermine agriculture. In his book *Speaking from Vermont*, written in 1938, Aiken

George Aiken was Governor from age 45 to 49. (Aiken Family Photo)

commented that "Grapevine communications tells me that the resettlement plan of moving out of the mountain has been a flop."

While Aiken was critical of the Old Guard in his own party, he was also a major opponent of federal flood control projects around New England, including those in Vermont. His focus was on keeping Vermont's resources for the benefit of Vermonters and not allowing them to be taken over by federal fiat. As Governor from 1937 through 1939, Aiken was a major thorn in the side of the federal government's plan for building federal flood control projects by leading other New England Governors in their opposition to a flood control plan that did not retain the rights for states to control their own resources. While the Roosevelt Administration wanted federal control without state interference, Aiken led the rear-guard battle against the federal flood control plan.

Ultimately, the federal government resolved that if Vermont did not want to have flood control projects that it wouldn't have any. One project, the Union Village Dam, on the Ompompanoosuc River in Thetford, was built by the Army Corps of Engineers, but it included only recreational and not power benefits. Gregory Sanford and Charles Morrissey's oral history of Aiken, published by the University of Vermont, suggested that his opposition to flood control projects pushed the opposing sides into a stalemate.

By contrast, Governor Aiken was a supporter of the New Deal program called the Civilian Conservation Corps (CCC). It should be noted that Vermont benefited significantly from the CCC, which resulted in the state park program that Vermont still has today.

George Aiken had enjoyed a rapid rise in Vermont politics from his first election in 1930 to the Vermont House and by his two terms as Governor in 1937 and 1939. He ran on sustained opposition to the Old Guard elements in the national and Vermont Republican Party, while vigorously supporting the working men and women, with his special affinity for farmers and laborers.

As Vermont Governor in 1936, Aiken presided over only one of two states (the other being the State of Maine) that had chosen to support Kansas Governor Alf Landon over President Franklin Roosevelt in the 1936

Presidential race. That decision gave Aiken national prominence and growing prestige within his own party. Additionally, his fight against aspects of FDR's New Deal raised Aiken's profile further and inspired some consideration of Aiken for President in the 1940 elections. At that time, the national Republican party was searching for candidates who could challenge the New Deal and FDR. Aiken was on that list.

The Vermonter made his first move toward a higher national profile when, in late 1937, he wrote an open letter to the Republican National Committee. The entire letter is printed in Aiken's *Speaking from Vermont* with one chapter heading titled: "A Voter Looks for a Party." The message in that chapter was blunt and very clear: either reform the national GOP or lose the opportunity to regain political power.

Aiken said that he had consulted with his Vermont constituency and concluded that "patriotic citizens" saw no hope for a party "offering no constructive policy or program, a party whose leaders are apparently more concerned with controlling party machinery than with American welfare, a party so torn by internal bickering, hopeless ambitions and lack of direction as to be in a nearly complete state of demoralization."

The first-term, 45-year-old Vermont Governor urged the Republican Party to "purge" the reactionary elements, inspired mainly by Southern GOP leaders, and "to focus its forces on the youth of our nation." Aiken's attacks continued in 1938, when he was the featured speaker at the National Republican Club's 1938 Lincoln Day Dinner at the Waldorf Astoria Hotel in New York City. At the posh black-tie dinner, Aiken told the audience, and the nation through a radio hook-up, that Lincoln "would be ashamed of his party leadership today."

This provocative speech was well covered by the press, and it drew angry responses from the Old Guard elements in the national party. The speech accomplished its purpose and propelled Aiken higher up on the list of potential GOP presidential candidates in 1940. In keeping with his common touch, after the speech, Aiken changed out of his formal attire and went to a local movie theater to see "Snow White and Seven Dwarfs."

Vermont Political Career

Aiken Flirts with Running for President

Fishing at Lake Averill, the four were discussing George Aiken running for President in 1940. Left to right: Ralph Flanders of Springfield, Kansas, Gov. Alf Landon, Governor George Aiken, and Sterry Waterman of St. Johnsbury. (Quimby Country Photo)

Aiken continued, throughout 1938, to flirt with the notion that he could be a candidate for President in 1940. According to Gregory Sanford, whose May 1977 UVM Master's Thesis, The Presidential Boomlet for Governor George D. Aiken, 1937-1939, or You Can't Get There From Here, served as the most complete and authoritative study of the topic. Aiken shut down his Presidential effort in early 1939. Years later, Aiken told me when I served as his Legislative Assistant that he was not comfortable turning over his campaign to big city handlers and money men. And, according to Sanford, Aiken's inexperience in international affairs made him an unlikely choice "in a world tottering on brink of war."

Stanford's thesis concluded that, "The boomlet had, however, served Aiken's purpose. From 1937-39, it allowed Vermont to assert its influence on the Republican Party and to offer to the nation an alternative to the New Deal's unending faith in federal planning." History will record that Wendell Willkie won the GOP nomination in 1940 over Sen. Robert Taft on the sixth ballot. Aiken, a delegate to the 1940 convention, supported Willkie, even though he was a former private utility executive. Willkie lost to Franklin Delano Roosevelt, who was elected to his third term.

Driving the Aiken boomlet had been his opposition to the New Deal Flood Control plans for Vermont and New England. Aiken had two main objections to the plan. The first, as previously mentioned, was that the federal government would exercise too much power over state resources, such as land and water. The second was rooted in Aiken's deeply held animosity towards the private utility interests that would have profited from the energy benefits, even though they would have been on the hook to pay for some of the infrastructure improvements.

Amidst Aiken's national presidential speculation, and despite his hints that perhaps a third party should be formed if the national Republican Party didn't change its ways, the Vermont Governor had his hands full running Vermont. His traditional enemies, the business interests in Vermont, still chafed under his leadership. They always thought that he leaned too far left, and by quickly adopting some New Deal programs that provided social welfare benefits, Aiken showed that he was too much of an unpredictable maverick, and certainly not an orthodox Republican.

His two terms as Governor were focused on protecting Vermont's natural resources, promoting the expansion of electric service to rural areas of the state, and supporting Vermont agriculture, primarily the dairy industry that was the major economic driver of the state's economy. During his first Inaugural message as Governor in 1937, Aiken had said:

> We wish to remain on good terms with our neighboring states, but the waterpower of Vermont is our heritage, a natural resource bestowed upon us even as other states have their natural advantages. I believe this gift should be used primarily for the benefit of our own state, and we should not surrender any of it without just recompense. I hope the time is not far distant when every Vermonter will be enabled to enjoy the use of electric power in his home or business at rates proportionate to our bounty.

In his Second Inaugural in 1939, Aiken continued his focus on protecting Vermont from federal control without compensation, and he also encouraged a relationship with the Province of Quebec:

> Friendly relations with one's neighbors go far toward promoting prosperity

and welfare. During the last two years, our relations with neighboring states and with the Province of Quebec have been of a most cordial nature. I believe this has resulted in mutual benefits received with an increase in business activity and the sustaining of public morale so necessary in these times of worldwide adversity.

We have also cooperated freely with the federal government in most matters and have found federal officials generally courteous, earnest in their work, and desirous of cooperating with us. With the desire of certain federal officials to remodel the lives and direct the ways of our people, we have felt obliged to disagree.

Nor has our state administration felt that it could recognize the claim of the federal government to take for itself the resources belonging to the people of our state without our consent and without making a just recompense. I intend to maintain this stand during the next two years. It is my earnest hope that we will continue to maintain and improve our friendly and neighborly relationship with the Dominion of Canada, our neighboring states and with the federal government.

But I believe Vermonters are still able to govern themselves and that we should be ready at all times to stand shoulder to shoulder with our neighboring states, or alone, if necessary, in resisting any attempts to take from us the right of self-government or to put upon us any form of oppression whether that oppression comes from within or without our national borders.

In 1939, after the legislature passed an Aiken proposal to make the state's Public Service Commission an independent state agency, free of utility control, did this shift in definition for the commission become a major cause of new friction between Aiken and the Republican State Committee. Aiken wanted a pro-consumer utility regulator. To accomplish that goal, he appointed the former president of the Vermont Farm Bureau, Ellsworth B. Cornwall, as Chair. Cornwall was a controversial figure in Vermont. Following his ascension to the Senate, Aiken continued to spur conflict between the Old Guard of the Vermont GOP and the younger progressive wing of the party.

Aiken did not consider running for a third term as Governor, but he had not made his plans widely known. It was clear, though, that the leaders of the Vermont Republican party were ready to replace him. In early 1940, party regulars openly supported Lt. Gov. William Wills as Aiken's replacement, even before Aiken revealed that he would not pursue a third term. Aiken's decision to only serve two terms, however, fell in line with the "Mountain Rule," which dictated that the Vermont Governorship would alternate within the Vermont Republican Party between candidates from either side of the Green Mountains. For the longest time, it was tradition for a governor to only serve a single two-year term, but that tradition had been amended after Governor John Weeks was elected to a second term in 1928. Not until 1966, when Democratic Governor Philip H. Hoff, the first Democrat to hold the office in over one hundred years, ran for a third term, did a Vermont governor break the unspoken two-term rule.

Vermont's political world dramatically changed on June 20, 1940 when Vermont Sen. Ernest W. Gibson, Sr. died in office. Aiken appointed his close friend and ally and the son of Gibson, Sr., Ernest W. Gibson, Jr., to the post, an interim position to be held until a special election could be held. The election was then scheduled for the fall of 1940. In essence, Gibson kept the Senate seat "warm" until Aiken could win the seat outright.

The Old Guard convinced Aiken's friend, Springfield industrialist, Ralph Flanders, to run for the Senate seat. It was a bitter campaign, but Aiken won with 55 percent of the vote. It was Flanders' first run for political office. Flanders did win a Vermont Senate seat in 1946 after President Truman appointed Vermont Senator Warren Austin as the first Ambassador to the United Nations. By then, Aiken was already the senior U.S. Senator from Vermont.

As Governor, George Aiken had been instrumental in starting the Vermont ski industry, in response to his Commissioner of Forests and Parks, Perry Merrill. Merrill had convinced Aiken to lease state-owned land to the Mount Mansfield Company for ski area development. As Aiken said in his 1941 farewell address to the Legislature, "There has been a great and profitable development in winter sports throughout the state, particularly in the

Vermont Political Career

Mansfield and Pico Mountain regions. Vermont is one of the few states that can sell four feet of snow and twenty below zero at a profit."

Anthony Marro, previously mentioned, wrote this about Merrill:

> In the Swedish winter of 1920, Perry Merrill had an epiphany that eventually would transform Vermont. At the time, he was a young worker with the Vermont Forest Service who was spending a year at the Royal College of Forestry in Stockholm and traversing the Swedish forests on eight-foot-long skis. Recreational skiing was almost unknown back in Vermont. The first ski lift, a rope tow powered by a Ford Model T engine wouldn't be installed at Suicide Six in Woodstock until 1934. But Merrill became convinced while in Sweden that skiing could become as popular in Vermont as it was in Scandinavia and that if ski resorts could be built on state lands, they could generate the revenue needed not only to pay for those resorts but also to fund many other state parks and state forests.
>
> The long story short is that Merrill made it happen, despite the opposition of many. He started out at a time when many Vermonters thought that spending tax dollars for public parks was both foolish and wasteful. By the time he retired in 1966, having served under nineteen governors and having been the head of the Department of Forests and Parks under thirteen of them, Vermont had gone from having no state parks at all to a sprawling empire that included 34 state parks and 32 state forests, with 85,039 acres of state forests, 11,288 acres of state parks, 8,520 linear feet of sand beach, 1,528 camp sites, 244 fireplaces, 311 grills and 1,093 picnic tables. Outdoor recreation had helped transform the entire economy of the state, and, as the *Rutland Herald* noted at the time of his retirement:
>
>> Merrill literally invented a government power base that... allowed him a dominant voice in the state's development. Merrill is generally recognized as a patron saint and guiding light of the multimillion-dollar Vermont ski industry, the man who preached its economic potential and used his power to nurture it when other Vermonters thought skiing, at least the downhill kind, was for showoffs, sissies and flatlanders.

In his autobiography, The Making of a Forester, Merrill himself wrote: "I always loved Vermont, and anything that I saw work well in other places,

I wanted to apply to Vermont. I was sure that her beauty was so great that people once experiencing it would want to return again and again. I wanted people to be able to swim in her lakes, canoe in her rivers, camp in her forests and drive through her hills and valleys. And especially, I wanted to know that her natural resources would be developed in a way that would preserve them for future generations."

During his last years in office, it often was said that Merrill was the last dictator left in state government, albeit a benevolent one, and that his oversight of the state's forests was so complete that "The leaves don't turn red until Perry gives them the word." He may not have been a dictator, in fact, but he had so much autonomy that Gov. Robert T. Stafford once complained that he couldn't find out how much the state had spent in building the base lodge at Killington because only Merrill knew, and Merrill wouldn't tell him.

Merrill was a legendary state commissioner who ran his department brilliantly, with autocratic rule. His legacy is a preserved recreational landscape.

Governor Aiken

Despite the 34 years George D. Aiken served as a U.S. Senator representing Vermont, he never preferred being called "Senator." What he really liked was the title "Governor." That title is what his staff always called him, or simply "Gov."

Aiken often told me, and others who asked, that he enjoyed his four years as Governor of Vermont more than being a Senator. Why?

"When you are Governor, you know fairly soon whether your decisions were right or wrong ones. When you are a Senator it may take 10 or 20 years before you even begin to know the answer," Aiken explained. In fact, when Aiken retired from the Senate to return to Vermont, he noted more than once that it was like "being let out of jail."

Aiken liked the fact that as Governor, he was one of 50 elected leaders in the United States whereas in the Senate he was one of 100 members. As

Governor, Aiken was used to being the sole decision-maker. As Governor, you would have to live or die by your decisions. As a legislator, Aiken's only power came with his one vote. Yet if the vote was very close, Aiken's vote amplified his voice on the issue.

Legislating, by its nature, is usually a slow, deliberative way to arrive at decisions. As a farmer, he was used to planting seeds in the springtime, which would then grow over the summer and be ready for harvest in the fall. In Congress, it could take a generation for ideas that were planted by Aiken, like the St. Lawrence Seaway, to turn into a reality. Patience was a prized commodity for a legislator. Aiken clearly understood the difference. By temperament, he preferred faster resolutions to issues. That said, though, Senator Aiken was very protective of the role of Congress in foreign policy matters when the Executive Branch would attempt to usurp the power of Congress.

8

Early Senate Career

A Champion for Overlooked Americans

While most well-known for his concentration on U.S. foreign policy during his later years in the Senate, George Aiken also had a determined focus on electric power issues prior to his appointment to the Senate Foreign Relations Committee in 1954. In fact, his efforts as a freshman member of the 1931 Vermont House, when he de-railed a plan to build some 80 dams on Vermont rivers and streams with downstream benefits going to the private utilities, was very likely the most important decision that propelled his long political career.

As a state legislator, Lieutenant Governor, and Governor, Aiken consistently opposed federal control of the natural resources of Vermont. As the Presiding Officer of the State Senate in 1935, he pushed the passage of the Vermont rural electric bill, and then, in 1939 as Governor, he threw the switch for the Washington Electric Co-op, which brought the first Rural Electrification Administration (REA) power to Vermont. Soon, two other REA co-ops would be formed to bring electricity to rural Vermont.

If federal government policies helped the average Vermonter and the nation, Aiken could and would be supportive despite his concerns regarding an increasingly dominant U.S. Executive Branch. This theme continued to inspire his state-rights-oriented approach to domestic policy. George Aiken was a pragmatist, not an absolutist.

For example, in 1959, when Aiken became a member of the Joint

Committee on Atomic Energy, the idea of a commercially powered plant was a gleam in the eye of those who wanted to make peaceful use of the atom. Aiken supported nuclear energy only as long as the public power systems were able to take advantage of its benefits along with the investor-owned utilities. In this effort, Aiken was later strongly supported by New York Sen. Robert F. Kennedy, D-New York.

As a result, Aiken and others led the legislative fight for making nuclear power available to public and private utilities. Fighting the legislation, however, was another archenemy of Aiken's: the oil industry, which he feared would take over the coal and uranium conglomerates.

As Senator, Aiken joined other public power interests to fight for legislation that would harness the tides at Passamaquoddy and the Dickey-Lincoln Project in Maine. While the bill to authorize the project became law, the private utility interests opposing a federal "yardstick," much like the Tennessee Valley Authority, for New England were successful in blocking appropriations to make the projects a reality. The Vermonter would often remark, years later, "If they [the oil industry] can control the fuel, they will control the economy of the world."

St. Lawrence Seaway Project

For Senator Aiken, as he often told me during the years I worked for him, his proudest achievement in the energy field was the St. Lawrence Seaway project. In 1943, Aiken introduced his first Seaway bill. From then until its enactment in 1954, Aiken constantly fought against railroad and private utility lobbies that opposed the bill.

The Seaway project was important to agriculture as it would allow the movement of grain and other goods between Canada and the United States in competition with the railroads. Up until the 1950s, so-called "milk trains" slowly hauled milk throughout Vermont, stopping at every little crossroads. At the time, Vermont dairy farmers felt that the railroads overcharged them for shipping their milk. As important as that was for Aiken, the real impetus for his Seaway support was the development of the power potential of the

St. Lawrence and Niagara Rivers. While New York State had prior claim to the power benefits, there would be a surplus available to neighboring states, such as Vermont.

In 1959, in a panel discussion at Georgetown University in Washington, D.C., Aiken spelled out the reasons for his long-standing support of the St. Lawrence Seaway project. His number one reason was that he was from a "power-starved area, in the highest priced power area of the United States." He also favored improved navigation of waterways to help facilitate the flow of commerce, especially feed grains for agricultural users. Aiken believed the Seaway would have a "profound effect upon the entire economy of the United States." Finally, he argued that in building the Seaway, the United States and Canada could "set an example to the rest of the world of international cooperation."

Another reason for Aiken's long support of the Seaway project is that he felt it laid the groundwork for the construction of the so-called "Champlain cut-off." The cut-off would enable cargo ships coming through Montreal by way of the St. Lawrence River to navigate south down the Richelieu River into Lake Champlain, then down the Hudson River into New York City. Additionally, other waterways to Philadelphia and Baltimore, as well as waterways into the heartlands of the United States, in the Great Lakes Region, would be more accessible, allowing ships to circumvent an extra 1,500 miles or more, Aiken believed. However, Senator Aiken never realized this aspiration of his when environmental concerns and logistical barriers made the project infeasible.

Vermont Electric Power

Thus, Vermont was allocated a share of the surplus, which was earmarked in 1959 and 1960 for the Vermont Public Service Commission. In order for Vermont to take advantage of this low-cost public power, a statewide transmission system had to be built. The power was distributed by the Vermont Electric Power Company, or VELCO. This project was unique since it was owned and operated by Vermont's public and private utility systems. The system was the first in the country of such joint ownership, and it continues today. The Vermont Public Service Commission allocated to all Vermont utilities a 200-kilowatt-hour block of low-cost power. This allotment quickly helped to move Vermont from having the most expensive power rates in New England to the lowest in the six-state region, a tremendous incentive for economic development and for the state's rural consumers. Therefore, it was a surprise to some when, in 1966, Aiken opposed a proposal by Governor Phil Hoff to import low-cost hydroelectric power from Canada, a move that would have lowered electric rates even more significantly. The legislature defeated the proposal using Aiken's opposition as a major reason. Aiken was against the idea because it would have involved Vermont making a $450 million pre-payment to the British-Newfoundland Corporation, which was developing the power source for resale to the Canadian province of Quebec. Hoff resented Aiken's opposition then and for a long time after.

Aiken also always kept a wary eye on the oil industry and suspected it of dominating the governments in the Middle East as it sought to control production quotas, which would, in turn, raise the price of oil. For Vermonters, the price of oil was a critical factor for the state's economy because many Vermonters, then as now, used oil to heat their homes and to run their vehicles.

In the winter of 1973, the Arab Oil Embargo began. It gave the oil sheiks the ability to control the production and price of oil imports. As a result, the New England region, which was then the most dependent region on oil imports, became the most vulnerable region.

Aiken's Influence on Agriculture

By the time Aiken served as Governor of Vermont, he had made agriculture a personal and professional priority. Although he tried unsuccessfully, while Governor, to avert a milk strike, he nonetheless urged Vermont dairy farmers to create and form milk bargaining cooperatives, thereby laying the groundwork for a more sustained dairy economy. Aiken also pushed for Vermont to have better highways so that the state's farmers could more easily ship their milk to a variety of markets and import their feed grains from other states.

Given his work with the dairy industry, as well as his general strong support for the promotion of agriculture, it was no surprise that when Aiken took his seat in the Senate in 1941, he became a member of the Senate Agriculture and Forestry Committee. As Aiken's former legislative assistant, Charles Weaver, (who served in that capacity from 1954 to 1972) would often tell me during the time I worked with Weaver from 1969 to 1972, "The imprint of Senator George David Aiken is clearly evident on every major agricultural law enacted in the last 30 years."

Weaver would cite Aiken's influence on such monumental legislation as the National School Lunch Act, The Special Milk Program, the Food Stamp Act, and the Rural Water and Sewer Act. Aiken was also the principal sponsor of Public Law 480, better known as the Food for Peace Program. It was here that Aiken's interest in sharing America's agricultural abundance to help eliminate famine in other parts of the world and his focus on foreign policy would intersect. As Aiken once wrote to a fellow Vermonter in 1966, "I have always felt that we could do more with food than bullets."

After Weaver retired in 1972, I was handed the Agriculture Committee portfolio as well as the Foreign Relations Committee assignment as Aiken's legislative assistant. From this vantage point, I witnessed first-hand Aiken's dual interest in world affairs, as well as his passion for making sure that Americans and others in the world had access to food supplies. One of his ongoing efforts was trying to figure how a barrel of oil could be traded for a bushel of wheat on the world market.

As a carry-over from his earlier days as a champion of farmer cooperatives, Aiken pushed for the adoption of such cooperatives on a nationwide basis. Aiken had an innate love of all living things, from the pigeons and squirrels he fed on the Capitol lawn to the wildflowers he propagated for commercial uses. It influenced his decision to advocate for agricultural research and public conservation practices, so citizens could enjoy their natural surroundings.

For the health of rural America as well as for people in the more populated towns and cities, Aiken focused on a strong and viable farm economy. To accomplish this primary goal, Aiken worked on a bipartisan basis. It was his long-held philosophy that he would never oppose programs or policies for partisan reasons if they helped people, no matter which party or groups proposed them.

One example of Aiken's legislative accomplishments in this area was the creation in 1972 of the Special Supplemental Nutrition Program for Women, Infants, and Children (WIC). The program was designed to provide nutrition and health care for low-income pregnant women, breast-feeding women, and children under the age of five. The WIC program was co-sponsored by Minnesota Senator Hubert Humphrey and Aiken. The two teamed up to create this federal feeding program much like they had in years past to push for Food Stamp legislation.

The WIC effort began as a two-year pilot program, with locations in various parts of the country, usually in cities and counties. Since Vermont only had a small state population, Aiken insisted that Vermont's WIC program be administered on a statewide basis. The experiment in Vermont proved highly successful and, in 1974, WIC became a permanent national program. Even today, many years after Aiken's death, there are signs in social agencies urging mothers to sign up for the WIC program, along with Food Stamps, now renamed the Supplemental Nutrition Assistance Program (SNAP). These two very successful domestic programs serve as meaningful highlights and lasting monuments to Aiken's Senate career.

Aiken's imprint on the natural world was another important theme in his political career. In the 1920s he had propagated wildflowers and ferns on his property. His fear was that unless a way was found to keep them alive in perpetuity, that the pressures of urban growth would render such flowers and ferns extinct. In the introduction to his 1933 self-published book *Pioneering With Wildflowers*, Aiken wrote:

> Constantly pushed back by immigrant people, immigrant animals, and even immigrant plants, many species are now making a gallant last stand in the face of extermination. If some of them are to be saved, it must be through the prompt action of our people. We must learn how to propagate

and grow all worthwhile species, and the purpose of this book is to give others, in plain, nontechnical language, some of the knowledge of wildflower requirements which I have learned.

In that same book, which eventually went through five printings, Aiken demonstrated his keen sense of humor with this dedication: "To Peter Rabbit, in the hope that flattery will accomplish what traps and guns have failed to do and the little rascal will let our plants alone from this time on."

Aiken's rural background and his concern for the wellbeing of the natural environment helped to set the scene for one of Aiken's last major legislative initiatives before his 1975 retirement. This effort was the Eastern Wilderness Act, which became law on Jan. 3, the day after Aiken retired. The new law allowed the Forest Service to establish wilderness areas in forest lands located east of the Mississippi River. The act was modeled after the Wilderness Act of 1964, which had given the Interior Department control over wilderness areas located west of the Mississippi River. It took Aiken nearly two years to work the legislation through the jurisdiction of the various competing congressional committees. It was done with the usual Aiken patience and good humor.

By the time the act passed the Democratic-controlled Senate in 1974, the legislation was proclaimed by colleagues to be a "perpetual monument" to Senator Aiken, and collectively bestowed upon him the title "Father of The Eastern Wilderness."

Part III

Author Perspective:
What Would George Aiken Do Today?

Stephen C. Terry

The process of writing this book about Senator Aiken led me to reflect once again on the special character and strength of the Vermont Republican. I first began writing in January 2017, just as Donald J. Trump was sworn in as President of the United States. The contrast between who Aiken was as a Republican and the Republican Party as it exists today remained at the forefront of my mind as I told Aiken's story.

I became convinced by late summer of 2019 that it was important for me to convey to readers how George D. Aiken, the venerable Vermonter, would likely react to events of today. My view, based on my long association with the Senator, is that George Aiken would be ashamed of his party's leadership and the supine way it has let Trump define what is now the Republican Party.

George D. Aiken first emerged as a national political figure when he criticized the Republican Party on February 12, 1938 as Governor of Vermont. Aiken, decked out in a tuxedo with tails and a formal white tie, appeared as the main speaker before the National Republican Club's Lincoln Day Dinner, held at The Waldorf Astoria Hotel in New York City.

This venue was not a usual place for the first-term Vermont Governor, who spoke with a trace of the rural accent of a native Vermonter and still considered himself a farmer. Aiken looked a little stiff in his formal wear, but he was ready to deliver a barn-burner of a speech that ripped into the

GOP establishment.

Looking across the well-heeled audience of party blue-bloods, Aiken got their immediate attention when he said: "The greatest praise I can give to Lincoln is to say he would be ashamed of his party leadership today."

The Lincoln Day Dinner was a coveted speaking assignment, usually reserved for a potential Republican Presidential candidate. At the time, there was a presidential boomlet attempting to draft Aiken as a challenger to New Deal President Franklin D. Roosevelt in the 1940 Presidential Election. He was seen across the country as the natural antidote to Roosevelt's big-government programs, having offered balanced-budget proposals with a strong appeal to working-class voters.

Aiken's speech and his "Lincoln" quote reverberated across the country. For the next eight months, he was in demand as a speaker at GOP events around the nation, before he decided that he would not become a presidential candidate and took his name out of the running.

Aiken took his name out of presidential consideration because he would not accept the reality of presidential politics, which, even then, meant that he would have to turn his campaign over to professional politicians and handlers, and he would have little control over what they did or said.

Aiken's Place in History

The question posed today, some 80 years after Aiken's 1938 speech, is how would the Vermont Senator react to President Trump and to Trump's total acquisition of the Republican Party with all its attendant turmoil in foreign and domestic policy? Would Aiken be silent? Would he speak out? Would he formally break from the Republican Party?

We have seen many Republicans in Congress unwilling to speak out when President Trump's policies have conflicted with values upon which they were elected. Their silence speaks volumes as to how tremendously the Republican Party has changed in the 35 years since Aiken served. The current philosophy of the Republican Party runs counter to George Aiken's core values.

Author's Perspective

Aiken would have been very outspoken about the current polarized atmosphere of Washington, where every decision appears based on partisan politics and where decisions have very little respect for the rule of law or the Constitution.

Based on my years associating with and working for Aiken and knowing in some detail his personality and philosophy, as well as his political history, I would observe the following:

- Given Aiken's Vermont upbringing and his early days as a dirt farmer in Putney, the Vermont native would have been dismayed by President Trump's impulsive behavior.

- An early supporter of protecting natural resources for public use, Aiken would be incredibly dismayed at the subordination of environmental policies to deregulation for the sole benefit of the private sector.

- Aiken would have been deeply disappointed at the unpredictability and cavalier use of social media to formulate government policy, all without consultation with Congressional leadership.

- Aiken would be disapproving of some of the White House staff and some of the current cabinet choices, just as he was of Nixon's.

- For his part, Aiken would never have been cowed by threats of primary opposition, big money opponents, or Presidential tweets. Aiken would be secure in his views because he had his finger on the pulse of Vermonters, and, by and large, they trusted him to make decisions on their behalf.

- If George Aiken were on the political scene today, I have no doubt that he would be very critical of President Trump's unorthodox, highly-partisan political style and his erratic behavior in office that has shaken confidence in the United States at home and around the world.

- Trump's lying would disgust George Aiken. Trump's disdain and disrespect for any Constitutional norms, and the rule of law he finds inconvenient in achieving his own goals would push Aiken beyond his breaking point—much like what transpired with Richard Nixon when it was revealed through the forced releases of White House tapes in 1974 that he had begun to cover-up the Watergate scandal soon after it had occurred, and then lied about it for nearly two years.

- Despite the issues present within today's Republican Party, Aiken would likely remain a member of the GOP, determined to not let the values he always associated with the Party disappear from its identity. He would fight to preserve the ideals he believed to be at the core of the Republican Party.

History will remember George D. Aiken with affection and respect, especially looking through the lens of the 35 years since his death. Aiken's place in Vermont history was foretold when Middlebury College President James I. Armstrong awarded him an honorary degree on June 1, 1970 with these words:

> Venerated and venerable Vermonter, as rugged as granite, as enduring as marble, he derives his power of statesmanship not from electric or nuclear sources nor from political manipulation but from a character of fierce integrity and shrewd independence, which deeply trusts both man and nature. His pioneering, life-long love of wildflowers confirms his belief that, like Voltaire's Candide, "We must cultivate our garden," in Vermont, not Vietnam. Acknowledged as neither hawk nor dove but wise old owl, he knows from a life's experience that there can perhaps be as much wit and wisdom learned in a red school house as in a white house. Vigorous protector of the environment and defender of individual rights not vested

interests, he seeks to heal the erosion of natural soil and national spirit. His farmer's instincts and kinship with Vermont's traditions recognize the need of the youthful educational community to help one's neighbors and old folks with their chores next fall by harvesting a fine political crop. He stands with Thucydides' ideal leader, Pericles: "We do not say that a man who takes no interest in politics is a man who minds his own business; we say that he has no business here at all." In a time of turmoil and torment, he understands that peace and patriotism are not irreconcilable ideals. Like Vermont's old poet laureate (Robert Frost in his 1928 poem "What Fifty Said"), her senior Senator listens to youth in peaceful protest:

> Now when I am old my teachers are the young.
> What can't be molded must be cracked and sprung.
> I strain at lessons fit to start a suture.
> I go to school for youth to learn the future.

Washington Today

The political atmosphere in the nation's capital is highly partisan and toxic amid a constant war of armed camps. Republicans and Democrats don't socialize with each other. They simply don't appear to like each other. The notion of such a close friendship between the Democratic Senate Majority Leader and a senior member of the Republican Party, like the bond shared by Mansfield and Aiken, would be implausible.

Granted, the world of George Aiken was well before the advent of the 24-hour news cycle, social media platforms, or a time when constant news was either generated or re-circulated by millions of Americans using Twitter, Facebook, and many other forms of digital communications. Now, truth itself is in peril, as many Americans have abandoned their trust in journalism as the arbiter of fact. Instead, many people in this country are turning to unreliable, often untrue, sources on social media for all their information.

For the most part, news in Aiken's time was what appeared on the front pages of the morning and afternoon newspapers. Print news was the coin of the realm. Television news was just coming of age during Aiken's final term. In those days, people had time to think and to reflect. They did not spend time constantly reacting to events, as people do in the political climate of today. The current second-by-second bombardment of news, and its addictive impact on society, was simply not present during Aiken's time.

During his long tenure in the Senate, Aiken waged a persistent fight to preserve the power of Congress as a co-equal branch of government, as set forth in Article I of the U.S. Constitution. In Aiken's time, Congress' power and independence was constantly under attack by an increasingly powerful Executive branch. During Nixon's presidency, the Senate passed the War Powers Resolution, limiting the President's ability to act unilaterally or to make commitments on behalf of the country. Congress would have to be consulted before a President took such steps.

Today, Executive power has never been more extensive. President Donald Trump has on multiple occasions sought to cut Congress out the decision-making process. He has even shut down the government and declared a national emergency to acquire funds for the construction of a massive border wall, funds that Congress refused to appropriate as part of the budget for that year.

Aiken would have been shocked that a sitting President would personally attack members of Congress with racial taunts and threats as Trump did in mid-summer of 2019. Aiken would have been deeply disappointed and embarrassed that fellow Republican Senators would refuse to publicly call-out such behavior. This current exhibition of political cowardice would not sit well with the Vermonter who, in 1950, joined other GOP members to sign a Declaration of Conscience to start the movement that ultimately led to the Senate censure of Republican Senator Joe McCarthy of Wisconsin.

If Aiken were in the Senate today, I believe he would surely be among the few Republicans challenging President Trump.

In Washington, during the 1960s and 1970s, there still existed, in my memory, a deep sense of decency and doing what was right, despite the political turmoil of the moment over Vietnam and Watergate. That atmosphere provided the background for a person like George Aiken to rise up and become an influential leader.

Common sense leadership, however, is not a deep reservoir that will

Author's Perspective

always replenish itself. It needs the support of educated voters in order for a democratic government to survive and be resilient enough to withstand those who are only intent on corrupting it.

One can certainly argue that politics today have dramatically changed since Aiken's era. Yet Vermont still remains an outlier compared to most other places in the country.

Vermonters maintain trust in their elected members of Congress. As a result, they give them a wide berth to make their own decisions without a constant threat of political retribution. Currently, both of the Vermont's Senators and its lone Representative enjoy that political freedom. In the recent past, Vermonters supported the decision of U.S. Sen. Jim Jeffords to leave the Republican Party in 2001 to become an Independent. His party shift handed control of the U.S. Senate to the Democrats at the time.

The consistent theme here is that Vermonters are ready and willing, through their ballots, to place trust in their top elected political leaders. That trait may change in the future, but it is hard to make the case it will change any time soon, based on a multi-year review of prior election results and the character of Vermonters.

Vermont still remains a place where moderate Republicanism continues to exist despite the state's transformation in the last generation to one of the deepest blue states in the Union. An anti-Trump Republican, Gov. Phil Scott, was easily re-elected in November 2018, while at the same time, voters increased the Democratic and Progressive majorities in the Vermont State House. Vermonters tend to vote their values irrespective of political labels.

It is against this current backdrop in Vermont politics that an Aiken-like Republican from Vermont could emerge to challenge the leadership of the Republican Party. Sadly, the reality is that few other states could produce a Republican candidate in the mold of Aiken, and even a moderate Vermont Republican seems unlikely to garner enough support to challenge the status quo within today's GOP.

George D. Aiken, however, would not be silent if he were still in the Senate representing Vermont. Vermonters would expect and want Aiken to speak truth to power once again just as he did with Lyndon Johnson on Oct. 19, 1966.

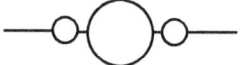

Appendix

Speeches, Post-Script, Bibliography, and Index

Appendix

Governor Aiken's Lincoln Day Address
The New York Times
February, 12, 1938

The text of the address delivered last night by Governor George D. Aiken of Vermont at the dinner of the National Republican Club in the Hotel Waldorf-Astoria:

Up in Vermont where I come from they understand me pretty well, but down in Washington where the Republican National Committee got a letter from me recently, I am not considered orthodox. If an orthodox Republican speech on Lincoln Day consists of reciting history which everybody knows, giving Lincoln a great deal of praise which he does not need, justifying all the Republican party has been doing and excusing everything it is not doing by that all-embracing phrase, "Lincoln would have had it that way," then I am afraid you will not hear a very orthodox speech from me tonight.

After all, the Republican party in its origin and Lincoln himself were distinctly not orthodox. The men who met in a little white school house at Ripon, Wis., eighty-four years ago were roughly garbed tillers of the soil. They had felt the oppression of slave labor crushing down their efforts to make a decent living for their families. Short years before they had rallied to the standard of Andrew Jackson, the man, as a means of obtaining righteous consideration. Their plight was desperate, and in desperation they had placed their faith in one whose outspoken sympathy for the poor and whose animosity toward would-be monopolists promised them happier days. But they were doomed to disappointment.

Birth of the Republican Party

The reign of the spoils system and the greed of opportunists who capitalized upon the voting power of the common people tarnished their hopes. So they met in the little frontier town of Ripon to organize the most powerful political force which America had known. The Republican Party had come into being.

Unsuccessful in 1856, the new party entered the 1860 campaign. Success at the polls depended on attracting to the Republican standard those men who resented the leadership of the old parties. Men whose families slept on beds of straw, which were renewed each year at threshing time; men who rose before daylight to cradle buckwheat while the dew was on so that it would not shell and waste the precious grain; men who wielded the axe or followed the plow until darkness fell and who after super, by the dim light of a candle lantern, did the chores and made preparation for the morrow, until weariness overcame them.

Hardships? Yes--misery, poverty, sickness, lack of education, beset by parasites and profiteers yet they were the strength of America, and the greatness of the nation is ever dependent on such as they. Forever the rise and fall of a political party must depend on its ability to attract those who spin and those who toil.

Present Leadership Criticized

Today the Republican party attracts neither the farmer nor the industrial worker. Why not? To represent the people one must follow them. Lincoln did. The Republican national leadership today does not. The greatest praise I can give to Lincoln on this his anniversary is to say that he would be ashamed of his party's leadership today.

Would not Lincoln have been ashamed of us when Frank Hague, the Democratic boss of Jersey City, forbade free speech and free assemblage and no responsible voice in the Republican national leadership was raised in protest against his high-handed procedure? The reason was that free speech and free assemblage were being denied the C.I.O., and Tom Girdlers of the Republican party want the C.I.O. crushed even if a corrupt political boss of the opposing party has to tear up the Bill of Rights to crush them!

Appendix

I hold no brief for the C.I.O. I have had little experience with labor organizations. I don't know as much about labor as I should like to. I never worked in a factory. I never owned a share of stock or had anything to say about the management of a corporation. The first money I ever earned was weeding gardens at 5 cents an hour. The most I ever earned was last year, thanks to my salary of $5,000 as Governor of Vermont--half of which I used in paying debts.

Gettysburg and Jersey City

But I do know that the rank and file of Republicans throughout the country are for the Bill of Rights no matter whether the poorest or the richest of our citizens are concerned. Do you think the voice that was heard at Gettysburg would have been silent when free speech was denied in Jersey City? He who did not ask the color of their skins would not worry if another and a later group carried C.I.O. or A.F. of L, F.D.R. or G. O.P. on their placards.

Now let's go back a few years. Before 1933 the Republican Administration in Washington was silent too long over the abuses of Wall Street. Too long did Washington neglect to give serious study to the farmers' plight. Too long did Washington turn a pious eye away from the unfair treatment of labor in many industries. Lincoln, I think, would have been ashamed of this.

Now, the Republican national leadership is seeking a new statement of principles through a Committee on Program. Let's look at the Committee on Program. It has 217 members. Of these--sixty-five, nearly one-third of the whole committee, represent banking, insurance, stock and bond selling, manufacturing and business.

There are fifty-three lawyers--one quarter of the whole membership. So in these two groups alone we find more than one-half of the committee.

Four Men to Speak for Millions

Our millions of organized and unorganized workers are represented by just four labor men.

In spite of the fact that 40 percent of the population of our country is located in rural areas, and with one-quarter actually living on farms, they are represented on the Program Committee by a total of twenty-one who are engaged in agriculture--and I am afraid few of these are dirt farmers.

A full third of the committee, moreover, represents the concentrated industrial and financial area around New York City in the seven States of Massachusetts, Connecticut, Rhode Island, New York, Pennsylvania, New Jersey and Delaware. Two-thirds of the members of the committee come from that tier of States which runs eastward from Illinois and Michigan to the Atlantic Coast. In contrast, only one-seventh of the members are from the great farm States on the plains of the Middle West; only one-seventh from the eleven States of the Rocky Mountains and the Pacific Coast.

Can such a committee as this, sincere as they may individually be, write a convincing statement of principles for the party of Lincoln? I think not.

Significance of 50-Cent Dinners

It is idle to think we can continue to fool the voters with fine sounding statements that mean nothing. I understand that in one city tonight a Lincoln Dinner will be served for 50 cents. That's fine. But if that dinner is served for 50 cents just as a matter of publicity and the 50-cent feeling is not in the hearts of the Republicans participating, then we can chock up another loss. We need 50-cent dinners in schoolhouses, grange halls and community clubs where they will be taken at face value.

The worker and the farmer don't have to be looked down upon and

Appendix

have those in control of political parties attempt to fool them in this way. The worker and the farmer are educated and a politician--who exchanges his tall silk hat for one of felt simply for the occasion is not fooling them.

Now let's take a look at the New Deal. The rank and file of the Republican party is not opposed to Federal leadership. The country needs it. We want it. We cannot tolerate Republican lip-service to the slogan of States' Rights simply to cover up abuses which backward States or backward big business refuse to exterminate.

The Itch for Acquisition

The States have rights--vital rights. As Governor of Vermont I have fought to preserve them for the people. To preserve these rights I have at times had to fight the public utilities. At the present time I am having to fight the Federal Government. Far apart as these two orces are, I find the palms of both have the itch for acquisition.

We must not make the mistake of thinking we are protecting States' rights when we protest against Federal leadership. States' rights need protection only against Federal domination. There is a difference between Federal leadership and Federal domination, and that difference is the issue today. Of late years the Republican party has not been successful in Federal leadership; the New Deal seeks to be too successful in Federal domination. Both these attitudes are wrong.

The Federal Government has not yet dominated my State but we welcome its leadership and cooperation. For instance, in approaching a solution to the problems of social security we in Vermont are going to see to it that our system, with Federal cooperation, works as well, and better if possible, than that of any other state.

Even though our record in Vermont in the matter of progressive government is good--and it is--I think it could have been better if long before the New Deal we had had a vigorous Federal leadership to point out to us how our problems tied in with the problems of other States and how we could all work together for the common good.

Attitude Toward the President

A word in closing: Forget your hatred for the President. Stop crying "Fascist" every time he makes a move. Stop worrying about Reds in the White House. Because of your reckless hatred the minds of many American men and women are shut against your honest criticisms. Remember, the people were hungry for leadership in those dark days of 1932 and 1933. Remember, he gave it to them. He dispelled the clouds of inaction with the bright sun of leadership. But now that sun has dazzled him, and confused him, and led him far afield. Inspiring leadership has given way to fumbling futility.

Hundreds of thousands of the same people who turned to Franklin Roosevelt in 1932 are turning away from him now.

The Quest for Leadership

But do not delude yourselves that these thousands looking for leadership have yet turned to the Republican party! The people are just as hungry for leadership now as they were then, and they are not getting the sort they want either from President Roosevelt or from the Republican party. Give them Republican leadership--warm, human, understanding, sound--and they will turn to us.

Fail them--and you will see a third party in this country just as sure as you saw it in 1912. And this time it will last--a party of ordinary folks, factory workers, farmers, office workers, business men, school teachers, lawyers, doctors.

It will not be a party of any one class but of men and women of all classes, who will stand for neither the erratic wanderings of the New Deal nor the self-satisfied smugness of Old Guard Republicanism.

Wealth and position will not be a qualification nor yet a bar to membership in this party. Labor will belong to it, but it will not belong to labor.

Appendix

I hope this party will be the Republican party. And it can be if the Republican leadership catches up with the millions of men and women now in our party -- and with those other millions who seek a party to turn to in these troubled times.

———————

Senator George D. Aiken
Lend-Lease
U.S. Congressional Record
February 25, 1941

Mr. President, after weeks of committee hearings and several days of debate upon this floor, it seems that almost everything has been said that could be said for or against the lend-lease bill. I readily confess that the decision we are called upon to make is a hard one.

I came to the Senate with the fullest intention of going a long, long way to aid Great Britain in her fight against the totalitarian governments. I still have that intention.

On the day I arrived in Washington, H. R. 1776 was introduced and advocated by its sponsors as the most logical way of extending such aid. An intense difference of opinion had developed as to this question, not only in Congress but also throughout the country.

I would give a great deal, as I feel nearly everyone else here would, to know that I am taking the right stand in this momentous matter. But the decision I have reached is in full accord with my conscience. Although I have heard statements made upon the floor since the debate began with which I cannot concur, yet I believe that they were made by each speaker in full sincerity. I hold no rancor toward anyone and I do not doubt the sincerity of anyone with whose conclusion I do not agree.

I spent what time I could at hearing of the Foreign Relations Committee. From day to day I listened to an impressive array of witnesses both for and against the bill. I heard great men who have been appointed to the Cabinet of the United States express their earnest beliefs. I heard great educators propound their theories. I heard businessmen, publishers, aviators, and ex-political candidates, all giving the committee the benefit of their judgement, but frequently disagreeing in their conclusions.

As I attended the committee hearings, I looked in vain to see on the witness stand just one of those people upon the ultimate safety and future of our country really depends; just one person like he ordinary folks that sent us here to represent them. I looked in vain to hear just one of the common people of America tell his story and give opinion on this matter which concerns his well-being, his family, his home, and his life.

There people do not own great industrial plants; but without them such plants could never operate. They do not run great insurance companies or banks dealing in securities of foreign countries or foreign corporations, yet without their labors the wealth represented by the money such establishments lend could never have been created. They are ordinary folks to whom a new suit, some new suit, some new furniture, or a college tuition is a big thing; but they are the most important people in the world.

There are plenty of such folks in America. Nearly 50,000,000 of them marched to the polls last November to vote for one of two Presidential candidates, both of whom pledged themselves to keep America out of foreign wars.

The Americans whom we have not seen here are men and women from fields and farm, from the mines, the shops, and the offices all over our great country. Perhaps they could not come. I do not think many of them had the money to come. Perhaps they do not belong in this picture anyway. Maybe they do not understand international affairs well enough.

Maybe they cannot see why it is so important to their welfare to have the great corporations of America protected by our soldiers and sailors in their exploitation of the natural resources of other lands. Maybe the common folks of America are just supposed to go on paying out wars and do not of the dying, as usual.

Through all the debates of recent weeks, in the committee room and on the chamber floor, we have heard few facts have been presented because facts as to the future--and we are discussing a matter that concerns the future--are extremely hard to ascertain and to present.

For the most part we have listened to the personal opinions of those who have testified and argued. I admit that all I have to guide me in casting my vote on this matter in my own personal opinion. But I have formed this opinion in the basis of my own observations and not on the basis of ideas of the great and near great which have been advertised as facts.

A great newspaper recently stated that I was one of the four Senators who had not made up their minds how to vote on this matter; and several thousand people have volunteered their assistance in helping me to do this. But, in order to relieve any further suspense regarding my vote, I want to say now that my mind is made up to note "No" on this bill.

I was up in the hills of Vermont on Sunday. I saw many of the folks who were missing from the Foreign Relations Committee hearings. Some of them were not dressed any too well. A good many of them have mortgages on their farms and homes which they are trying to pay off with 70-cent dollars.

Every one of them would defend his country and his flag to the death; and there would not be and "cost plus" condition to their patriotism, either. The farm and village folks of my State do not want war. Their sympathies are with Great Britain. They would all the way, down to the last dollar and the last man, to protect Canada. But they do not see why American boys should give their lives to define the boundaries of African colonies, or to protect American promoters and exploiters in Indo-China or New Guinea. Neither do I.

But they are confused. Many persons are confused. We do not have to go outside Washington to find persons who are confused. They were told at first that House bill 1776 was a peace bill. They read it in the newspapers, some of which are owned and controlled, in one way or another, by great corporations. They heard it on the radio. They received propaganda circulars, and it has been impressed upon them by able speakers at rallies and other places.

Yet, upon reading the bill it seems to be nothing more or less than authorization--some might even interpret is as a direction--to the

President of the United States to put out country not only into Britain's war, but into any and every war on the face of the globe that he thinks should be out war too. It does not look so much like a peace bill to them now. It is not a peace bill. In our hearts nearly everyone of us knows this. The pending bill is the final step before the armed forces of the United States are scattered over the waters of the seven seas and the lands of four continents.

Lately there have been a tendency on the part of proponents of the bill to label it exactly what is it, "an act to provide for the intervention of the United States in other people's wars." They have presented plausible arguments why we should thus participate in the wars of other countries; but, as the junior Senator from North Carolina [Mr. Robert B. Reynolds] pointed out last Thursday, their arguments are as old as American history itself.

When I cast my vote on this bill, I shall regard it as a vote to determine whether or not America shall go to war now. To all those who, like myself, earnestly desire a British rather than a German victory, I put this question: Does this bill, H. R. 1776, aid England in the most effective way possible? I have not heard that England has asked for the enactment of this bill. I know only that she asked for help. This bill gives the President of the United States complete control over the blood stream of supplies which we are told is vitally necessary to the life of the British Empire. After this bill is enacted into law, the President of the United States can control this flow of goods even to the extent of depriving England of war materials now on order in this country unless England conducts this war as he thinks she should. Is it not possible that England might prefer to run her own war without this constant threat hanging over her? Do we know that England would rather have assistance granted in this manner than an outright grant of cash or credit.

We have been told no less an authority than the Secretary of Treasury himself that England cannot continue to carry on the war because her credit and cash resources have become exhausted. We are told 6 weeks ago that England might fall in 60 to 90 days unless we came to her assistance. The proponents of the bill have now used almost all those 60 days to put through a bill giving the President unlimited powers to meddle in all foreign affairs, if he is so minded, rather than to take 2 days to grant England the credit and cash upon which they said her life depended.

...Mr. President, are we to understand that if the bill fails, its proponents will not consider any other way of aiding England? Is it any wonder that a hundred million people have become confused, and are asking if aid to England is the real purpose of the bill?

From time to time the advocates of the bill have made gestures tending to placate and reassure an awakening American public. Several amendments have been added to it. So far as I can see, the amendments are mostly in the form of window dressing, and provide very little real restriction upon the acts of the Executive office.

It has been suggested to us on this floor that we should know what England's aims may be. If those who make the suggestions really want to know what England's war aims or England's peace aims may be, I suggest to the proponents of the idea that they get behind a resolution requesting the President to ascertain and make known these war aims.

There is something more important the people of America want to know, something the people of America should know. The matter that concerns out people more than England's war aims is this: What are our Government's aims for war? What are our aims for our Government for peace? Will we sit in at the council table when the armistice between nations is declared, and in what capacity? Will we sit in as a nonbelligerent or will we sit at the peace table as a belligerent? Who will sit there with us?

It is said we can have no peace with Hitler. With that assertion I have no quarrel. The only aim of peace or war that I have heard thus far is to "crush Hitler, kill Hitler". It sounds like an appeal to the neighborhood of nations to attend a first-class lynching party. We of America want something more definite than such statements. When we have crushed Hitler, when the bodies of American boys lie rotting in foreign lands, with whom shall we make peace? Do we intend to set up a puppet government in Germany? I understand that we shall restore the little nations of Europe and set up new governments for them. What kind of governments? Have we so much admiration for Hitler that we would emulate him? Is it out business to tell these countries under what form of government they should live?

What do we plan for the countries we expect to crush? What are we going t do with the 79,000,000 German people living in an area the size of Texas? Imagine with 263 Members in the United States House of Representatives; yet that is the number she would have were she as densely populated as is Germany. What shall we do with the 44,000,000 Italians living in an area the size of New Mexico? What shall we do with the 71,000,000 Japanese who live in a country so small that there is scarcely standing room for them? Are we going to put rings of steel around these nations; or do we expect to do with them, as I have heard supposedly sane people seriously suggest, "kill off half the population" while a large proportion of the world's surface is underdeveloped?

What about Holland? What about Belgium, France, Luxembourg, Norway, Denmark, and the other small nations of Europe, many of them densely populated, all of them starving? We say we intend to restore democracy to them; but is it necessary first to starve them to death? England says "No" when ex-President Hoover suggests feeding these unfortunate people and in America the great minds of our Government echo "No." These little nations have always regarded America as their best friend, and one to whom they could turn for encouragement and rescue and life for their people.

I ask now, Can we let them starve while a surplus of food rots in the United States? Can we let them freeze while 11,000,000 bales of cotton are in storage on this side of the Atlantic without a market in sight? Is this the kind of America we want to be? Is this the way we want to take to crush Germany? Must we become the most hated nation on earth?

Some have expressed the belief that Hitler would confiscate the food we would send to save the lives of people in the small occupied countries. Only the other night ex-President Hoover told us that if Germany should confiscate every bit of food and clothing which we would send to save the lives of millions of people who love and trust America, it would only last the German Nation 3 to 4 days. But he also told us that during the first World War, when Germany promised not to interfere with the feeding of starving and helpless people, that she kept that promise. Mr. Hoover ought to know best. He was there.

We are doing all we can, and would do more if it could be done feasible, to take care of the children of England. I doubt if any town of similar size in the United States is doing more in that respect than my own home town in Vermont. I wish we could feed and clothe and take to the heart of America every single one of these little homeless folks, who had nothing to do with bringing the war upon their country, but who are in danger of malnutrition, disease, and death. I am not much of a Bible student, but I have read it more or less. In all my readings I have never found any place where Christ said, "Suffer little British children to come unto Me."

We in America should not rest, we should not sleep, so long as there is any child in this wide world starving and suffering, regardless of the tongue he speaks or the color of his skin, while food and clothing accumulate and rot in America. Mr. President, the foremost influence in the United States today is fear. I am not proud of this. Wherever we turn, whatever we hear, it is fear, fear, fear. We are the greatest nation in the most protected position, and we are crying "fear."

This cry of fear did not originate with the common folks of the country. It has been put upon them by those who really do fear, not for their country, not for the lives of our people, but for their dollars. Unless they can arouse our people to the fighting pitch, unless they can mislead and fool them into a declaration of war, or a war without a declaration, they are going to lose money.

They want the American flag to float triumphantly in battle around the world. But as they envision their flag waving in glory over the oil fields of Asia Minor and the plantations of the East Indies they see on its field of blue not stars but dollar signs.

The part being played by some American industrialists and corporate interests in world affairs today should fill our hearts with shame. It may be that the reason they fear Germany, that they fear Russia, that they fear Japan, that they fear even smaller nations is that they know all too well how thoroughly they have prepared these nations to war against us.

The junior Senator from Oregon [Mr. Rufus C. Hollman] read upon the floor of the Senate not long ago a statement to the effect that the Russian steamer Angastroy was at the moment loading $400,000 worth of tin plate for export to Russia. Tin is a vital necessity for out defense, a commodity which we do not produce at home, and yet "dollar patriots" were reported to be selling it where they must have known it would likely be used against us whenever we enter this world struggle.

It was also brought out by our colleague from Oregon that carloads of airplane beacons, needed in this country, were on the way to Japan. There alleged facts have never been denied.

Even as recently as 1940 a majority--in fact, nearly all--the exports of copper, iron, and manganese from the Philippines have been delivered to Japan. We must not let little things like the lives of American boys and the hearts of American parents interfere with business. It is said that the success of the Nazi government in crushing Poland, in overrunning Holland, Belgium, Denmark, and France was due largely to the superiority of Hitler's equipment made on American machines. But do not think I am questioning the legality of selling vital materials to nations with whom we may be at war next week.

Thirty dollars a month is good enough pay for the boys in our Army. Of course it is. All they have to do is to leave their jobs, their homes, their future, and, it may be, die or come back blind or without their legs or arms or minds. This is not much so long as we can save money for our "dollar patriots" who are driving America into war today.

Let us stop and think a moment, though. We have a million men in the Army now for the first time in out peace-time history. These boys thought they were going for 1 year. They begin to wonder now. They expected to give up a year of their life willingly, gladly, patriotically. They are not coming back at the end of a year if this bill passes. Some will never see those homes up in the hills or on the prairies again.

The million now in the Army will be greatly increased. I would not be surprised if within the next 3 years we should have 4,000,000 young Americans under arms. Then what? Unless America becomes a military nation, unless war goes on and on and on, unless we unite with or inherit the British Empire and undertake to police that far-flung Empire on which the sun never sets, most of these boys will come back some day.

They will come back just as their fathers did a quarter of a century ago. What will they find when they get back? Will they find the jobs we promised to keep them? Will they find the Nation ready to do them justice for the sacrifices they have made for their country?

Or will they find the forces which are now urging America into war organized and lined up against them just as their fathers did after the last war? And will it take them 15 years of constant struggle to secure that which is rightly and honorably due them?

I tell you now, Mr. President, that if I had my way, every blood-soaked dollar made by American profiteers during wartime would be taken from them and given to the men whose loyalty to flag and country prompted them to give of themselves.

Besides the human sacrifice, we might as well understand now that war is not free. War will mean national bankruptcy for America within 3 years. At the rate we are going, war or no war, we will have a national debt of over $100,000,000,000 in that time. What will we do about that? Is not that something to fear as well as Mr. Hitler?

Not long ago we had 13,000,000 unemployed in America. War orders and defense order for ourselves and our potential enemies have reduced that number. But the problem of unemployment has not been solved. Will we, like Hitler, make war forever on nation after nation in order to keep our men employed? Or will we look forward to the day when we will have not 13,000,000 unemployed but twice that number? Is not that something to fear?

We know what the first World War did to American agriculture. We know that it had never recovered. We know, too, that in an effort to solve the problems of the rest of the world American agriculture had been sacrificed year after year. Germany used to take a third of American agricultural exports; but we are going to destroy Germany. England, Norway, Belgium, and Japan were all markets for American agriculture; but those markets are pretty well gone, for one reason or another.

Now we are headed for war. We are going to make America an industrial nation as no nation in the world has ever been industrialized before. If and when this war ends, American industry is going to try to place its goods in every country on the globe and may expect out farmers' markets to be further sacrificed to make this possible. America has already sacrificed part of the greatest market for industrial goods there is in the world by reducing the buying power of American agriculture in order to sell machines to Patagonia and Bohemia.

If America enters another world war now, the greatest economic sufferer will be the American farmer. Is that anything to worry about or not? Have we not enough trouble at home, anyway, without looking for more in Abyssinia and Siam? This conflict all over the world is primarily caused by the failure of governments to meet their domestic problems. When they fail in every other way they are forced to choose war as the only way out. Are we admitting failure, too? And will war solve our problems?

Will it restore permanent employment to those who would work? Will it restore solvency to an insolvent nation? Will it provide security for the individual? Will it be means of adequately regulating monopolies? Will it result result in the conservation of the natural resources of this great Nation? And will it bring about a fair and adequate monetary system?

Perhaps the answer to some of these questions is "Yes." If that is true, then there will be some benefit derived from war, but I cannot conceive of these benefits in any way counterbalancing the horrible cost. There is one thing more. Call this bill "Aid to Britain," "Defense of America," or any other title you want to give it; there is no disputing the fact that it gives the Chief Executive of out Nation the greatest authority any President ever had. In fact, I believe it gives him the greatest power any person in the whole world has ever had. The arguments to this effect have been made so often that I shall not repeat them here.

I can stand here before you and tell you truthfully that I have a great admiration for the President of the United States. I think he has brought about many reforms in our country that no one else would or could have brought about. He is a man of exceptional courage. I stand back of most of his program, much to the disgust of my own party organization. But we are asked to delegate this authority to an office, not to a man. Even if it were to a man, there is no man on earth who should have the power which this bill conveys to the President of the United States. This delegation of authority is a sign of woeful weakness on the part of Congress.

The passing of this bill will be the longest step toward a one-party government and one-man Government that has yet been made. During the past few years exceptional powers have been granted to the Chief Executive as emergency powers. With the exception of those ordered returned by the Supreme Court, such as the N. R. A., none of these powers has been surrendered, and none of them ever will be.

I know we are following a trend. I know that distances are getting short, that nations are being brought together, and that greater centralization of government is more applicable and more inevitable than it has been before; but the question is, How far are we going in this respect? We have before us ghastly examples of European nations that went too far. Will we follow in their footsteps?

I think this bill, H. R. 1776, goes too fat in giving the President authority to form alliances with other nations, htus obviating the necessity of negotiating treaties which require the approval of the Senate. It is said that out national safety depends upon this bill, and that unless we enact it, England will fail and we shall be invaded; that free enterprise will be destroyed, as we have heard here this afternoon; that we shall have to fight alone and possibly meet defeat.

Mr. President, let me say to you that I would rather see my country go down to defeat fighting gloriously all the nations of the earth, if need be, than to see it go down to defeat through the passive establishment here of a form of government we abhor.

Mr. President, perhaps I should apologize for taking so much time on this floor. I have already taken more time than expected to take; but I cannot feel at peace with myself unless I speak against the enactment of proposed legislation which I feel will not serve the best interests of my country.

All about us we hear talk of war, war, war. I do not think it is a sign of weakness to want peace throughout the world. I have believed for the past 3 years that if Americans would devote the effort toward promoting peace throughout the world that has been devoted to sowing the seeds of war, our influence would have been very great, and that we would almost, if not quite, at the doors of peace today.

There are those who honestly and sincerely fear a German invasion of this country; but let me call attention to the fact that when America was a young, struggling, united Nation, weak in arms and weak in everything but the desire for liberty, an invasion of this country was attempted, and we defeated both England and her hired German allies.

My little State of Vermont, which at that time was an independent republic, for 2 years held back the forces of Britain from invading the Colonies by way of the Richelieu River and the Champlain Valley. This has been pointed out as the route Hitler would likely take when he attempted to invade us. When England finally attempted to invade our young Nation by that route she was thoroughly thrashed at Bennington and Saratoga and Hubbardton, and the Revolutionary War was soon over. Never yet has an invasion of this country by way of the St. Lawrence River and the Champlain Valley been successful.

Today the common folks of America who did not appear at our hearings are looking to the Senate. They are looking to us, expecting that while we will give aid to our English cousins we will think and act for America first, last, and all the time. They are not looking to us to lead them into war.

Are we going to turn our backs on them and say that we have to send our men to Germany to collect unpaid royalties; that we have to protect foreign investments for financial concerns that turned their backs on the small business interests of America and put their trust in foreign governments? Are we going to say to them that we have to make worldwide markets for guns and oil and materials of war because new crop of war millionaires is necessary for our well being, and that the sons of the common people must die in order to being this about?

What I have said will not be liked by some persons in my State, but I would rather go home now and face the wrath of the money powers of my State than to go home a few years later and face the empty chairs and the empty hearts in the homes of my neighbors.

Appendix

Senator George D. Aiken
Vietnam Analysis - Present and Future
U.S. Congressional Record
October 19, 1966

Mr. President, now that the President is well on his way to Manila for a meeting with our allies in arms, it seems appropriate to review briefly event leading up to our present position in Vietnam, the status of that present position, and what possible courses are available for the future.

The President has stated repeatedly that the Manila conference is being held in the quest for peace.

I have never doubted the desire of President Johnson for peace in southeast Asia--a peace which would permit the withdrawal of U.S. troops from that area and greater concentration of our aid in the political, economic, and social fields.

I know I speak for the great majority of Americans in wishing him progress toward this objective at Manila.

Passing over the early years of our Vietnam involvement, the record of which is already abundantly clear, I would like to present the situation as it existed in February 1965, when the total of American combat troops in South Vietnam was less than 20,000.

In spite of confident reports by our highest military authorities at that time, there actually existed a clear and present danger of military defeat for the American forces.

In the face of this imminent danger, a detachment of marines was dispatched to Da Nang, and a program of building up military forces in Vietnam was launched.

The administration chose not to identify the danger of military defeat as the reason for escalation, but rather the aggression of the North Vietnamese military forces against South Vietnam.

Aggression is a word with two meanings: one is quasi-legal meaning which has in the past--in the case of North Korean aggression across the 38th parallel and Hitler's many aggressions in Europe--served as a formal rallying point for collective action; it also has a looser meaning, simply the determination of one country of a hostile act by another.

The United States has been unable to sustain "aggression" as a basis for collective action.

Even the countries most affected by our commitment in Vietnam did not increase their own commitment until the escalation of U.S. military power had proceeded beyond any point where outright military defeat was a credible alternative.

In short, our allies, like Korea, felt it was in their interest to follow our lead if only in respect for U.S. power.

Therefore, whatever merits of the U.S. charge of aggression, the word cannot be employed in its quasi-technical sense.

However, there is no reason to doubt that wide support exists in the world to the proposition that the military power of the United States should not be questioned or compromised.

This is the honor our gallant allies in Korea, Thailand, the Philippines, Australia, and New Zealand pay us by placing their soldiers alongside ours in Vietnam and in Thailand.

Insofar as our commitment to Vietnam represented an effort to sustain the credibility and integrity of the U.S. Armed Forces, the act of escalation cannot brook any serious dissent.

In February of 1965 and for some months thereafter, such a situation persisted.

However, at the present time it is no possible to sustain a clear and present danger of military defeat facing U.S. Armed Forces.

The enemy had apparently dismissed any idea of engaging in major formal combat with superior U.S. forces, and has resorted to a war of harassment and surprise guerilla tactics.

Faced with the harassment of the Vietcong and the North Vietnamese military forces, casualties to American forces in Vietnam are inevitable.

The more American troops in active combat, the more casualties from such harassment there will be.

Appendix

But these casualties in no way sustain the prospect of a military defeat.

Today, the American commitment in Vietnam no longer involves the fundamental objective of preserving the credibility and integrity of U.S. Armed Forces--provided that the war is not extended in time or in geography to that point where a wholly new threat to U.S. military power exists.

The new threat might take either the form of Chinese intervention, or, more pertinent, the form of a prolonged erosion of the credibility of U.S. power through harassment in a political context--namely, through the disintegration of the South Vietnamese society.

The U.S. Government has asserted frequently and emphatically that there is no military "solution" or objective in this war.

We do not seek to destroy North Vietnam nor its government.

This assertion is shared by virtually every type of observer--allied, official, and hostile.

The greater the U.S. military commitment in South Vietnam, however, the less possibility that any South Vietnamese Government will capable of asserting its own authority on its home ground or abroad.

The size of the U.S. commitment already clearly is suffocating any serious possibility of self-determination in South Vietnam, for the simple reason that the whole defense of that country is now totally dependent on the U.S. armed presence.

This was also true in Korea in 1954, but then the United States was operation under the umbrella of collective U.N. action, and along a well-defined battlefront which permitted organization of the rear areas.

None of this is true in South Vietnam.

Considering the fact that as every day goes by, the integrity and invincibility of the U.S. Armed Forces is further placed in question because there is no military objective, the United States faces only two choices: Either we can attempt to escape our predicament by escalating the war into a new dimension, where a new so-called aggressor is brought into play or we can deescalate the way on the ground that the clear and present danger of a military defeat no longer exists and therefore deescalation is necessary in order to avoid any danger of placing U.S. Armed Forces in a position of compromise.

Faced with these alternatives, the United States could will declare unilaterally that this stage of the Vietnam war is over--that we have "won" in the sense that our Armed Forces are in control of most of the field and no potential enemy is in position to establish its authority over South Vietnam.

Such a declaration should be accompanied, not by announcement of a phased withdrawal, but by the gradual redeployment of U.S. military forces around strategic centers and the substitution of intensive reconnaissance for bombing.

This unilateral declaration of military victory would herald the resumption of political warfare as the dominant these in Vietnam.

Until such a declaration is made, there is no real prospect for political negotiations.

The credibility of such a unilateral declaration of military victory can only be successfully challenged by the Vietcong and the North Vietnamese themselves--assuming that the Chinese remain aloof.

There is nobody in the United States or in the Europe or in Russia that is at all likely to challenge a statement by the President of the United States that our military forces have discharged their duty in their usual competent manner and occupy the field as victors.

Any charge against such an assertion directly challenges the ability of U.S. military power and makes the prospect of a wider war clear and present.

Right now in the eyes of most of the world, only the United States suggests that possibility.

Once the burden of suggesting a wider war is shifted from us to others--others who question the integrity of U.S. military power--the United States is again in the position of leading from collective strength politically.

This suggested strategy is not designed to solve the political

Appendix

problem of Vietnam.

It is simply designed to remove the credibility of U.S. military power--or more loosely the question of "face"--as the factor which precludes a political solution.

Again, it is important to stress that no politician in the United States, in Europe, or even Russia is likely to challenge a unilateral declaration of military victory onour part.

Even if such a challenge were made, the United States would be in a stronger position than it is today, for it would have established "aggression" again as a means of collective, rather than essentially unilateral action.

I have not discussed this possible course of action with President Johnson, but firmly believe that it presents a feasible course of action which ought not to be lightly dismissed.

Its adoption would not mean the quick withdrawal of our forces in southeast Asia.

In all probability, our military strength would have deployed in that area for many years to come.

We are a Pacific power, and no nation in southern Asia--possibly not even North Vietnam itself--would feel at ease were we to announce a withdrawal from that responsibility.

"Impeach Him or Get Off His Back"
U.S. Congressional Record
November 7, 1973

Mr. AIKEN ------ Mr. President, ever since last March when the series of events, real and imagined, wrapped up in the word "Watergate" began to dominate our public life, I have issued no prepared statements on this subject.

I have not spoken out because, in company with millions of others, I have not discovered an easy way of escaping our present predicament.

I do not want to contribute in any way to the destruction of the third Presidency in a row.

At the same time, the White House has handled its domestic troubles with such relentless incompetence that those of us who would like to help have been like swimmers searching for a way out of the water only to run into one smooth and slippery rock after another.

Under our Constitution, the duties and responsibilities of each of the three branches of our Government are set forth.

Congress tasks are to legislate and to hold the President and the executive branch accountable for administering laws.

These are highly technical tasks, demanding above all else cool heads and a strict adherence to established procedures.

Submission to the politics of righteous indignation makes it impossible for Congress to do its job.

It tends to make us look foolish and incompetent.

I am speaking out of now because the developing hue and cry for the President's resignation suggests to me a veritable epidemic of emotionalism.

It suggested that many prominent Americans, who ought to know better, find the task of holding the President accountable as just too difficult.

It suggests that the procedures laid down in the Constitution are just too complicated.

Appendix

It suggests that most of the American people cannot be trusted to keep their cool because some of them cannot keep theirs.

Those who call for the President's resignation on the ground that he has lost their confidence rish poisoning the wells of politics for years to come.

Within less than 10 years we have seen one Presidency destroyed by an assassin's bullet; another by a bitter and divisive war.

To destroy the third in a row through politics of righteous indignation cannot possible restore confidence either at home or abroad.

It can only sow the seeds of suspicion and cynicism in our lands, inviting a harvest of whirlwinds such as mankind has never seen.

The man who wrote our Constitution were fully aware how waves of emotionalism, if given an easy electoral outlet, could reduce any political system to anarchy.

That is why in a nation governed by its laws they provided that Presidents should rule for 4 years.

They laid down that that period of rule could be interrupted only after Congress had framed a change of high crimes and misdemeanors and had conducted a trial itself based on those charges.

To ask the President now to resign and thus relieve the Congress of its clear congressional duty amounts to a declaration of incompetence on the part of Congress.

If I read correctly the signals sent out by the judicial branch of Government, they are also saying that Congress is the place where this crisis must be resolved.

The President hoped to get from the Supreme Court a "definitive" ruling on executive privilege, but the judicial system is telling us that much and evidence must pass before any such ruling will be forthcoming.

That is how I read the decision of the court of appeals over the questions of taped evidence.

The court clearly directed all parties to seek compromise before coming back.

It follows as night does day that the Supreme Court was and is not ready to accept this case now.

I wish Archibald Cox had enlightened us a little on this situation in his press conference.

He gave us a masterful lecture on the rules of evidence and on how, if he seeks, persons who had violated the law might not get a just punishment.

But above and beyond the punishment of individuals lies the question of the President's fitness to serve.

Only the Congress can judge that--the Congress and the voters at duly scheduled elections.

The desperate search for a special prosecutor, with the virtues of Caesar's wife and unfettered authority of her husband, only represents another effort to escape responsibility.

It makes sense to me to ask the President to prosecute himself, yet any special prosecutor in the Justice Department will find himself in that ridiculous position.

I was not at all surprised that Archibald Cox was fired; I was more surprised that such an intelligent and experienced man did not quit first, or turn down the job in the first place.

Aside from the fact that it will take a lot of time and litigation to establish the constitutionality of such an act, the result is not likely to change matters one whit.

So long as the judicial branch does not want to render a "definitive" decision on the executive privilege, ways will be found to avoid such decision.

And the longer the process, the more obvious it will become that it is the Congress that has the duty.

But I fail to see any great act of patriotism in such of our duty.

On the contrary it is the President's duty to his country not to resign.

That which the American voter has done, let no man undo except through due process.

That should be the President's guiding command.

It has been suggested that the President appear as a witness before the Senate select committee or, perhaps, some other.

This would appear to be another desperate search for means of evading congressional responsibility.

The President's public explanations of the Watergate mess have been astonishingly inept.

Bu this is not of itself an impeachable offense, nor does it suggest that the President be scolded, publicly, in the presence of a congressional committee.

If Harry Truman were alive today, I would know what he would say to the Congress.

He would say the buck stops right here, on Capitol Hill.

It is the clear duty of the House, through whatever procedures it chooses to frame a changes of impeachment and to set itself a deadline for the task.

If no agreement can be reached by that deadline, the leaders of the House should tell the American people that no agreed charge could be found.

That is the way to begin to restore confidence.

If a charge is framed and voted, the Senate's clear duty is to proceed to a trial with all deliberate speed.

Since I would be a juror in such a trial, I intend to say nothing in advance about any possible indictment or any possible verdict.

I am not going to call for the President's resignation.

Quite the contrary, I urge the President to do his duty, and that is inconsistent with resigning.

Nor am I going to try to fool my constituents into believing that any special prosecutor outside of Congress itself can determine the President's ability or worthiness to govern.

Only Congress can do that now.

I was reminded recently of the short story Mark Twain wrote called "The Man Who Corrupted Hadleyburg."

Mark Twain hated self-righteousness, and in this story he told of how a very self-righteous New England town was brought to grief by a clever outsider who set the town's leading citizens to exposing the frailties and venalities of one another.

Politicians I have known are no greater or lesser sinners than the average person listed in the telephone book.

Nor do I have any reason to believe that the level of sin in our public life is higher than elsewhere.

What bothers me much more are those who now would have us believe that President Nixon and his associates alone are the ones who corrupted America.

It is a truly subversive idea, for what would happen if a clever outsider did to us what Mark Twain's hero did to Hadleyburg?

Again I come back to the vital importance of following prescribed procedures.

If the politics of righteous indignation succeeds in persuading the President to resign and relieving the Congress of its clear duty, how long will it be before our politics is corrupted by competitive self-righteousness?

Will it become the accepted fashion to run for public office on the skeletons in your opponent's closet?

Will we after all be corrupted not by real crimes, but by our own incompetence when faced with large issues of justice and morality?

And what will the rest of the world do if we get ourselves in such a state?

Will the word of the U.S. Government be trusted still?

Or will all other powers try to get something at our expense in every forum they can?

I have spoken before of the grave dangers of moral aggression in foreign policy.

That danger is clear and present now that the feuding families of the Middle East at war again.

It is a great tragedy, because both sides have a legitimate cause.

Appendix

Israel is fighting for its existence, accepting the sacrifice of another generation of soldiers, against the day when her neighbors will have enough confidence to accept her claim to nationhood.

The Arabs are fighting for that most elemental of all contemporary social needs, the confidence to see themselves as nations, rather than a primitive babble of tribes.

Only a fool would preach the politics of righteous indignation in the face of this grave tragedy,

And that kind of fool is perhaps the greatest threat to the peace of the Middle East today.

Painfully, delicately, against great odds, the community of nations, led by the United States and, hopefully still, the Soviet Union, are trying to establish procedures that will keep those feuding families from engulfing us all in a third world war.

There being no solution, there only being hope for a progressive chain of settlements, the procedures become literally a matter of life and death.

Congress task in following the impeachment procedures set down in the Constitution should be far easier.

The procedures exist.

They do not have to be invented.

But moral aggression here at home is hardly less dangerous than moral aggression in the Middle East.

It threatens to make an epidemic out of the incompetence that the word "Watergate"has come to stand for.

I hope the leaders of the House of Representatives will rise to their duty.

I hope they will set a deadline, of weeks or months, in which to come up with an impeachment charge.

If the deadline passes without an agreed charge, votes by a simple majority of the House, I expect that the leaders will then tell the American people that no agreed impeachment charge can be found.

If a charge is framed and passed, it is the clear duty of the Senate to initiate a trial with all deliberate speed.

If the president is convicted, so be it.

If not, there will be no legitimate reason for calling for the President's resignation or questioning his right to serve out his term.

As a potential juror in such a trial, I will not have anything to say about guilt or innocence.

None of us was elected to be a megaphone for the loudest voices in out constituencies.

We were elected to legislate and to hold the President and his administration accountable for their actions.

We cannot afford at this critical time to practice the politics of outraged emotions in carrying out these vital tasks. Confidence will never be restored that way. It will only be restored by a determination on our part to follow procedures laid down in the Constitution.

May I now pass on to this Congress advice which I received recently from a fellow Vermonter-

"Either impeach him or get off his back."

Mr. President, I ask unanimous consent to have printed in the Record an editorial on resignation which appeared in Wall Street Journal this morning.

There being no objection, the editorial was ordered to be printed in Record, as follows:

On Resignation

We note that demanding President Nixon's resignation is the latest sport among out newspaper colleagues and even a few responsible politicians. Without denying that Mr.Nixon has maneuvered the Republic into quite a fix, the demands for resignation strike us as hasty and indeed a bit unserious.

Whether or not a President ought to resign, and under what conditions, is something that needs to be thought through carefully. Mr. Nixon is only out 37th President after all. A single precedent would be no trifling matter for the future development of our political institutions. It is foolish to assume that if Mr. Nixon resigned his replacement could pick up the presidency as if nothing had happened. Before demanding such a step, serious men ought to stop to speculate about its future institutional consequences.

Yet we find little or nothing of this in typical demand for resignation. Among the ground for its demand, *The New York Times* included the bombing of Laos, the impoundment of funds, and the President living "beyond his means by borrowing heavily from two millionaire friends." But the *Times* managed to ignore the question of whether Mr.Nixon's resignation should await the confirmation of the vice-presidential choice, surely a matter of no small moment and indeed of no small bearing on the advisability of resignation itself.

Even when the resignation demand is couched in terms that recognize its gravity, as in Time magazine's craftsmenlike editorial, the grounds turn out to be amorphous and ambiguous. The President hired a lot of people who are under indictment. He probably know of the cover-up., Time concludes but the fact of the matter is immaterial because those perpetuating it were appointees. He authorized and then rescinded a plan including illegal acts in the name of national security. He fired Archibald Cox. The effect of all this was "to subvert the constitutional system itself."

A President who subverted the Constitution, we should think, ought to be impeached. We would be quite surprised, though, if the editors of Time believe that plausible grounds for impeachment currently exist, or that the President's knowledge of the cover-up would be immaterial to sucha. step. For our part, we still very much want to learn what is on the Oval Office tapes; even with the two of them suspiciously absent there ought to be plenty to test the key point of John Dean's credibility; if he is not credible the President has no accuser.

We would need to know such facts to remove a President by impeachment. Is a public fervor culminating in his resignation a.less grave and serious step? The resignation demands arise because impeachment would be a long and wearing process. A major reason it would be a long and wearing process is that it requires evidence and due process. The appeal of resignation is precisely that it requires no charge, no evidence, no investigation, no due process, no specific grounds. 'Is that the kind of constitutional precedent we want to set?

Now, we would not say there are no circumstances under which a President ought to consider resignation. We would hope that a President faced with solid grounds for impeachment would not insist on formalities. We can even envision arguments to the effect that resignation might help protect the presidency. As we suggested in the editorial to which readers respond today, Mr. Nixon is without legal or political defenses against a fishing expedition through his whole administration, itself a sorry present for the presidency. If he concluded that his attack would eventually make it impossible to serve out his term, he might want to use the opportunity of the vice presidential vacancy to name a successor chosen to defend the prerogatives.

We suppose, too, that there comes a point at which a President is so discredited he cannot function. But we see no evidence that any such point has been reached. Mr. Nixon has dealt with the Middle East crisis. His vetoes are being sustained in Congress. No doubt some will say he is only trying to distract the nation from Watergate if he goes on television to plead for energy conservation. But such a plea is so clearly appropriate the public would probably respond to the substance of his message.

Thus, we are mostly suspicious of the demand that the President resign because he has lost the confidence of the people. The very words smell of the French Fourth Republic rather than the American Constitution. Especially since we are moving ever deeper into a world where rapid change and instant communication are likely to afflict any national leader with crisis after crisis, we doubt that our institutions ought to evolve toward changing Presidents with every change in the public mood.

The House of Representatives ought to proceed with its impeachment, and indeed make it a more serious investigation than it currently promises to be. If grounds for impeachment are found, so be it. But we are suspicious indeed of having a President forced from office in some extralegal, extra-constitutional manner. The important thing is not whether

Appendix

Mr. Nixon stays in office or leaves, The important thing is that whatever is done is done in a grave and responsible way.

The Presidency

Mr. MANSFIELD ------ Mr. President, I have, as always, listened with attention to what the distinguished Senator from Vermont (Mr. AIKEN) has had to say this morning.

Insofar as the question of impeachment is concerned, that is a matter for the House only to decide in the first instance.

Insofar as the question of the President's resignation is concerned, that is a question on which the President, and the President only, can arrive at a decision.

I note that during the course of the distinguished Senator's speech he stated:

The President hoped to get from the Supreme Court a "definitive" ruling on Executive Privilege, but the Judicial system is telling us that much time and evidence must ask before any such ruling will be forthcoming.

That, I think, is a matter of opinion open to question because, based on the issue of the tapes and the rulings handed down by Judge Sirica in the distinct court, and by five to seven judges sitting on the Court of Appeals for the District of Columbia, it appeared to me that the courts were deciding the question of executive privilege, even though the tapes may have had an indirect bearing on it.

Furthermore, I would disagree with the President of the United States when he said that in his opinion, he felt that his position would have been upheld by the Supreme Court. I think that, too, is merely an opinion and that the Supreme Court could have gone either way.

The distinguished Senator also refers to Mr. Archibald Cox, a man he has known for years and in whom he has known for years and in whom he has a great deal of confidence, as do I. The Senator states:

I was not at all surprised that Archibald Cox was fired; I was more surprised that such an intelligent and experienced man did not quit first

Say We Won and Get Out

or turn down the job in the first place.

May I say that I was pleasantly surprised when Mr. Cox took on the job of special prosecutor, under certain conditions laid down before the Committee on the Judiciary in connection with the nomination of Mr. Elliot Richardson to be Attorney General. I was disappointed, and still am, that Mr. Cox was fired summarily from a job which he was undertaking on the basis of obligations, commitments, and policies made to the Committee on the Judiciary, which represented the Senate as a whole; and I think that this man of such great dedication, quiet dignity, and great patriotism was done a great disservice.

However, I think that he, Mr. Richardson, and Mr. Ruckelshaus, because of their decency, integrity, and their honor, are bigger men now than they were before they were discharged or resigned.

As far as the question of the President appearing as a witness before the Senate Select Committee is concerned, I would concur with the remarks of the distinguished Senator from Vermont. I do not think that any President should be subjected to such a procedure.

The distinguished Senator stated:

If Harry Truman were alive today, I know what he's say to the Congress.

He's say the buck stops right here, on Capitol Hill.

Well, some of the buck stops here as far as various constitutional procedures are concerned, but now all. I recall to my distinguished friend that wehn Harry Truman was President of the United States he had on his desk in the oval room in the White House a placard which proclaimed, "The buck stops here." So it not only stops here, but also it stops down at the White House.

As far as a special prosecutor is concerned, I frankly feel that a special independent prosecutor not beholden to either the executive or the legislative branch should be chosen. I think he should be a man of complete independence, not a man who can fired by a President of the United States, and not a man whom we have to take on the basis of promises made, either implied or express, because this man must be fired. This man must represent, as an appointee of the court, the people of the United States.

After all, it is the people of the United States who happen to be the Government of the United States. I hope we will never lose sight of that fact. The President is transient just passing through, but the institution of the Presidency is something permanent and all enduring. We Senators are just transients passing through, but the institution of the Senate and the Congress is all-enduring. When you get right down to it, it is not a matter of personalities, it is not a matter of legislative branch, the executive branch, or the judicial branch; it is a matter of the people and their concerns.

Like the distinguished Senator from Vermont, I want to see the people given the attention which they deserve because they are the ones who are most concerned, they are the ones who will make the decisions eventually, and that is as it should be and that is as it must be. "The people" is not an empty term. "The people" means something in this country; and "the people" will make the decision on the basis of the evidence laid before them by the so-called Ervin Select Committee of the Senate and by the findings of the grand juries and by the actions of the special prosecutor, and that will be done in due time, because regardless of the travail, the malaise, the difficulties which confront this country today, this Republic is going to survive, and out of the purgatory which this Nation and its people are undergoing today will come a better, cleaner, and more upright Nation. So while we are going through this period let us keep in mind that we are paying a price for mistakes which can be attributed to all of us, that in paying that price, in undergoing this confession, in going through this purgatory, we will in the end reach the promised land.

Several Senators addressed the Chair.

Mr. MANSFIELD ------ I yield to the Senator from Vermont.

Say We Won and Get Out

Mr. AIKEN ------ Mr. President, I would like to add to what the majority leader has said that what is going on today comprises a powerful argument for the constitutional amendment which he and I have been proposing for some years and which has received very little, if any, consideration either by Congress or the public up to this time.

That amendment would provide for a single 6-year term for the President.

In view of the fact that the President carries a bigger load every year, I am not sure but what a single 5-year term, such as is in vogue in a great many of the other leading countries of the world, would be more appropriate. If we had a single 5-year term for the President at this time, I very much doubt that a good deal of the emotionalism which we are going through today would be existing. There would be emotionalism, because folks have to have something to be emotional about at all times, but it would probably apple to a different subject, particularly as to what would happen to the next President. In closing, let me say I do not envy the next President, whoever he may be.

Mr. MANSFIELD ------ Mr. President, if the Senator will yield, let me say that, once again, I am in wholehearted accord with what the Senator has just said. I do not envy the President because whoever occupies the Office of the Presidency, the burdens and the pressures are too great for any one man to undertake for.

Appendix

**George Aiken
Cabot High School Graduation Speech
Cabot, Vermont
June 17, 1969**

The reason I am here today is that having spent three years of High School in a class of three members, I felt honored to be with you ten graduating Seniors in this small but lively town to share with you this memorable occasion.

While small towns like Cabot are finding it more difficult to compete with the great urban areas of our country, the fact remains that the community is still the basis of good government.

In many ways the thousands of our Nation's small towns and cities are still the strength of our democracy.

People can get involved in local affairs and know that they have an influence over the direction of their government.

I am frequently asked how to get active in politics.

The best way I know is to participate in your community affairs.

If people think you're doing a good job, they will support and promote you.

I'm not here to talk politics with you, however.

But I did want you to know that all decision-making, all wisdom, all knowledge doesn't come from Paris, London, Washington or even Montpelier.

Sometimes good ideas come from places like Cabot and other small towns off the beaten path.

With that off my chest – and I like to do that every so often with the hope that some of my Washington friends hear it – I would like to talk with you tonight about the world you are facing today.

It is a world where changes often come without warning but nevertheless a world where human instincts have shown little change over the centuries.

I understand that some of the graduates of tonight are going to college, others into military service and some will take part in the Vermont economic system.

Perhaps some of you will even help out at the Cabot Cheese Plant.

I hope so because Cabot Cheese has wide reputation for quality.

The important thing is that all of you will continue your education in your own way.

The secret of knowledge is really nothing more than trying to find out answers to crucial questions.

The problems affecting the world tonight face all men collectively regardless of race, creed or color.

In a nutshell the problem is over the issue of power, political and economic.

Who will control it?

Who will have it?

How will it be exercised?

There are factors which relate to the great struggle for power.

The world is getting smaller and spheres of influence are getting larger.

Our influence may someday extend to other planets.

The great frontiers of space are already being explored and mapped out.

As the world gets smaller and more crowded, man's problems get more complex and he sometimes gets more irritated.

He also gets envious.

Then "he's-got-it" and "I-want-it" instinct is a human trait that is still prevalent in the world.

Granted we don't fight wars over beaver pelts anymore like the American French-Indian War in the 18th Century.

But we still get involved and I suspect we will continue to get involved in wars of varying degree over the natural resources and territory.

The hunger for power of the emerging nations will have to be balanced by the need to control the power and influence of the strong.

Appendix

Today we get concerned over the so-called "hippies" but we have always had young people unhappy with life and that catch-all bugaboo called the "establishment."

But now we have something more serious than the historical impatience of youth.

We are now seeing some of our young people radicalized because of world events – primarily the war in Vietnam.

The values of American Life – equality, justice and liberty – have lost their meaning for many of them.

Many of our young men are morally outraged by the great paradoxes of our times

They can't understand why young people have to fight wars which are promoted by those who would increase their own influence and power.

They are unhappy, and frequently with justification, that our country has tried to force its ways upon other people.

The majority of our youth feel deeply about these problems, but still respect the laws of the land.

But there is a lesser segment of youth who have little respect for the law.

They see no harm in trespassing on private property and destroying it or infringing upon the rights of others.

There should be a clear and firm distinction made between the campus liberal and the campus outlaw.

We need the ideas of our young people.

They are refreshingly candid, although sometimes not too practical.

But these ideas should be forged on the anvil of peaceful discussions, not from the platform of mob rule where confrontation replaces conciliation, compromise and common sense.

No society can prosper if chaotic conditions are permitted to exist in its great institutions of higher learning.

The end of the Vietnam War will help take some of the pressure off continued alienation of youth from traditional American values.

Perhaps, we should also consider what Abraham Lincoln once said when he called for a new birth of freedom for each generation to keep the torch of liberty alive.

This current generation – perhaps never so insistent before – is asking for a larger stake in the decision making.

What they really want is more power.

But the young aren't alone.

Red China wants more power.

France under DeGaulle thought it should have more than it had.

Fortunately, the two great super powers – Russia and the United States – are at least thinking about ways to control their own power to destroy each other.

We are now living in an age when both Russia and the United States have the military capacity to inflict total destruction on the other.

We are also living in an age when our defense planners use such grisly terms as "assured destruction", "mutual deterrent", or "the balance of terror."

The desire for power is a thirst that we haven't learned yet how to quench.

What we call one man's ambition is sometimes nothing but another man's greed.

I got my first lesson in the fine line between what is greed and ambition when I was about your age.

In those days a powerful publishing empire printed the Boston American.

There was a cartoon on page one in which the North American Continent was covered by an American Flag.

Beneath the cartoon ran a caption which went something like this: "Eventually, why not now."

This desire to spread American influence as far as possible isn't dead.

We still have people who would resolve all international problems by the show or use of force.

Appendix

Now that our interest in Vietnam is beginning to wane, the next areas of concern for this country will likely be Latin America.

In the future, our relations with these Latin countries will be important, and may well dominate our future foreign policy.

We must watch ourselves in Latin America and keep cool.

This won't be easy as we see both Russia and now Red China trying to exert more influence.

I hope we can pause long enough to remember that the Monroe Doctrine was promulgated in December 1823, 146 years ago, and if other countries now try to extend their trade in Latin America, this isn't always "dangerous to our peace and safety."

Today, we are the greatest military power on earth.

We have a responsibility to protect other friendly countries from tyranny and outside oppression if they ask us to.

But this doesn't mean we can also tell them how to live or what they should eat, or how they should dress, or that Coke is better than wine.

With a few glaring exceptions we have controlled our military might reasonably well.

I hope we will continue to do so and not succumb to those who are urging us to play King of the Mountain at every turn in our relations with other countries.

If I could leave one thought with you tonight it is that learning how to get along with people and governing ourselves is still one of our fundamental jobs.

It takes talent to run a good club meeting.

It takes skill to run a good school board meeting and it take tolerance and understanding to be successful at either.

These same skills that are needed to run the Congress of the United States or the United Nations are also needed to run a town meeting or farm cooperative.

Only the scale is different.

If we are to be a successful nation and live in a peaceful world, we still have to figure our wats to live together.

This means changing old ways of doing things.

It may mean giving the younger generation more control over its own destiny.

It may mean instilling more human compassion in our big institutions where it is government, labor unions, business, or big schools.

Lincoln must have had this in mind when we called for a new birth of freedom for every generation.

It was a philosophic way of saying we should be able to change with the times.

We cannot stop changes from taking place but we can try to direct them.

A changing world demands changing viewpoints and attitudes.

The old order, the old answers and the old priorities aren't always the best answers to new questions, though we should not always consider the solutions to problems inadequate simply because they served our ancestors well.

It is not always easy to accept change, particularly for those have achieved success under old-time practices.

But unless our society keeps up with our social and technological advancements we will always be facing troubles.

One of our most fundamental tasks us to get along with our neighbors individually and as a nation.

As Vermonters, we have always had to exercise tolerance, understanding and ingenuity.

But we should also remember the words of one of our fellow Vermonter, Robert Frost, when he said:

"Good fences make good neighbors."

I am honored that you invited me here tonight.

Furthermore, I am envious of each and everyone of the members of the graduating class.

You have learned much during your years at Cabot High School.

You will learn far more in the future than you have learned to date.

Appendix

I trust you will use the knowledge acquired to make a better life for yourselves and will also share it with others.

For that alone will make a better world.

———————

An Interview with Senator Aiken
Vermont Life
Spring 1973

This article was originally published in the Spring 1973 issue of Vermont Life, reprinted with permission from Vermont Life through the Vermont Department of Tourism and Marketing, credit to Bernie Sanders and James Soper:

> *Forty years now a revered and independent leader in Vermont and the Nation's Capital, is*
> AIKEN OF VERMONT
>
> *Here interviewed*
> By BERNARD SANDERS

George David Aiken, the ranking Republican in the U.S. Senate, is a Vermonter of 80 years, forty-one of them devoted to political office, the past 32 in Washington. But Aiken's intimate knowledge and understanding of Vermont and Vermonters still is matched by none.

In our independent tradition, he always has voted as his conscience dictated. As it is in Washington, Vermonters have returned to George Aiken an affection, admiration and support unparalleled in the long political annals of the State.

—Ed.

SANDERS — *Could you describe a little bit the Vermont that you knew as a child? Where you grew up and the style of life that existed then?*
AIKEN — Well, I think I described that in a speech that I gave at the World's Fair in New York in 1938. After several governors had spoken and told of the wonderful things they had in their states, it came my turn, and I said that Vermont may not have as much as some of these

other states do, but what we have is paid for.

Of course, in the flood of 1927, when 80 people drowned and there were millions of dollars in damage, the state did have to go into debt. But we were on a pay-as-you-go basis up until a few years ago when we were really forced into indebtedness. You can't keep up with your competition really without offering some of the things that they do.

S. — *Did you grow up on a farm?*

A. — Oh yes, yes. I never lived off the farm until I came to Washington. It was up on West Hill in the town of Putney. A small farm. You could learn quite a lot there. Got most of my education, my formal education, in a little red schoolhouse — No. 5. And we learned quite a lot of things you didn't learn in town.

S. — *How far was your home from the schoolhouse?*

A. — Then I had to go down to Putney Village. That was not quite four miles away.

S. — *How did you get to school?*

A. — Walked.

S. — *Through the snow?*

A. — Yes, sometimes snow up to your knees. Of course we didn't have busing, but we didn't have recreational facilities either. We got our exercise going to school and back.

I took three years of high school in Putney's new schoolhouse. It cost the town $12,000, and everybody said how in the world are they ever going to pay for it? But they did. And I had one teacher for three years of high school in one room. I think there were the three of us who finally got through the junior year there

Then I went to Brattleboro for the final year of high school. That meant walking an extra mile to the depot and taking the train from Putney to Brattleboro. I think it cost us nine cents each way, every day. Of course that was a lot of money, but I finally made it. I do recall coming to Washington with the Senior Class — just before we graduated. President Taft was in the White House then and he shook hands with every one of us personally. Presidents don't do that anymore.

S. — *What are some of the strongest memories that you have from your childhood?*

A. — Oh, all of them, all of them. A big oak tree in back of the house on the top of the hill. Supposed to be about 550 years old. It was on the next farm but I own that tree now. I imagine it's the largest tree in Vermont and maybe the largest in New England. It's about seven feet in diameter two feet from the ground. And you learn a lot from that. You learn a lot that you don't get out of books.

S. — *You wrote a book, I believe, on wildflowers.*

A. — That was in 1933. I dictated it. The book still sells.

S. — *Where did you develop your interest in wildflowers? Did it come naturally?*

A. — Naturally. My father and mother always raised things. My father raised vegetables and peddled them down in the village. My mother always had a bigger flower garden than she could take care of. And then, in the District School, we had wildflower contests. We would see who could find them first and the most varieties. And that came naturally. I suppose I started when I was about five- or six-years-old in that field.

S. — *Let me ask you a question. Vermont, over the years, has changed considerably, of course...*

A. — Yes, it has changed. Of course the population has increased. More people are coming into Vermont now than are leaving it by several times over, I understand. And the situation has changed. Land values have changed. Land that used to be $5 or $10 an acre is $5 or $10 thousand an acre now, if it's rightly located, has a view or water on it anywhere.

S. — *How do you view the change? Does it make you sad?*

A. — Why I view the change as inevitable. You can't stop that change. The best we can do is try to guide it so that we can derive the most benefit and the least harm from the change. But certainly, when people say we won't permit any more people to come into the state, that's nonsense. They can't stop it.

S.— *How did you get drawn into politics? Were your parents involved in politics?*

A. — I think there was an Aiken in the State Legislature as far back as they had state legislatures. My father got into politics almost by accident in 1912. That was a Bull Moose year. He was a supporter of Teddy Roosevelt and somebody persuaded him to run for town representative from Putney. And he was elected, much to his surprise.

And I ran for the House in 1923 and didn't make it. Somebody said I would do away with our little district schools and I was so mad I wouldn't answer — so I lost by a few votes.

S. — *What happened between 1923 and 1931?*

A. — I tended the business — the nursery and the farm. And just got over losing the election. In 1923 I suppose I could have changed the course of my political career, but I never was any hand to deny accusations. But I got up there, to Montpelier, in 1931 and that was the year Vermont established a statewide highway system and put a state income tax into effect. And at that time — in the year 1931 — there was a proposal in the Legislature to construct about 80 dams on all the streams in Vermont, primarily on the Connecticut River system. Ostensibly they were for flood control purposes. Actually they were to benefit the power companies. And about that time I got the idea that somebody besides politicians ought to get involved in politics. In 1933 some of my friends thought I ought to run for Speaker of the House.

S. — *This was after one term in the legislature?*

A. — After one term in the legislature. And I don't know why I did it, but my two opponents were both bankers and, you know, in 1933 a banker couldn't have been elected dog catcher anywhere. Everybody was mad at them. So I did get to be Speaker. Had a very good session. I recall I didn't have to rap for order at any time. Had no lawyers — oh yes, had two lawyers in the House — out of 248 members.

S. — *That's what I would like you to talk a little about. Now, in Vermont, as in all the states, legislatures are getting to be kind of professional, in that there are now relatively few farmers or small businessmen. What was the Legislature like in 1933?*

A. — Every town, large and small, had a representative. Of course we had the 30-member Senate then as we do now. But it so happens that it was the representatives from the small towns that usually had the experience, headed the committees and ran the Legislature. The larger towns were not in the habit of returning their members.

S. — *Was the composition of the Legislature then mostly farmers?*

A. — I'd say they predominated. As I say, in 1933 there were just two lawyers — three lawyers, but one died. Just two lawyers and, of course, they offset each other beautifully. So you might say we had no lawyers in the House. And two years later when I presided over the Senate as Lieutenant Governor we didn't have any lawyers in the Senate. In the House I'd say there were more farmers than anything else, because I know when sap started running they wanted the Legislature to wind up so they could go home. In the Senate, though, you'd get more business people, store-keepers. I've forgotten exactly, but they were a good cross-section.

S. — *Is there any truth to the rumor that in the old days the small towns used to send to the Legislature those people who were on relief so that the town could save money?*

A. — Occasionally, yes, it was true. I remember when my father was a member of the House, one member from a nearby town didn't show up, and they found him down on the Winooski River cutting ice. Of course that wouldn't be permitted now because of the pollution.

S. — *Do you have any feelings about the quality of life in those days as compared to now? Do you think people were living better then? Were they happier than they are today?*

A. — No, no. They're better off now. The better off they get the more discontented they get. The more educated they get, the more they get discouraged with public life. The people are better off now. They wouldn't go back to the "good old days."

I have a standard answer to those who complain about not being able to attain their objectives right off. I say if you're not satisfied look over you shoulder and see where you came from. Do you want to go back 5 years, 10 years, 20 years — maybe 500 years? Do you want that? No, none of them wants to go back. They are — and that's a worldwide occurrence — living better than the human race has ever lived before. You can go into old cemeteries in Vermont and see rows of little headstones where a family of children was wiped out by a contagious disease — scarlet fever, diphtheria or something like that.

"The Pentagon wasn't telling [Truman] what was going on."

S. — *What about the difference in politics in Vermont, say, from 1923 when you first began, and now? How has it changed?*
A. — Well of course the Legislature's been reduced in size. I think that probably was inevitable. But it takes away from the identity of the towns. And here's another thing we'd better be careful about. The smaller the state legislature, the more the members become sitting ducks for lobbyists and big business.
S. — *What year did you first come to the U.S. Senate?*
A. — After I was Speaker in 1933-35 I was elected Lieutenant Governor and in 1937 Governor for 4 years (two terms), and then I came down here to the Senate.
S. — *So you've served under quite a few presidents: Roosevelt, Truman, Eisenhower, Kennedy, Johnson and now Nixon. What personal reminiscences do you have of the various presidents?*
A. — Well, President Roosevelt didn't like me very well when I was Governor of Vermont because I objected to the federal government taking over everything in the state.

At that time they were going to move people off the land that couldn't support them properly, and take them off the hills and put them in the valleys, and take jurisdiction over the water and land everywhere. And I objected very strenuously to that. In fact so many of us objected that it was not done. Then I know that President Roosevelt was very much upset because he proposed a highway over the tops of all our mountains, an extension of the Appalachian Highway, and we, Vermont, voted that down. He regretted that. After he was elected, though, for the fourth time in 1944, the White House called up and asked me to come down, He just wanted to visit.

S. — *Had you met him personally before that?*

A. — Oh, yes. I'd met him before that, but not on favorable conditions. And I went down there and stayed quite a while. I remember that his aide, General Watson, kept trying to get me out and the President wouldn't let him. After that, until he died, we got along very well indeed.

He was very strong for the St. Lawrence Seaway and power project, which the utility companies were very much opposed to. And I well recall that after he went down to Hot Springs that winter and I had constantly put in amendments and so forth — and bills — he sent a wire to me urging the Senate to approve the St. Lawrence Seaway project. And, of course, the Democratic leadership didn't think very much of that. So, we got along very well from the last, shall I say, the last November to April that he lived. And then Harry Truman, whom I worked pretty closely with, came on as President.

S. — *You knew Truman in the Senate, I imagine?*

A. — Yes, yes indeed. And I used to go down there at least once a week, just to talk with him. He was having very difficult times.

S. — *In what sense?*

A. — Well, for one reason, the Pentagon wasn't telling him what was going on with the war, although he was, constitutionally Commander in Chief of all our forces. So that was one thing. Another thing I recall is that Japan was trying to get out of the war, and he didn't know whether the American public would stand for our letting them get out of the war without invading Japan at an estimated cost of about 200,000 killed or wounded. So he called me down there in May. I had a couple of Memorial Day talks to give and I told him I'd sound the people out and see what they thought about letting Japan out of it, which I did. And there was no objection so far as I could see. And I reported back to him. But after that the bombs on Hiroshima and Nagasaki came later in August, and the war ended.

S. — *Did you have any idea that the atom bomb was ready for use?*

A. — No, and at that time I don't think that he did either. I don't think that the Pentagon had even told him that the atom bomb was about ready. At that time Ernest Gibson was a Colonel in the Pentagon. I told the President that Ernest was over there and he said to bring him in, that he'd like to talk with him. So we went in one morning, and then he arranged with Ernest Gibson to fix things up through the Commanding Officer of G-2, General Clark, so that he would get a report every day on what was going on in the war.

S. — *You mean that he was that far away…?*

A. — Oh, the Pentagon didn't think that Harry Truman had any business knowing about that war for the first two or three months he was President.

S. — *So he had to work outside of channels to get information about what was happening?*

A. — He got it, finally. He had to find the channels because, as I say, the Pentagon felt that it was the United States, or the whatever you want to call it, and that didn't think that the President had to know these things. I think times have changed a little in that respect.

S. — *And what about Eisenhower?*

A. — Ike was good. When he first came in as President I told him that I was not going to be telling him what he ought to do all the time, but that if I could help him at any time to let me know. He had Sherm Adams with him. Sherm was good. Sherm was born and raised in Windham County, Vermont, and his wife in Windsor County. I found him good. But, unfortunately, Sherm said "no" two or three times when the boys wanted him to say "yes" and, of course, they got him out of the White House.

But Ike was one of the better presidents. You could talk with him on the telephone, call him up, and he'd almost answer the telephone himself. He'd say: "I'll tend to that right away," and that was it. We look back on it now and find that we had eight years with no American killed in foreign countries because of war, no inflation during those eight years. He looks better every day.

Jack Kennedy, of course, had the office next to me and Jack and I got along fine, until he decided he wanted to run for President. And then, of course, he had to do things that we couldn't work together on very well.

S. — *You mean for political reasons?*

A. — Yes, when he got to be President he thought it was a grand social affair or about two or three months. And then they had the Bay of Pigs episode down in Cuba which didn't work to our advantage. The next day he called up and asked me to come down to visit and talk.

For the last six months before he was assassinated I talked with him very frequently. In fact I went to Moscow for him for the signing of the test ban treaty. He said he wouldn't send a Congressional delegation unless I did go, so I had to go.

> *"Lyndon... loved to be asked but he didn't like to be told."*

After that, of course, we had Lyndon Johnson who was different from any of the others. I think I can describe Lyndon in a single sentence. He loved to be asked, but he didn't like to be told.

S. — *Was this true of him as a Senator as well as a President?*

A. — I think so. He was different. But he was awfully good in some respects. As far as rural development — the rural water bill, which the Budget Bureau was deadly against. He just snapped them into line one day and that legislation went through.

He used to ask me to go places for him. I went to Mexico I think twice. I went to Canada with him once... He came up to New England on my birthday one year. Finally, I went around the world to visit the heads of state in 16 different countries with Senator Mansfield and three other members of the Senate at the request of President Johnson...

And now we have Richard Nixon. I think he's doing pretty well — and I'll use the old Vermont escape clause — so far. Certainly he's had the benefit of his predecessor's mistakes. I want to say this: Although we got into a bad situation over in Indo-China, we went in with the

Appendix

"We can't stop people from coming into Vermont."

best of intentions to keep the North Vietnamese from slaughtering several hundred thousand more Catholics and people they considered persona non grata. We had a responsibility for those refugees we had moved, and we got into that war by trying to exercise that responsibility. And every time that President Kennedy or Johnson committed more troops and got us further involved, I'm sure they thought they were doing the right thing to bring the situation to a satisfactory conclusion. But it didn't work out that way.

S. — *Have any things happened in your political life which you've regretted — decisions which you've made which, in retrospect seem basically wrong, that you'd re-do if you had the chance?*

A. — That's a hard question to answer. I think everybody's made mistakes. I have found it good policy if you make a mistake to admit it right away and let people forget it. But so many people that make a mistake spend the rest of their lives trying to justify the mistake. It just doesn't work — it doesn't pay. I've often said that anyone in high position in government ought to make at least one mistake so that could admit it.

When Jack Kennedy said that he was to blame for the fiasco at the Bay of Pigs, his stock went right up high in public estimation. Jack was not to blame for the fiasco at the Bay of Pigs. I know that. But he said he was. And then when the U-2 spy plane was brought down over Russia and President Eisenhower said; "Yes, that was our plane. We got caught." That was the end of it. Nobody blamed him anymore. We knew perfectly well that the Russians had their own system too — but when Ike said we got caught that was the end of it.

S. — *You talked a lot, in the book you wrote called Speaking From Vermont back in 1938, about the philosophy of self-reliance. Could you go into that a bit? Do you still feel the same basically or have you changed your views?*

A. — I have a copy of every talk I've given since 1936. I've got them bound, and once in a while I look back to see if I've changed my mind. I don't think so. Not the philosophy. You have to change your mind with changing circumstances — but I feel about the same now as I did then.

S. — *What does the philosophy of self-reliance mean to you?*
A. — Well, I don't think I'm the one to point that out. As I say right now, I'm concerned with the widening spread between the haves and the have-nots. Even though the have-nots are having better medical attention, better food, better clothing, better education than they ever had before, the spread is widening.

S. — *There was a time when Vermont was populated by small farmers who really ran their own farms, and sank or swam, depending on how well they did on their own efforts. That's not really the case anymore. People are now more dependent on employers or government.*
A. — I had a letter the other day from a person living in Vermont who wound up saying; "It's about time that some hard-headed businessmen ran this government." And I had to write back and tell him that when the shoe pinches those hard-headed businessmen are the first ones in Washington looking for federal assistance. And that is true.

S. — *Could you talk a little bit about your political campaigns and the fact that you are known to spend very little money on them?*
A. — Well, if I spent a lot of money in Vermont it would have reacted against me. I think what helped me in state-wide elections in Vermont at first was that I had about 10,000 customers for trees and plants in the state of Vermont. And I never talked politics to any extent. I simply talked about things of interest to the community. One big mistake that political parties make is trying to make all candidates subscribe to the same platform and the same ideas. And you just can't do it and win elections.

Although I've always run on the Republican ticket I feel when I get down here I represent all the people of the state and I've been very fortunate in my relationship with the Democratic Party in Vermont.

S. — *There's been some discussion lately about the state of Vermont being, in a sense, dominated or over-run by out of state interests. For example, a lot of the large Vermont industries are selling out to out of state corporations.*

A. — As I say it's something that's inevitable. We can't stop people from coming into Vermont. They're coming more and more and more — and land values have gone up, and up and up. We can't stop it. We are trying to guide the influx so that we will keep Vermont as it was as far as we can, but still realize that changes are inevitable... I hate to see Vermont industries sell out to the conglomerates, but that is the order of the day... We've paid a little price there. On the other hand we've got a lot of small industries still in Vermont, and coming into Vermont. We've got the recreational industry which is probably the fastest growing industry in the world. So that's a change you can't help. We do hate to see the old homeowned, home-grown industries fall into the hands of a giant corporation. But it's something we can't stop and it's a worldwide situation.

When you can't stop it — you've got to guide it. I used to say that if you stand on the track and see a train coming down you can do one of two things. You can stand still and get run over, or you can hop on it and try to control it. We've done pretty well in Vermont.

Post Script

Jeff Danziger

Non-Americans often miss the difference between the states and think of Americans as all pretty much the same. America for them is a blend of bombast, braggadocio, and overweight. The differences between a Mainer and a Los Angeleno are invisible to them. Oddly, this is true even for many Americans. Are Vermonters different from Southerners, Westerners? And in what particulars? I'll repeat the old creak: to a foreigner, a Yankee is an American, to an American a Yankee is a Northerner, to a Northerner a Yankee is a New Englander, to a New Englander a Yankee is a Vermonter, and to a Vermonter a Yankee is a man who eats pie for breakfast.

Some years ago, the Mormons sent a fresh-faced young man named Jim Mullin to Vermont to run for the Senate. He showed up, declared residency, and began spending money in his campaign. The money was from his Mormon backers, including Orin Hatch, still with many rotten tricks in his future. Needless to say, young Mr. Mullin did not appeal to Vermonters, and he failed to be nominated. But some wondered what had given him the idea or had given his backers their hopes of getting him elected. They had looked at the map, seen an opening, and assumed that states were all pretty much alike. In a small place like Vermont, they reasoned, anyone with some cash could get elected.

And not long ago another transplant, propitiously named McMullen, who was from Massachusetts, made the same mistake. Some will remember that he not only misread the Vermont mind, but he didn't know how many teats a cow had.

The difference between states is a result of history, industry, climate, religion, and a kind of political fog that rises from the earth itself. The same traits are found here and there, but it's the blend of such traits that marks a state's distinctiveness. Vermont's blend is fairness, simplicity, and a strong desire to be left alone. Even the Vermont stereotype is a blend of traits: a laconic sense of humor, taciturn speech, financial tightness, and so on. Most of these are erroneous. But the greatest of these, at least from my observation, is fairness.

Not to patronize my neighbors, but nothing displeases Vermonters more than seeing someone screwed by wealth or power. And this is all the more true when other people are taken advantage of, rather than the Vermonter himself—if that makes sense. If unfairness does occur, then something should be done. If there's no redress, then at least there's widespread rejection.

How then does the state deal with the advance of someone like the current president?

I was living in Plainfield, Vermont, during the Vietnam War, and I received a draft notice in 1966. For reasons I can't remember I obeyed the order, perhaps in part because I had been raised to be an obedient child. I had been taught to think that the United States usually took actions that were fundamentally right, even if the underlying morality was not obvious. I wasn't patriotic, but I wasn't unpatriotic either.

What I wanted most to avoid was the infantry, the destination of nearly all draftees. To escape life slogging around with a rifle, I enlisted and signed up for an assignment to a year-long language school to learn the southern dialect of Vietnamese. The school was housed on a lonely air force base in Texas, on the Mexican border in the most un-Vermont area of the country. At the end of the year, the war was still going on, and my assignment using my new language skills was assured. I had hoped that that the war would end, and I would not be needed. But it didn't end.

Post Script

Thus, I would up in hot, stinking, noisy Vietnam. The army, by that time disorganized and resentful, assigned me to the task I was least capable of, mechanical maintenance. My unit fixed all sorts of things mechanical, mostly repairing artillery, changing tubes in the guns on the far-flung firebases that were accessible only by helicopter. One can quickly grow uncharmed by helicopters. They are dangerous.

I wrote a letter to George Aiken, as Vermont a person as ever lived. I pointed out that this was a provable waste of taxpayer money, since at some cost and time I had studied the language of our allies, and if we were ever to turn the war over to the South Vietnamese nation, someone would have to tell them. Me, just to take an example. Senator Aiken was famous at the time for suggesting that the way out of the Vietnam quagmire was to simply declare that we had won, and then come home. There was a desperate wit in this solution, and many were impressed by its immediate value.

But the army did not, and still does not, appreciate soldiers getting special attention from their congressmen. I was called into the commander's hut and yelled at. On the table was a letter from George Aiken asking for an explanation or a rectification of this constituent's obviously valid objection. My commander sneered about what would happen if everyone wrote letters to their senator, adding a few sneers about my fitness as an officer. I was a smart guy, wiseass, and so on. Which was pretty accurate. I was hoping to be reassigned to the much safer and air-conditioned headquarters in Saigon, translating stuff. The commander was in a vengeful mood. I wound up working with POWs and intelligence operations, not far from the Cambodian border. So, after all my scheming, I was walking around in the jungle with the infantry. And a rifle.

Even so, I will always be grateful to George Aiken. This episode showed me that there was a Vermont identity and that Vermont took care of its own. And since I wasn't killed or wounded, it actually worked out. I wrote a letter of appreciation to Aiken but kept it brief. No reason to thank someone effusively for doing his job.

I had first fallen in love with the physical beauty of Vermont, but after the war I came home to love the spirit of the place. I taught high school for a number of years, and I noticed that although students left for a while, they often came back. Not for the money, and not for the opportunities to succeed, but for fairness and the shared opinion about what was important in life. Money was not unimportant, as a friend said, but at best it was just helpful.

So, if there is any value in the comparison between, on the one hand, Vermont and its people, and, on the other, a thuggish grifter like Trump, it's that Americans are not all like Trump. Even the people who voted for him are not all like him. Some maybe, but not that many. And for Vermont, a state that, per capita, voted against Trump more than any other state, the way forward is cloudy. If the Trump thugs cut money for schools, kill Obamacare, neglect the infrastructure, and insult Canada in the years to come, how do we react? Many propose that we pay no attention to him. We'll get through the next four years somehow, with inventiveness, cooperation, care for one another, and the sure knowledge that someday it will end and be forgotten, like a storm, powerful but transient.

In other words, as George Aiken advised, we simply declare victory, and come home.

Vietnam War Timeline

The Vietnam War started in the 1950s, according to most historians, though the conflict in Southeast Asia had its roots in the French colonial period of the 1800s. The United States, France, China, the Soviet Union, Cambodia, Laos and other countries would over time become involved in the lengthy war, which finally ended in 1975 when North and South Vietnam were reunited as one country. The following Vietnam War timeline is a guide to the complex political and military issues involved in a war that would ultimately claim millions of lives.

Vietnam Background: Uneasy French Rule

1887: France imposes a colonial system over Vietnam, calling it French Indochina. The system includes Tonkin, Annam, Cochin China and Cambodia. Laos is added in 1893.

1923-25: Vietnamese nationalist Ho Chi Minh is trained in the Soviet Union as an agent of the Communist International (Comitern).

February 1930: Ho Chi Minh founds the Indochinese Communist Party at a meeting in Hong Kong.

June 1940: Nazi Germany takes control of France.

September 1940: Japanese troops invade French Indochina and occupy Vietnam with little French resistance.

May 1941: Ho Chi Minh and communist colleagues establish the League for the Independence of Vietnam. Known as the Viet Minh, the movement aims to resist French and Japanese occupation of Vietnam.

March 1945: Japanese troops occupying Indochina carry out a coup against French authorities and announce an end to the colonial era, declaring Vietnam, Laos and Cambodia independent.

August 1945: Japan is defeated by the Allies in World War II, leaving a power vacuum in Indochina. France begins to reassert its authority over Vietnam.

September 1945: Ho Chi Minh declares an independent North Vietnam and models his declaration on the American Declaration of Independence of 1776 in an (unsuccessful) effort to win the support of the United States.

July 1946: Ho Chi Minh rejects a French proposal granting Vietnam limited self-government and the Viet Minh begins a guerrilla war against the French.

March 1947: In an address to Congress, President Harry Truman states that the foreign policy of the United States is to assist any country whose stability is threatened by communism. The policy becomes known as the Truman Doctrine.

June 1949: The French install former emperor Bao Dai as head of state in Vietnam.

Vietnam War Timeline

August 1949: The Soviet Union explodes its first atom bomb in a remote area of Kazakhstan, marking a tense turning point in the Cold War with the United States.

October 1949: Following a civil war, Chinese Communist leader Mao Zedong declares the creation of the People's Republic of China.

January 1950: The People's Republic of China and the Soviet Union formally recognize the communist Democratic Republic of Vietnam and both begin to supply economic and military aid to communist resistance fighters within the country.

February 1950: Assisted by the Soviet Union and the newly Communist China, the Viet Minh step up their offensive against French outposts in Vietnam.

June 1950: The United States, identifying the Viet Minh as a Communist threat, steps up military assistance to France for their operations against the Viet Minh.

March-May 1954: French troops are humiliated in defeat by Viet Minh forces at Dien Bien Phu. The defeat solidifies the end of French rule in Indochina.

April 1954: In a speech, U.S. President Dwight D. Eisenhower says the fall of French Indochina to communists could create a "domino" effect in Southeast Asia. This so-called domino theory guides U.S. thinking on Vietnam for the next decade.

The Geneva Accords

July 1954: The Geneva Accords establish North and South Vietnam with the 17th parallel as the dividing line. The agreement also stipulates that elections are to be held within two years to unify Vietnam under a single democratic government. These elections never happen.

1955: Catholic nationalist Ngo Dinh Diem emerges as the leader of South Vietnam, with U.S. backing, while Ho Chi Minh leads the communist state to the north.

May 1959: North Vietnam forces begin to build a supply route through Laos and Cambodia to South Vietnam in an effort to support guerrilla attacks against Diem's government in the south. The route becomes known as the Ho Chi Minh Trail and is greatly expanded and enhanced during the Vietnam War.

July 1959: The first U.S. soldiers are killed in South Vietnam when guerrillas raid their living quarters near Saigon.

September 1960: Ho Chi Minh, facing failing health, is replaced by Le Duan as head of North Vietnam's ruling communist party.

December 1960: The National Liberation Front (NLF) is formed with North Vietnamese backing as the political wing of the antigovernment insurgency in South Vietnam. The United States views the NLF as an arm of North Vietnam and starts calling the military wing of the NLF the Viet Cong—short for Vietnam Cong-san, or Vietnamese communists.

May 1961: President John F. Kennedy sends helicopters and 400 Green Berets to South Vietnam and authorizes secret operations against the Viet Cong.

January 1962: In Operation Ranch Hand, U.S. aircraft start spraying Agent Orange and other herbicides over rural areas of South Vietnam to kill vegetation that would offer cover and food for guerrilla forces.

February 1962: Ngo Dinh Diem survives a bombing of the presidential palace in South Vietnam as Diem's extreme favoritism toward South Vietnam's Catholic minority alienates him from most of the South Vietnamese population, including Vietnamese Buddhists.

January 1963: At Ap Bac, a village in the Mekong Delta southwest of Saigon, South Vietnamese troops are defeated by a much smaller unit of Viet Cong fighters. The South Vietnamese are overcome despite their four-to-one advantage and the technical and planning assistance of U.S. advisers.

May 1963: In a major incident of what becomes known as the "Buddhist Crisis," the government of Ngo Dinh Diem opens fire on a crowd of Buddhist protestors in the central Vietnam city of Hue. Eight people, including children, are killed.

June 1963: A 73-year-old monk immolates himself while sitting at a major city intersection in protest, leading other Buddhists to follow suit in coming weeks. The United States' already declining confidence in Diem's leadership continues to slide.

November 1963: The United States backs a South Vietnam military coup against the unpopular Diem, which ends in the brutal killing of Diem and his brother, Ngo Dinh Nhu. Between 1963 and 1965, 12 different governments take the lead in South Vietnam as military coups replace one government after another.

November 1963: President Kennedy is assassinated in Dallas, Texas. Lyndon B. Johnson becomes president.

Say We Won and Get Out

America Enters the Vietnam War

August 1964: USS Maddox is allegedly attacked by North Vietnamese patrol torpedo boats in the Gulf of Tonkin (the attack is later disputed), leading President Johnson to call for air strikes on North Vietnamese patrol boat bases. Two U.S. aircraft are shot down and one U.S. pilot, Everett Alvarez, Jr., becomes the first U.S. airman to be taken prisoner by North Vietnam.

August 1964: The attacks in the Gulf of Tonkin spur Congress to pass the Gulf of Tonkin Resolution, which authorizes the president to "take all necessary measures, including the use of armed force" against any aggressor in the conflict.

November 1964: The Soviet Politburo increases its support to North Vietnam, sending aircraft, artillery, ammunition, small arms, radar, air defense systems, food and medical supplies. Meanwhile, China sends several engineering troops to North Vietnam to assist in building critical defense infrastructure.

February 1965: President Johnson orders the bombing of targets in North Vietnam in Operation Flaming Dart in retaliation for a Viet Cong raid at the U.S. base in the city of Pleiku and at a nearby helicopter base at Camp Holloway.

March 1965: President Johnson launches a three-year campaign of sustained bombing of targets in North Vietnam and the Ho Chi Minh Trail in Operation Rolling Thunder. The same month, U.S. Marines land on beaches near Da Nang, South Vietnam as the first American combat troops to enter Vietnam.

June 1965: General Nguen Van Thieu of the Army of the Republic of Vietnam Governmental Military (ARVN), becomes president of South Vietnam.

Vietnam War Timeline

More Troops, More Deaths, More Protests

July 1965: President Johnson calls for 50,000 more ground troops to be sent to Vietnam, increasing the draft to 35,000 each month.

August 1965: In Operation Starlite, some 5,500 U.S. Marines strike against the First Viet Cong Regiment in the first major ground offensive by U.S. forces in Vietnam. The six-day operation diffuses the Viet Cong regiment, although it would quickly rebuild.

November 1965: Norman Morrison, a 31-year-old pacifist Quaker from Baltimore, sets himself on fire in front of the Pentagon to protest the Vietnam war. Onlookers encourage him to release his 11-month-old baby daughter, whom he is holding, before he is engulfed in flames.

November 1965: Nearly 300 Americans are killed and hundreds more injured in the first large-scale battle of the war, the Battle of la Drang Valley. At the battle, in South Vietnam's Central Highlands, U.S. ground troops are dropped onto and withdrawn from the battlefield by helicopter, in what would become a common strategy. Both sides declare victory.

1966: U.S. troop numbers in Vietnam rise to 400,000.

June 1966: American aircraft attack targets in Hanoi and Haiphong in raids that are among the first such attacks on cities in North Vietnam.

1967: U.S. troop numbers stationed in Vietnam increase to 500,000.

February 1967: U.S. aircraft bomb Haiphong Harbor and North Vietnamese airfields.

April 1967: Huge Vietnam War protests occur in Washington, D.C., New York City and San Francisco.

September 1967: Nguyen Van Thieu wins the presidential election of South Vietnam under a newly enacted constitution.

November 1967: In the Battle of Dak To, U.S. and South Vietnamese forces resist an offensive by communist forces in the Central Highlands. The United States forces suffer some 1,800 casualties.

January-April 1968: A U.S. Marine garrison at Khe Sanh in South Vietnam is bombarded with massive artillery by communist forces from the People's Army of North Vietnam (PAVN). For 77 days, the marines and South Vietnamese forces fend off the siege.

North Vietnam Shocks America

January 1968: The Tet Offensive begins, encompassing a combined assault of Viet Minh and North Vietnamese armies. Attacks are carried out in more than 100 cities and outposts across South Vietnam, including Hue and Saigon, and the U.S. Embassy is invaded. The effective, bloody attacks shock U.S. officials and mark a turning point in the war and the beginning of a gradual U.S. withdrawal from the region.

February 11-17, 1968: This week records the highest number of U.S. soldier deaths during the war, with 543 American deaths.

February-March 1968: Battles at Hue and Saigon end with American and ARVN victory as Viet Cong guerillas are cleared from the cities.

March 16, 1968: At the U.S. massacre at Mai Lai, more than 500 civilians are murdered by U.S. forces. The massacre happens amid a campaign of U.S. search-and-destroy operations that are intended to find enemy territories, destroy them and then retreat.

Vietnam War Timeline

March 1968: President Johnson halts bombing in Vietnam north of the 20th parallel. Facing backlash about the war, Johnson announces he will not run for reelection.

November 1968: Republican Richard M. Nixon wins the U.S. presidential elections on the campaign promises to restore "law and order" and to end the draft.

May 1969: At Ap Bia Mountain, about a mile from the border with Laos, U.S. paratroopers attack entrenched North Vietnamese fighters in an attempt to cut off North Vietnamese infiltration from Laos. U.S. troops eventually capture the site (temporarily), which would be nicknamed Hamburger Hill by journalists due to the brutal carnage of the 10-day battle.

September 1969: Ho Chi Minh dies of a heart attack in Hanoi.

December 1969: The U.S. government institutes the first draft lottery since World War II, prompting ever more young American men—later disparaged as "draft dodgers"—to flee to Canada.

Gradual Withdrawal from Vietnam

1969-1972: The Nixon administration gradually reduces the number of U.S. forces in South Vietnam, placing more burden on the ground forces of South Vietnam's ARVN as part of a strategy known as Vietnamization. U.S. troops in Vietnam are reduced from a peak of 549,000 in 1969 to 69,000 in 1972.

February 1970: U.S. National Security Advisor Henry Kissinger begins secret peace negotiations with Hanoi politburo member Le Duc Tho in Paris.

March 1969-May 1970: In a series of secret bombings known as "Operation Menu," U.S. B-52 bombers target suspected communist base camps and supply zones in Cambodia. The bombings are kept under wraps by Nixon and his administration since Cambodia is officially neutral in the war, although *The New York Times* would reveal the operation on May 9, 1969.

April-June 1970: U.S. and South Vietnamese forces attack communist bases across the Cambodian border in the Cambodian Incursion.

May 3, 1970: In a bloody incident known as the Kent State Shooting, National Guardsmen fire on anti-war demonstrators at Ohio's Kent State University, killing four students and wounding nine.

June 1970: Congress repeals the Gulf of Tonkin Resolution to reassert control over the president's ability to use force in the war.

Vietnamization Falters, America Exits

January-March 1971: In Operation Lam Son 719, ARVN troops, with U.S. support, invade Laos in an attempt to cut off the Ho Chi Minh Trail. They are forced to retreat and suffer heavy losses.

June 1971: *The New York Times* publishes a series of articles detailing leaked Defense Department documents about the war, known as the Pentagon Papers. The report reveals the U.S. government had repeatedly and secretly increased U.S. involvement in the war.

March-October 1972: The People's Army of Vietnam launches the large-scale, three-pronged Easter Offensive against the Army of the Republic of Vietnam and U.S. forces. While North Vietnam gains control of more territory in South Vietnam, the offensive isn't the decisive blow its military leaders had hoped for.

December 1972: President Nixon orders the launch of the most intense air offense of the war in Operation Linebacker. The attacks, concentrated between Hanoi and Haiphong, drop roughly 20,000 tons of bombs over densely populated regions.

January 22, 1973: Former President Johnson dies in Texas at age 64.

January 27, 1973: The Selective Service announces the end to the draft and institutes an all-volunteer military.

January 27, 1973: President Nixon signs the Paris Peace Accords, ending direct U.S. involvement in the Vietnam War. The North Vietnamese accept a cease fire. But as U.S. troops depart Vietnam, North Vietnamese military officials continue plotting to overtake South Vietnam.

February-April 1973: North Vietnam returns 591 American prisoners of war (including future U.S. Senator and presidential candidate, John McCain) in what is known as Operation Homecoming.

The Vietnam War Ends

August 1974: President Nixon resigns in the face of likely impeachment after the Watergate Scandal is revealed. Gerald R. Ford becomes president.

January 1975: President Ford rules out any further U.S. military involvement in Vietnam.

April 1975: In the Fall of Saigon, the capital of South Vietnam is seized by communist forces and the government of South Vietnam surrenders. U.S. Marine and Air Force helicopters transport more than 1,000

American civilians and nearly 7,000 South Vietnamese refugees out of Saigon in an 18-hour mass evacuation effort.

July 1975: North and South Vietnam are formally unified as the Socialist Republic of Vietnam under hardline communist rule.

The War Dead: By the end of the war, more than 58,000 Americans lose their lives. Vietnam would later release estimates that 1.1 million North Vietnamese and Viet Cong fighters were killed, up to 250,000 South Vietnamese soldiers died and more than 2 million civilians were killed on both sides of the war.

This timeline is reprinted here courtesy of History.com

History.com Editors. "Vietnam War Timeline." History.com. A&E Television Networks, September 13, 2017. https://www.history.com/topics/vietnam-war/vietnam-war-timeline.

George D. Aiken Chronology

1892: George David Aiken born at Dummerston, Vermont, August 20, son of Edward W. and Myra A. (Cook) Aiken.

1909: Graduated from Brattleboro (Vermont) High School.

1910: Became Master of the Putney (Vermont) Grange.

1913: Helped organize the Windham County Farm Bureau, the second farm bureau in Vermont.

1914: Married Beatrice Howard (deceased). Children: Dorothy Aiken Morse (deceased), Marjorie Aiken Cleverly (deceased), Howard Aiken (deceased), Barbara Aiken Jones (lives in Vermont).

1917: Elected president of the Vermont Horticultural Society, marking his contribution to gardening and to preservation and propagation of native plants, especially wildflowers.

1920: School Director, Town of Putney; served until 1937.

1930: Elected to the Vermont House of Representatives as the Member from Putney; served until 1935.

1933: Began a two-year term as Speaker of the Vermont House of Representatives. His *Pioneering with Wildflowers* published (revised edition, 1968).

1935: Elected Lieutenant Governor of Vermont, served two years. G.D.A. was instrumental in bringing rural electric co-operatives into Vermont; secured passage of enabling legislation that brought REA benefits to the state. President of the Windham Country Farm Bureau.

1936: His *Pioneering with Fruits and Berries* was published.

1937: Elected Governor of Vermont. For four years in office, he successfully resisted the federal government's claim to jurisdiction over Vermont streams and watersheds. He also initiated action to establish the Connecticut River Flood Control Compact (finally approved when he introduced the bill as a U.S. Senator in 1953). G.D.A. the first governor to sign the Interstate Parole and the Probation Compact.

1938: Received national attention for his call to end the "hate-Roosevelt campaign." His *Speaking from Vermont* published.

1940: Elected (November 5) to fill the unexpired term (ending January 1945) of U.S. Senator Ernest W. Gibson, Sr., who died in office; at that time G.D.A. was one of the youngest men ever elected to the U.S. Senate. Re-elected November 7, 1944; November 7, 1950; November 6, 1956; November 6, 1962; and November 5, 1968.

George D. Aiken's Senate Committees

Aeronautical and Space Sciences 1965-67.
Agricultural and Forestry 1941-75; chairman 1953-55. Ranking

member of the subcommittee on Agricultural Credit and Rural Electrification; member of subcommittees on Environment, Soil Conservation and Forestry, and on Agriculture Appropriations.

Joint Committee on Atomic Energy 1959-75. Became ranking Senate member of the committee, and of five subcommittees – on Communities, on Legislation, on Research, Development and Radiation, on Energy, and on Licensing and Regulation.

Civil Service 1941-47.

Education and Labor (since 1946 Labor and Public Welfare) 1941-46.

Expenditures in the Executive Departments (later Government Operations) 1941-49; chairman 1947-48.

Foreign Relations 1954-75. Chairman of Senate Delegation of Canada-United States Interparliamentary Group for ten years; chairman, subcommittee on Canada 1958-69. Became ranking member of four subcommittees – on U.S. Security Agreements Abroad, on Far Eastern Affairs, on Western Hemisphere Affairs, on Near Eastern Affairs.

Labor and Public Welfare 1947-54; chairman, subcommittee on Education 1947-48.

Pensions 1941-47.

1941: Opposed Lend Lease to Great Britain in his first major speech before the U.S. Senate. He saw Lend Lease as vesting unlimited authority in the hands of the executive branch to make international arrangements, bypassing Congress in the process.

1943: Introduced his first bill for the construction of the St. Lawrence Seaway, a major project that would involve dams, locks and canals to allow oceangoing ships access to the Great Lakes; also, at the international rapids, a hydroelectric project capable of producing 1.5

million kilowatt hours was planned. Opposition of the St. Lawrence Seaway came from railroads, utilities and seaboard harbor interests, all of whom feared economic disadvantage from the Seaway. G.D.A. and other Seaway proponents continued to work for implementation of the project every year for eleven years, at the end of which time the necessary legislation was finally passed.

Also in 1943 G.D.A. introduced the first Food Allotment bill to distribute surplus agricultural commodities among low-income people.

1944: Spoke of consumer co-operatives as the "greatest single force for effectively regulating private industry." He opposed Congressional delegation of power to the President: "Congress has given the President enough power to do about anything he wants."

1945: Called on Republican Senators to support the legislative program proposed by President Truman.

Co-sponsored a dental aid bill that would give federal aid to non-profit private groups for dental studies and demonstration programs.

With Senator Robert LaFollette of Wisconsin, proposed a food-coupon program for low-income families, and a hot-lunch program for schools.

Re-introduced the St. Lawrence Seaway bill, which was again defeated.

1946: Criticized a speech by Winston Churchill in Fulton, Missouri, in which Churchill proposed a United States-Great Britain military alliance. G.D.A. said, "I am not prepared to enter a military alliance with anyone. England, the United States and the Soviet Socialist Republics should work together for assuring the efficiency of the United Nations Organization"; also queried why the United States should support British foreign policy, pointing out that Britain and Russia had been at odds for two hundred years, and that the U.S.A. should "steer clear of this conflict and work instead to bring the two nations together."

On the United Nations, G.D.A. said "With public opinion as it is, we've got to take one step at a time toward an orderly world. The U.N. may not be working very smoothly or making much of a splash right now, but it's working better than our own government did in the first year of its existence."

Was instrumental in enacting the Farmers Home Administration law.

In November became eligible for the chairmanship of the Senate Labor and Welfare committee but he was opposed by conservative Republican Senator Robert Taft because of his frequent support for labor and opposition to strike-control legislation.

1947: In a Senate speech, said that there was no mandate "for this Congress to block the development of atomic energy for industrial purposes, or to turn the benefits of such development over to a little group of ruthless men who would control all the sources of power of the United States and the world if possible."

In another speech he called for an extension of food shipments to Greece and other European countries, calling food "our most potent weapon" against totalitarianism.

As Acting Chairman of the Agriculture committee, guided the first pesticide bill through the Senate – the Federal Insecticide, Fungicide and Rodenticide Act.

Questioned a Navy requisition for $97,252.50 worth of silver-plated fingerbowls and matching plates; Secretary of the Navy Forrestal said such purchase would be reviewed in the future.

In an article about G.D.A. in *The New York Times*, Arthur Krock said that many of the Senator's colleagues thought his roll call record placed him with New Deal Democrats: of 123 roll calls in the 79th Congress, G.D.A. voted with Republican majorities 21 times, against them 82 times, and was paired of did not vote 20 times.

Was appointed to the Commission on Organization of the Executive

Branch, also known as the Hoover Commission, which was formed to study ways to simplify the structure of the federal government, and to define and limit "executive functions, services and activities."

1948: Co-sponsored the permanent Crop Insurance Act; also sponsored the Agricultural Act, which established price supports for basic farm commodities and laid the foundation for dairy-price supports.
Co-sponsored the St. Lawrence Seaway project.

1950: Proposed a dairy-support plain, including easier credit for low-income farmers and expanded consumption of dairy products through public education, school-lunch programs, and food coupons.
Joined Henry Cabot Lodge, Jr., in trying to strengthen the Republican platform on civil rights by including a pledge to enact civil rights legislation in the current Session and to break a filibuster if necessary; this effort overruled.
Received the annual award of the American Parents Committee for his outstanding service to the nation's children.

1951: Co-Sponsored a voluntary medical insurance bill in which states would get federal grants to provide care to the poor.
Served as a member of the Douglas Committee to study ethics in government.

1953: Was author of the Farm Credit Act, the first in a series of new laws allowing the farm credit system to be farmer-owned.

1954: Co-sponsored Public Law 480, widely known as "Food for Peace," one of the major instruments of on-going United States Foreign Policy.
The St. Lawrence Seaway and Power Project, which he had sponsored since 1943, was signed into law on May 13.
Sponsored the Water Facilities Act, which extended loans for the

development of water facilities to all areas, not just arid and semi-arid regions; also sponsored the Aiken-Hope Small Watershed Act, which provided for flood prevention and watershed management on smaller streams.

1955: Received the Distinguished Service Award from the American Farm Bureau Federation for meritorious service to American agriculture.

1957: Member of a study mission to the Caribbean as a member of the Consultative Subcommittee on the American Republics.

1958: As chairman of the Subcommittee on Canada of the Foreign Relations committee, he inaugurated the Canada-United States Interparliamentary Group to establish a forum for discussion of mutual problems between lawmakers of each country.

1959: Visited Latin America as a member of the Foreign Relations committee.

1960: Appointed by President Eisenhower as a representative of the United States to the fifteenth session of the General Assembly of the United Nations: was assigned to Committee V, Administration and Budgetary Matters.

In a speech in Boston, G.D.A. said the primary task of the United States in the 1960's "is to protect the nationalist revolution, with its subsidiary social and economic aspects, from scavengers, whether of the communist left or the totalitarian right."

1961: Received the Congressional Distinguished Service Award of the American Political Science Association.

1962: Aiken-Talmadge bill enacted, authorizing co-operation between state departments of agriculture and the federal government in the administration and enforcement of federal meat and poultry regulations.

Opposed President Kennedy's request for United States' purchase of $100 million in United Nations bonds, saying the U.N. already owed the United States $32 million, and urged that U.N. finances be scrutinized "in order to bring home to all members of the United Nations that their relationships with that organization itself are to be financially responsible."

Was appointed to the President's Commission on the Status of Women.

Helped defeat the Northeast Water and Related Land Resources Compact, which would have given southern New England utilities control over Vermont streams and adjacent lands.

1963: Appointed by President Kennedy as a member of the United States delegation to Moscow to witness the signing of the Nuclear Test Ban Treaty.

Co-sponsored the Land and Water Conservation Fund bills to improve rural recreational facilities (the bills authorized establishment of the Bureau of Outdoor Recreation in the Department of the Interior).

1964: The historic Civil Rights bill of 1964 passed Congress as a result of intensive revision work and support by a bi-partisan committee of seven Senators – Aiken, Dirksen, Humphrey, Kuchel, Magnuson, Mansfield, and Saltonstall – cooperating with the office of Attorney General Robert F. Kennedy.
Sponsored legislation requiring registration of all pesticide chemicals.

1965: Joined Senator Mansfield and three other Senators on a special study mission to Europe and Asia, the mission including a period of time in Vietnam. Their report, published on January 6, 1966, was called "The Vietnam Conflict: The Substance and the Shadow." The report warned that Vietnam was an "open-ended" conflict and that the war's end was not in sight, either through negotiation or through increased military pressure.

The Aiken Rural Water and Sewer Act, providing for improvement of rural water and sewer systems, enacted.

Was a principal co-sponsor of the bill authorizing the Corps of Engineers to construct, operate and maintain a tide-harnessing power project at Passamaquoddy, Maine (subsequent appropriations bill blocked, but the project remains under study).

1966: By October, he concluded (in a statement called "Vietnam Analysis – Present and Future") that the time had come for the United States to begin a withdrawal program. His plan for ending the war became known as the Aiken Formula: "Declare ourselves winners and get out."

Sponsored a bill to establish national recreation areas in the Connecticut River Valley.

1967: Married Lola Pierotti on June 30.

1968: The Aiken Fair Practices Act was passed, protecting farm co-operatives from coercion by urban processors of perishable farm commodities.

Drafted legislation to protect small utilities against regional monopoly of the generation and distribution of electricity by the nuclear-power plants of private utilities; bill redrafted and passed in 1970 as Public Law 560.

Named an honorary member of the Soil Conservation Society of America, one of the most coveted honors in American conservation.

In an interview in U.S. News and World Report, he said: "There has been too much tendency on the part of the public to look to government to solve all its problems – including its morals."

1969: Co-sponsored, with Senator Alan Cranston of California, Senate Resolution 205, which stated that recognition of a foreign government does not necessarily imply that the U.S. approves the character of that government.

Helped stop Senate Approval of the Foreign Aid Appropriations bill because it contained an unauthorized $54.4 million item for jet aircraft for Nationalist China.

Received the distinguished service citation from the Experiment in International Living.

Persuaded the Department of Agriculture to establish in Vermont one of five pilot programs for feeding infants and expectant mothers.

1970: The Senate adopted on June 30 the Cooper-Church-Aiken-Mansfield amendment to the Foreign Aid Military Sales bill, which said, in effect, that the executive branch could not wage further war in Cambodia without consent of Congress. This was the first legislative move against the widening of the Indochina war; the first time in nearly twenty years that the Senate reasserted its foreign policy authority under the Constitution.

He guided the first egg inspection act through the Senate.

Was ranked number three on a list of twenty-one legislators who have led in promoting conservation.

1971: With Senator Mansfield, re-introduced a Constitutional amendment providing for a single Presidential term of six years. The move sparked national debate.

Early in the year he suggested that the United States convene an Indochina peace conference that would include the United States, the People's Republic of China, the Soviet Union, and other nations.

In a Senate speech urging Asian nations to do more to promote peace in Indochina, he declared he was "convinced that neither the Senate nor the American people are of an isolationist mind, for we all know that the self-righteousness of isolationism is as dangerous to our security and prosperity as is the self-righteousness of misguided intervention."

George D. Aiken Chronology

1972: Secured passage of the Federal Environmental Pesticide Control Act, which set up new regulations for pesticide use in interstate and intrastate commerce.

Had a leading role in formulating and writing the Rural Development Act, which he called "the single most important piece of domestic legislation approved by the 92nd Congress." The law provided loans and grants for developing small rural business enterprises.

Initiated a drive that led, in 1974, to the Eastern Wild Areas legislation, which established sixteen wilderness areas and seventeen wilderness study areas east of the 100th Meridian.

1973: Worked for successful enactment of the Agriculture and Consumer Protection Act of 1973, which established the "target price" concept for agricultural commodities, a major change in farm policy.

Worked closely with Senator Humphrey in enacting Public Law 93-189, which directed foreign aid programs to concentrate on improving the health, education, and agricultural development of poor countries.

In a Senate speech about the Presidency and Watergate, he declared that Congress should "either impeach President Nixon or get off his back." In another speech to the Senate he spoke of the need for bipartisan foreign policy in the Senate to make the President accountable. He warned that if the President ignores Congress, "instead of accountability he will get partisan investigation; instead of consultation, he will have confrontation."

Sponsored legislation to revise the Rural Electrification Act, which insured that rural areas and small co-operatives would be able to obtain loans to expand their facilities to meet energy demands.

The George D. Aiken Sugar Maple Laboratory was dedicated in South Burlington, Vermont, making Vermont the maple research center of the United States.

1974: In a critique of Congress published in U.S. News and World

Report, he said, "We duck too many issues. Somebody said we should take the eagle off the seal and put the duck on instead."

On Valentine's Day he announced he had much unfinished business at home and would not be a candidate for re-election to the United States Senate.

1975: Completed his final term in the U.S. Senate in January; returned home to Vermont.

1976: Began residence as scholar at the University of Vermont in Burlington, where he met with students and faculty, and participated in an oral history; he continued this relationship with the university until 1981. Additionally, all of Senator Aiken's papers from his time in Congress were donated to the UVM library's special collections.

Senator Aiken was in high demand as a speaker for many organizations and special events and did so frequently until 1983. Meanwhile, he actively tended his garden in Putney and with Lola, divided their time between Putney and Montpelier, Lola's home town.

1984: George David Aiken dies on November 19 in Montpelier (Vermont), aged 92; survived by his wife Lola, and his three daughters (with Beatrice).

This timeline is recreated from entries in Senator Aiken's Senate Diary:

Aiken, George D. *Aiken: Senate Diary, January 1972-January 1975*. Brattleboro, VT: Stephen Greene Press, 1976.

Bibliography

Aiken, George D. *Pioneering with Fruits and Berries.* Brattleboro, VT: Stephen Daye Press, 1936.

Aiken, George D. *Aiken: Senate Diary, January 1972-January 1975.* Brattleboro, VT: Stephen Greene Press, 1976.

Aiken, George D. *Pioneering with Wildflowers.* Putney, VT: Author, 1933.

Aiken, George D. *Speaking from Vermont.* New York: Frederick A. Stokes Company, 1938.

Arlen, Michael J. *The Camera Age.* New York: Farrar, Straus & Giroux, 1981.

Arnett, Peter. *Live From the Battlefield.* New York: Simon & Schuster, 1994.

Aronson, James. *The Press and the Cold War.* New York: Bobbs-Merrill, 1970.

Bermer, William. *William Fulbright and the Vietnam War.* Kent, OH: Kent University Press, 1988.

Berman, Larry. *Lyndon Johnson's War: The Road to Stalemate in Vietnam.* New York: Norton, 1989.

Braestrup, Peter. *Big Story: How the American Press and Television Reported and Interpreted the Crisis of Tet 1968.* Boulder, CO: Westview Press, 1977.

Browne, Malcolm W. *Muddy Boots and Red Socks: A Reporter's Life.* New

York: Times Books, 1993.

Clifford, Clark. *Counsel to the President, Clark Clifford: A Memoir*. New York: Random House, 1991.

Dallek, Robert. *Flawed Giant: Lyndon Johnson and His Times, 1961-1973*. New York: Oxford University Press, 1998.

Esper, George, and the Associated Press. *The Eyewitness History of the Vietnam War, 1961-1975*. New York: Villard Books, 1983.

Fall, Bernard B. *Last Reflections on a War: Bernard B. Fall's Last Comments on Vietnam*. New York: Doubleday, 1967.

Fall, Bernard B. *Two Vietnams: A Political and Military Analysis*, rev. ed. New York: Praeger, 1967.

Farrell, John. *Richard Nixon: The Life*. New York: Doubleday, 2017.

FitzGerald, Frances. *A Fire in the Lake: The Vietnamese and the Americans in Vietnam*. Boston: Atlantic-Little, Brown, 1972.

Fulbright, J. William. *The Arrogance of Power*. New York: Random House, 1966.

Halberstam, David. *The Best and the Brightest*. New York: Random House, 1972.

Halberstam, David. *The Powers That Be*. New York: Alfred A. Knopf, 1979.

Hallin, Daniel. *The Uncensored War: The Media and Vietnam*. New York: Oxford University Press, 1986.

Hess, Gary. *Vietnam and the United States, Origins and Legacy of War*. New York: Twayne Publishers, 1998.

Hersh, Seymour. *The Prince of Power: Kissinger in the Nixon White House*. New York: Summit, 1983.

Hilsman, Roger. *To Move a Nation*. New York: Doubleday, 1967.

Hoopes, Townsend. *The Limits of Intervention*. New York: McKay, 1970.

Johnson, Lyndon B. *The Vantage Point*. New York: Holt, Rinehart and Winston, 1971.

Just, Ward. *To What End, Report from Vietnam*. Boston: Houghton Mifflin, 1968.

Karnow, Stanley. *Vietnam: A History*. New York: Penguin Books, 1991.

Kearns, Doris. *Lyndon Johnson and the American Dream*. New York,

Harper and Rowe, 1976.

Knightley, Phillip. *The First Casualty: From Crimea to Vietnam: The Correspondent as Hero, Propagandist, and Myth Maker.* New York: Harcourt Brace Jovanovich, 1975.

Lederer, William, and Eugene Burdick. *The Ugly American.* New York: W.W. Norton & Co., 1958.

Manchester, William. *American Caesar: Douglas MacArthur, 1880-1964.* Boston: Little, Brown, 1978.

Mann, Robert. *A Grand Delusion: America's Descent into Vietnam.* Princeton, NJ: Basic Books, 2001.

Matthews, Chris. *Jack Kennedy: Elusive Hero.* New York: Simon & Schuster, 2011.

McNamara, Robert S., and Brian VanDeMark. *In Retrospect: The Tragedy and Lessons of Vietnam.* New York: Doubleday, 1995.

McPherson, Harry. *A Political Education.* Boston: Little, Brown, 1972.

Morris, Edmund. *The Rise of Theodore Roosevelt.* New York: Coward, McCann, 1970.

Newman, John M. *JFK and Vietnam.* New York: Warner Books, 1992.

Nguyen, Viet Thanh. *The Sympathizer.* Corsair, 2015.

Nixon, Richard. *No More Vietnams.* New York: Arbor House, 1985.

Nixon, Richard. *RN: The Memoirs of Richard Nixon.* New York: Grosset & Dunlap, 1978

Olson, Gregory. *Mansfield and Vietnam: A Study in Rhetorical Adaptation.* East Lansing, MI: University Press, 1995.

Olson, James and Randy Roberts. *Where the Domino Fell: America and Vietnam, 1945-1990.* New York: St. Martin's Press Inc., 1991.

Prochnau, William. *Once Upon a Distant War.* New York: Times Books, 1995.

Reeves, Richard. *President Kennedy: Profile of Power.* New York: Simon & Schuster, 1993.

Reston, James. *Deadline: A Memoir.* New York: Times Books, 1992.

Robertson, Nan. *The Girls in the Balcony.* New York: Random House, 1992.

Salinger, Pierre. *With Kennedy.* New York: Doubleday, 1966.

Salisbury, Harrison E., ed. *Vietnam Reconsidered: Lessons From a War.* New York: Harper & Row, 1984.

Schlesinger, Arthur M., Jr. *The Bitter Heritage: Vietnam and American Democracy, 1941-1966.* Boston: Houghton Mifflin, 1967.

Schlesinger, Arthur M., Jr. *A Thousand Days: Thirty Years of the Asian Revolution by a Correspondent for The New Yorker.* New York: Random House, 1979.

Shaplen, Robert. *The Lost Revolution.* New York: Harper & Row, 1965.

Shawcross, William. *Sideshow: Kissinger, Nixon, and the Destruction of Cambodia.* New York: Simon & Schuster, 1978.

Sheehan, Neil. *A Bright Shining Lie: John Paul Vann and America in Vietnam.* New York: Random House, 1988.

Sheehan, Neil, et al. *The Pentagon Papers.* New York: Quadrangle Books, 1971.

Sorenson, Theodore C. *Kennedy.* New York: Harper & Row, 1965.

Talese, Gay. *The Kingdom and The Power.* New York: Anchor Books, 1978.

Parsons, David L. *The Vietnam War: 1945-1975.* New York: New York Historical Society, 2017.

Ungar, Sanford J. *The Papers and The Papers.* New York: E.P. Dutton and Co., 1972.

White, Theodore H. *The Making of the President 1960.* New York: Atheneum, 1961.

Wicker, Tom. *On Press.* New York: Viking Press, 1978.

Articles

Stoler, Mark. "Aiken, Mansfield and the Tonkin Gulf Crisis" Vermont History, Montpelier, Spring 1982

Stoler, Mark. "What Did He Really Say? The "Aiken Formula" for Vietnam Revisited", 1978.

Bibliography

Interviews

Aiken Tapes, LBJ Library, University of Virginia, Miller Center.
Carl Marcy, Chief of Staff, Senate Foreign Relations Committee, 1983, Senate Historical Office Oral History Interview, Washington, D.C.
George D. Aiken, interview by Paige Mulhollan, Oct. 10, 1968, LBJ Oral History Project, LBJ Library.
George D. Aiken, George D. Aiken Oral History Memoir, interview by Charles T. Morrissey and D. Gregory Sanford, University of Vermont, March 1981.
Pat Holt, Deputy Chief of Staff of the Senate Foreign Relations Committee, 1980, Senate Historical Office Oral History Interview, Washington, D.C.
Stephen C. Terry, personal notes and material from 1965 to 1984, including interviews as a reporter, conversations with Senator Aiken as his staff assistant, 1969- 1975, and conversations until 1984.

Congressional Hearings Footage

Vietnam Senate Foreign Relations Hearings in 1966 and 1968, American History TV, C-SPAN 3
Retired General James M. Gavin at the Senate Foreign Relations Committee, February 1966. American History TV, C-SPAN 3
John F. Kerry Testimony at the Senate Foreign Relations Committee, April 1971. American History TV, C-SPAN 3.

Films

Dateline: Saigon. Northern Light Productions, 2016.
Hearts & Minds. The Criterion Collection, 1974.
Last Days in Vietnam. Moxie Firecracker Films, 2014.
The Vietnam War: A Film by Ken Burns & Lynn Novick. Florentine Films, 2017.

Government Documents

Glennon, John P., and Edward C. Keefer. Foreign Relations of the United States: Vietnam, 1961-1963, Vols. 1-4. Washington, D.C.: U.S. Government Printing Office, 1988-1991.

U.S. Congress. Senate. Foreign Relations Committee, 1954-1956, Vols. 6-18.

Index

1938 Presidential Boomlet 163
1940 U.S. Senate Campaign 162, 163, 166, 180

A

Aiken, Beatrice Howard (wife) 148, 151, 153, 263, 274
Aiken, Edward Webster (father) 145, 146, 149, 150
Aiken, George D.
  agricultural legislation 34, 171, 173
  and electric power 155, 164, 170, 172, 271
  and farm cooperatives 173, 174
  and his Senate Diary 114, 115, 118, 119, 120, 122, 127, 128, 129, 132, 140, 274, 275
  and rural electric cooperatives 157, 158
  and the "Old Guard" 107, 137, 154, 155, 156, 161, 162, 165, 166, 194
  and the rural water and sewer program 65, 66, 174, 271
  and weekly troop levels 114
  as Governor of Vermont 20, 136, 168, 173, 179, 191, 193, 264
  as House Speaker 160, 264
  as Lieutenant Governor 158, 160
  death 140
  opposition to FDR's New Deal 55, 136, 157, 158, 160, 161, 162, 163, 164, 180, 193, 194, 267
  opposition to Vermont dams 155, 170
  retirement 140, 155, 168
  siblings 145
Aiken, Lola Pierotti (wife)
  10, 25, 27, 67, 79, 80, 81, 82, 93, 94, 97, 99, 107, 109, 114, 119, 121, 127, 128, 140, 271, 274
Aiken, Myra (mother)
  145, 146, 263
Aiken Nursery 152
Armstrong, James I. 182
Augeri, Louis 13, 288

B

Ball, George W. 48, 54, 60
Bay of Pigs 43, 47, 242, 243
Blair, James P. 37, 38
Brandt, David 13
Brattleboro High School 146
Burlington Free Press 63, 82, 83, 101, 105

Butterfield, Fox 41

C

Castro, Fidel 18, 43
Chicago Democratic Convention, 1968 76, 77
Church, Frank 40, 61, 103
Coffin, Howard 127
Coffin, Rev. William Sloan, Jr. 64
Cooper-Church-Aiken-Mansfield Amendment 104, 105, 108, 123
Cooper, John S. 103
Cronkite, Walter 71, 72
C. Turner Joy (ship) 51

D

Danziger, Jeff 6, 14, 247

E

Eastern Wilderness Areas 115
Eisenhower, Dwight D. 18, 33, 35, 36, 37, 42, 43, 59, 84, 239, 241, 243, 253, 269

F

Flanders, Ralph E. 34, 163, 166
Food Stamp, WIC legislation 174, 175
Fulbright, J. William 40, 53, 60, 61, 62, 68, 84, 90, 110, 135

G

Gavin, James 36
Geneva Accords 36, 41, 253
Giap, General Vo Nguyen 35
Gibson, Ernest W. Jr. 80, 156, 166, 241
Gibson, Ernest W. Sr. 80, 166, 264
Giles, Eliza 14
Giuliani, Peter 126
Goldwater, Barry M. 50, 51, 52, 118, 132

Green Mountain Parkway 158, 159
Gulf of Tonkin 14, 51, 52, 61, 256, 260
  Resolution 52, 61, 256, 260

H

Hackett, Luther F. 106
Hand, Samuel 10, 154, 156, 160, 286, 288
Hatfield, Mark. 103
Hayes, Thomas L 102
Ho Chi Minh 32, 36, 39, 40, 54, 56, 59, 67, 78, 84, 87, 89, 91, 251, 252, 254, 256, 259, 260
Hoff, Philip H. 51, 65, 74, 77, 108, 125, 166, 173, 286
Humphrey, Hubert 40, 60, 75, 76, 77, 78, 83, 96, 175, 270, 273

J

James, Norman 82
Johnson, Lyndon B. 5, 7, 18, 25, 26, 27, 28, 29, 30, 31, 35, 36, 40, 45, 46, 47, 50, 51, 52, 53, 54, 55, 57, 59, 61, 62, 63, 64, 65, 66, 67, 68, 70, 71, 72, 73, 74, 75, 77, 78, 84, 88, 91, 94, 95, 96, 112, 113, 120, 133, 137, 138, 139, 186, 209, 213, 239, 242, 243, 255, 256, 257, 259, 261, 275, 276

K

Kennedy, John F. 5, 18, 35, 40, 42, 43, 45, 46, 47, 48, 49, 50, 57, 61, 73, 74, 76, 88, 95, 112, 171, 239, 242, 243, 254, 255, 270, 277, 278
Kennedy, Robert F. 48, 73, 76
Kerry, John F. 107, 111, 279
Krebs, Albin 29
Ky, Nguyen, Cao 56, 110

L

Landon, Alf 161, 163
Laos 35, 39, 42, 43, 103, 104, 109, 121, 221, 251, 252, 254, 259, 260
Leahy, Patrick J. 128
Lend-Lease legislation 5, 106, 136, 196
Lodge, Henry Cabot, Jr. 46, 58

M

Maddox (ship) 51, 256
Maerki, Vic. 63, 83
Mahoney, John 77
Mansfield, Mike 7, 19, 25, 27, 28, 40, 44, 45, 47, 49, 52, 53, 55, 57, 58, 59, 60, 65, 70, 82, 90, 98, 104, 106, 111, 123, 135, 138, 139, 166, 183, 242, 270, 272, 277, 278
Marro, Tony 11, 34, 83, 129, 167, 286
Marx, Leonard 73
Matthews, Chris 48
McCarthy, Joseph 34, 35, 70, 74, 76, 137, 184
McGovern, George 90, 103, 117
McNamara, Robert, S. 45, 48, 60, 72, 112, 277
Merrill, Perry 166, 167, 168, 275
Meyer, Karen 116
Miami Republican Convention, 1968 76, 77
Mitchell, John 112
Mitchell, Robert W. 127
Morrissey, Charles 14, 30, 58, 140, 150, 153, 161, 279
Morse, Burr 40, 53, 62, 154, 263

N

Nelson, Garrison 14
Newman, John M. 42
Nixon, Richard 5, 7, 10, 19, 29, 35, 40, 43, 46, 53, 76, 78, 79, 83, 84, 85, 86, 87, 88, 89, 90, 91, 92, 93, 94, 95, 96, 97, 98, 99, 100, 101, 102, 103, 104, 105, 106, 107, 108, 109, 110, 111, 112, 113, 114, 115, 116, 117, 118, 119, 120, 121, 122, 123, 124, 125, 126, 127, 128, 131, 132, 133, 135, 138, 139, 181, 182, 184, 218, 220, 221, 222, 223, 239, 242, 259, 260, 261, 273, 276, 277, 278
North Vietnam 15, 26, 36, 37, 39, 52, 53, 54, 56, 57, 59, 62, 63, 65, 66, 67, 68, 70, 77, 78, 85, 90, 91, 98, 114, 116, 117, 119, 120, 121, 124, 138, 211, 213, 252, 254, 256, 257, 258, 260, 261

O

O'Donnell, Kenneth 48
Olsen, Gregory Allen 66

P

Pentagon Papers 41, 42, 43, 44, 53, 54, 84, 112, 113, 260, 278
Porter, Bill 10
Putney Grange 146

Q

Quinn, Elizabeth 80, 82

R

Ridgway, Matthew 36, 59
Rogers, William P. 84, 97, 100
Rusk, Dean 60, 72, 73, 74
Russell, Richard B. 73, 138
Rutland Herald 9, 10, 76, 79, 81, 82, 83, 102, 125, 127, 129, 167, 286

S

Salmon, Tom, P. 128
Sanford, Gregory 14, 140, 156, 161, 163, 278, 279

Scott, Phil 185
Senate Foreign Relations Committee 9, 18, 21, 26, 30, 32, 33, 34, 37, 39, 40, 41, 57, 60, 61, 62, 67, 70, 73, 82, 84, 100, 101, 103, 104, 107, 109, 112, 115, 118, 123, 136, 137, 170, 174, 196, 198, 265, 269, 279, 280
Smith, Margaret Chase 34, 51, 95, 117, 118
Sorensen, Ted 278
Stine, Patrick 67
St. Lawrence Seaway 18, 169, 171, 172, 240, 265, 266, 268
Stoler, Mark 14, 30, 31, 52, 278

T

Taft, William Howard 235
Terry, Faith 15,
Terry, Stephen C. 3, 4, 5, 65, 177, 279
Tet Offensive 70, 116, 258
Trigg, Sophia 14
Truman, Harry S. 17, 18, 47, 72, 166, 217, 224, 239, 240, 241, 252, 266
Trump, Donald J. 179, 180, 181, 182, 184, 185, 250

U

University of Vermont 3, 10, 13, 30, 52, 105, 140, 154, 161, 274, 279, 286, 288

V

Vermont House 148, 149, 150, 155, 156, 159, 161, 170, 263, 264
Vermont Senate 149, 156, 159, 166
Viet Cong 28, 39, 44, 45, 54, 55, 56, 58, 60, 67, 68, 69, 70, 71, 76, 77, 85, 87, 92, 98, 99, 120, 254, 255, 256, 257, 258, 262
Vietnamization 85, 86, 90, 93, 99, 259, 260

W

Watts, Richard 13, 288
Weaver, Charlie 81, 174
Wicker, Tom 50, 278
Wilson, Woodrow 152, 159
Windham County Farm Bureau 263
Worthy Debtor Law 157

Stephen C. Terry. (Photo by Faith Terry)

Stephen C. Terry of Middlebury served from 1969 to 1975 as Legislative Assistant for Senator George D. Aiken. Terry spent 16 years as a reporter and Managing Editor at the *Rutland Herald* where he often reported on Senator Aiken. Terry and the University of Vermont historian Sam Hand co-authored in 2004, "The Essential Aiken" a compilation of Senator Aiken's important speeches. He also wrote with Hand and Anthony Marro in 2011, "Philip Hoff: How Red Turned Blue in the Green Mountain State."

After a long career in business and service on non-profit Board of Directors, Terry was named 2014 Citizen of the Year by the Vermont Chamber of Commerce. He is a 1964 University of Vermont graduate, and Chair of the George D. Aiken Lecture Series at UVM.

Louis Augeri. (Photo by Richard Watts)

Louis D. Augeri, originally from Lawrenceville, New Jersey, is a Senior at the University of Vermont studying History and Political Science. This is Augeri's second book project after working with historian Nick Muller on another Center for Research on Vermont publication, *Samuel B. Hand: Green Mountain Scholar* (2018).

Augeri is the winner of the 2018 Green Mountain Scholar Award for outstanding student research and a member of the Phi Alpha Theta History Honor Society.

www.ingramcontent.com/pod-product-compliance
Lightning Source LLC
Chambersburg PA
CBHW031431160426
43195CB00010BB/693